Women's Cinema in Contemporary Portugal

Women's Cinema in Contemporary Portugal

Edited by
Mariana Liz and Hilary Owen

BLOOMSBURY ACADEMIC
NEW YORK • LONDON • OXFORD • NEW DELHI • SYDNEY

BLOOMSBURY ACADEMIC
Bloomsbury Publishing Inc
1385 Broadway, New York, NY 10018, USA
50 Bedford Square, London, WC1B 3DP, UK
29 Earlsfort Terrace, Dublin 2, Ireland

BLOOMSBURY, BLOOMSBURY ACADEMIC and the Diana logo are trademarks of
Bloomsbury Publishing Plc

First published in the United States of America 2020
This paperback edition published in 2021

Volume Editor's Part of the Work © Mariana Liz and Hilary Owen

Each chapter © of Contributors

For legal purposes the Acknowledgements on p. ix constitute an extension
of this copyright page.

Cover image: *Batrachian's Ballad* (Leonor Teles, 2016) © Leonor Teles

All rights reserved. No part of this publication may be reproduced or transmitted
in any form or by any means, electronic or mechanical, including photocopying,
recording, or any information storage or retrieval system, without prior
permission in writing from the publishers.

Bloomsbury Publishing Inc does not have any control over, or responsibility for,
any third-party websites referred to or in this book. All internet addresses given in
this book were correct at the time of going to press. The editors and publisher
regret any inconvenience caused if addresses have changed or sites have
ceased to exist, but can accept no responsibility for any such changes.

Library of Congress Cataloging-in-Publication Data
Names: Owen, Hilary, 1961- editor. | Liz, Mariana, editor.
Title: Women's cinema in contemporary Portugal / edited by Hilary Owen, Mariana Liz.
Description: New York: Bloomsbury Academic, 2020. | Includes bibliographical
references and index.
Identifiers: LCCN 2019040299 | ISBN 9781501349720 (hardback) | ISBN 9781501349737
(epub) | ISBN 9781501349744 (pdf)
Subjects: LCSH: Women motion picture producers and directors–Portugal. | Women
in the motion picture industry–Portugal. | Women in motion pictures. | Feminism
and motion pictures. | Motion pictures–Portugal–History and criticism.
Classification: LCC PN1995.9.W6 W73 2020 | DDC 791.43/6522–dc23
LC record available at https://lccn.loc.gov/2019040299

ISBN: HB: 978-1-5013-4972-0
PB: 978-1-5013-8688-6
ePDF: 978-1-5013-4974-4
eBook: 978-1-5013-4973-7

Typeset by Deanta Global Publishing Services, Chennai

To find out more about our authors and books visit www.bloomsbury.com and
sign up for our newsletters.

Para a Rosa
Para Big M and Little M

Contents

Acknowledgements ix
List of contributors xi

Introduction: Portuguese cinema, women's cinema, world
    cinema *Mariana Liz and Hilary Owen* 1

Section One Histories

1 Unfinished: The cinema of Noémia Delgado *Manuela Penafria* 23

2 Four decades on screen: The fiction films of Margarida Gil
    Ana Isabel Soares 43

Section Two Feminisms

3 Monsters, mutants and maternity: The politics of the posthuman in
    Teresa Villaverde, Raquel Freire and Solveig Nordlund *Hilary Owen* 65

4 Urban homes and urban families: Teresa Villaverde's *Colo* and
    Susana Nobre's *Ordinary Time* *Mariana Liz* 88

5 Natural women? Nature and femininity in Noémia Delgado's
    Masks and Teresa Villaverde's *Trance* *Patrícia Vieira* 107

Section Three Archives

6 Image, historical memory, politics: Margarida Cardoso's *Kuxa
    Kanema* and Susana de Sousa Dias's *48* *Estela Vieira* 129

7 Affect and the archival turn: Documentaries by Inês de Medeiros
    and Susana de Sousa Dias *Alison Ribeiro de Menezes* 150

8 The essay film and Rita Azevedo Gomes's *Correspondences* *Ana
    Cabral Martins* 169

Section Four Transnationalisms

9   Women's cinema, world cinema: Margarida Cardoso's *Yvone Kane* Sally Faulkner   191

10 Portugal's year zero: Emergent women directors, 2013–17
    Filipa Rosário   212

Bibliography   231
Index   245

Acknowledgements

First, we would like to thank Fundação Calouste Gulbenkian for their financial support over almost two years, which enabled this book to be written, and which supported a roundtable on Women in Portuguese Film in 2017, a workshop with contributors in 2018; and the 'Mostra: Realizadoras Portuguesas' in 2019, which were a vital part of this project. We are also very grateful to ICS (Instituto de Ciências Sociais, Universidade de Lisboa) for hosting us in 2018 for our contributors' workshop, particularly, Margarida Bernardo, for brilliantly coordinating the workshop. To Joana Ferreira, Susana de Sousa Dias, Cíntia Gil, Rita Benis, Cristina Matos Silva and Ana Sousa Dias, thank you for agreeing to take part in the Gulbenkian roundtable in 2017, and for making it such a lively event. We thank the filmmakers who came to the 'Mostra' and took part in Q&A sessions, as well as everyone who led these sessions and offered insights into the films: Margarida Cardoso, Margarida Gil, Catarina Mourão, Raquel Freire, Susana de Sousa Dias, Leonor Teles, Marta Mateus, Karin Wall, Ricardo Vieira Lisboa, Raquel Ribeiro, Ana Isabel Strindberg, Tiago Baptista and Ana David.

We would also like to thank all the contributors to this book for being such wonderful colleagues to work with. We would particularly like to thank Ana Cabral Martins for her cheerful, efficient and always insightful commitment to the project behind this book, from its very early stages.

Thank you to the staff at the Cinemateca Portuguesa library, particularly Teresa Borges. For permission to reproduce images, we are very grateful to Cinemateca Portuguesa, Portugal Film, C.R.I.M. and Ar de Filmes. For allowing us to use images from their films, we also thank Teresa Villaverde, Susana Nobre, Cláudia Varejão, Salomé Lamas, Leonor Teles and Joana Pimenta. For the translation of Chapters 1, 2 and 10 into English we thank Ana Rita Martins, and for her additional work on the translations of Chapters 2 and 10, we thank Rhian Atkin.

We very much appreciated the conference on 'Transnational Portuguese Women Artists' which Cláudia Pazos Alonso and Maria Luísa Coelho co-organized with Hilary Owen at Wadham College, Oxford, UK in March 2017, and where much of the early planning for this book came together. We are also very grateful for the encouraging and pertinent feedback at the book proposal stage from Ginette Vincendeau, Duncan Wheeler, Chris Perriam and Christopher T. Lewis. In the course of this project, we have benefitted from some lively and stimulating discussions of our work with Paulo Cunha, Raquel Freire, Olga Kourelou, Ana Margarida Dias Martins, Inês Ponte, Ellen Sapega, Fernando Vendrell and Belén Vidal. In addition to this, Hilary would particularly like to thank Chris Perriam, Núria Triana-Toribio and Darren Waldron for their generous sharing of experience and ideas over the years teaching cinema at the University of Manchester.

We both owe a debt of gratitude to Katie Gallof at Bloomsbury for believing in this book project and offering tireless support and encouragement for its completion.

Finally, Mariana would like to thank Pete, and Hilary would like to thank Till, for their endless patience and loving support.

Contributors

Sally Faulkner is Professor of Hispanic Studies and Film Studies at the University of Exeter, UK, where she is Associate Dean for Internationalization and Development in the College of Humanities. She has published widely on Iberian audiovisual cultures, and her books and edited volumes include *A History of Spanish Film: Cinema and Society 1910-2010* (2013), which appeared in Spanish translation in 2017, *Middlebrow Cinema* (2016) and 'Portuguese Film: Colony, Postcolony, Memory' (2016), a special issue of the *Journal of Romance Studies*, co-edited with Mariana Liz. She has organized public screenings and festivals of Iberian and Latin American cinema in the UK, and currently co-runs a 'Subtitling World Cinema' Digital Humanities project at Exeter.

Mariana Liz is a postdoctoral research fellow at ICS-ULisboa, the Institute of Social Sciences at the University of Lisbon. Her research interests are Europe and European cinema, contemporary film in Portugal, gender and urban studies. She completed a PhD at King's College London in 2012 and taught at King's, Queen Mary and the University of Leeds in the UK before moving to Portugal in 2016. She is the author of *Euro-Visions* (2016), editor of *Portugal's Global Cinema* (2018) and co-editor of *The Europeanness of European Cinema* (with Mary Harrod and Alissa Timoshkina, 2015).

Ana Cabral Martins worked as a research assistant for the 'Portuguese Women Directors' research project at ICS-ULisboa, Portugal. She has a PhD in Digital Media, and her thesis was titled 'Cinema in the Age of Digital Technology: A New Architecture of Immersion'. Her recent work includes a chapter on comics and movies in the volume *Visions of the Future in Comics: International Perspectives* (2017) and an article on 'A Bridge and a Reminder: *The Force Awakens*, Between Repetition and Expansion', published by *Kinephanos – Journal of Media Studies and Popular Culture* (2018).

Hilary Owen is Professor Emerita of Portuguese and Luso-African Studies at the University of Manchester and Research Fellow in the Sub-Faculty of Portuguese at the University of Oxford, UK. She is the author of *Mother Africa, Father Marx:*

Women's Writing of Mozambique, 1948-1992 (2007), co-author with Cláudia Pazos Alonso of *Antigone's Daughters?: Gender, Genealogy and the Politics of Authorship in 20th-Century Portuguese Women's Writing* (2011), co-editor with Anna M. Klobucka of *Gender, Empire and Postcolony: Luso-Afro-Brazilian Intersections* (2014) and co-editor with Claire Williams of *Transnational Portuguese Studies* (forthcoming 2020). She publishes on feminism, gender and postcolonial theory in Portuguese and Lusophone African literatures and film.

Manuela Penafria is Associate Professor at the Universidade da Beira Interior, Portugal, and a research member of Labcom.IFP-Communication, Philosophy and Humanities. She teaches film theory and practical courses on documentary film. Her most recent publications focus on 'filmmaker' theory', a research strand she is developing with Portuguese, Brazilian and Spanish colleagues. She is co-editor of the journal *DOC On-line* (Portugal/Brazil), co-coordinator of a work group at AIM (the Portuguese Association of Moving Image Researchers), and a member of AIM's Advisory Board.

Alison Ribeiro de Menezes is Professor of Hispanic Studies at the University of Warwick in the UK. She has written widely on literature, culture and memory in Spain and Portugal, including the books *Juan Goytisolo: The Author as Dissident* (2005), *A Companion to Carmen Martín Gaite* (with Catherine O'Leary, 2008) and *Embodying Memory in Contemporary Spain* (2014). She has co-edited *Legacies of War and Dictatorship in Contemporary Portugal and Spain* (with Catherine O'Leary, 2011) and most recently *Public Humanities and the Spanish Civil War* (with Antonio Cazorla Sánchez and Adrian Shubert, 2019). She is currently completing an AHRC-funded project on Chilean refugee and exile experiences in the UK following the 1974 *golpe de estado* and writing a monograph on cultural representations of the disappeared in transnational perspective.

Filipa Rosário is a research fellow at the Centre for Comparative Studies, University of Lisbon, Portugal, where she coordinates the cluster 'Cinema and the World – Studies in Space and Cinema'. Her research interests are filmic landscape, filmic space, Portuguese cinema, 1960s and 1970s cinema. She is the vice-president of the Portuguese Association of the Moving Image Researchers (AIM), where she coordinates the work group 'Landscape and Cinema' (with Iván Villarmea Álvarez). Rosário is the author of *O Trabalho do Actor no Cinema* *de John Cassavetes* (2017). She co-edited *New Approaches to Cinematic Spaces* (with Iván Villarmea Álvarez; 2018) and *ReFocus: The Films of João Pedro Rodrigues and João Rui Guerra da Mata* (with José Duarte, 2020).

Ana Isabel Soares holds a PhD in Literary Theory (University of Lisbon, Portugal, 2003), and completed a post-doctorate in the same programme on Portuguese documentary films and poetry (2009–10). She has taught undergraduate and postgraduate courses on English Literature and Film Studies at Universidade do Algarve, Portugal, since 1996. A full member of the Centre for Research in Arts and Communication (CIAC), she was one of the founders and the first president of AIM (Portuguese Association of Moving Image Researchers). Her publications range from literary to film studies. She has translated literary theory and poetry.

Estela Vieira is Associate Professor in the Department of Spanish and Portuguese at Indiana University Bloomington, USA. Her research focuses on Lusophone literature, culture and film, including postcolonial and feminist studies, cultural memory, nineteenth-century realism and modernist poetics. She recently co-edited a special number of the *Journal of Lusophone Studies* on Portuguese cinema (with Clara Rowland, 2017). She is the author of *Interiors and Narrative: The Spatial Poetics of Machado de Assis, Eça de Queirós, and Leopoldo Alas* (2012), and her current book project studies nineteenth-century Portuguese women writers.

Patrícia Vieira is Associate Research Professor at the Centre for Social Studies (CES) of the University of Coimbra, in Portugal, and part-time Associate Professor of Spanish and Portuguese at Georgetown University, USA. Her most recent book is *States of Grace: Utopia in Brazilian Culture* (2018). She has published numerous articles in the fields of Comparative Literature, Literature and Film, Postcolonial Studies, Literary Theory, Ecocriticism, and Literature and Philosophy, as well as op-eds in *The New York Times*, the *LA Review of Books* and *The European*, among others.

Introduction: Portuguese cinema, women's cinema, world cinema

Mariana Liz and Hilary Owen

Noémia Delgado
Margarida Gil
Teresa Villaverde
Raquel Freire
Solveig Nordlund
Susana Nobre
Margarida Cardoso
Susana de Sousa Dias
Inês de Medeiros
Rita Azevedo Gomes
Joana Pimenta
Salomé Lamas
Cláudia Varejão
Leonor Teles

This, in order of appearance, is the cast of our book: fourteen Portuguese women directors active between the 1970s and the present day, working on fiction and documentary, short and feature-length films, with varying degrees of visibility, within and beyond Portugal. Some are established prizewinners, some are relatively new to the profession, some have battled for decades to get the resources they need and some of them will play more than one 'role', and be explored from various different angles, in the chapters that follow. *Women's Cinema in Contemporary Portugal* problematizes current understandings of Portuguese cinema, women's cinema and world cinema. It analyses the relationship between these three concepts, and the ways in which, taken together, they offer a productive theoretical framework for the study of contemporary film, at a time when questions of scale and territory, marginality and centrality, and nationality and gender are more relevant than ever in the realm of cinema.

Our intention in this work is to discuss films made by Portuguese women. The selected case studies simultaneously illuminate the question of how to frame a dual focus on 'small cinemas' and 'women's cinema' in analytical terms, which remains sufficiently alert to the historical, cultural and political embeddedness of Portugal's transnationalized cinema production. In continuing to interrogate the working concepts of 'small nation cinema' and 'women's cinema' we suggest that, rather than fixing geographical minority and smallness, and indeed gender issues, as potential 'setbacks', it might be more productive to think about how the cinema made by contemporary Portuguese women directors can occupy, and eventually create, new territories altogether. To this end, we borrow Patricia White's idea of 're-territorialization',[1] to ask what spaces and temporalities contemporary Portuguese women's cinema occupies in the era of transnational cinemas, world cinemas and global cinematic practices.

Small cinemas: Re-territorializing women's filmmaking

It would be difficult, on various levels, not to regard Portugal as a 'small nation'. The country occupies a small geographical territory with only ten million inhabitants, and it has limited geopolitical influence at an international level along with a low GDP. The Portuguese language is the sixth most widely spoken in the world, but it is still, within the European context at least, considered a 'minor' language, and the nation's film output is extremely low.[2] Seen in this light, Portuguese cinema is easy to label as 'small cinema'.[3] While a number of Portuguese films have reached major film festivals in recent years, and have even won some of its top awards, Portuguese cinema is known abroad mostly through the work of specific high-profile directors, such as Manoel de Oliveira, Pedro Costa and Miguel Gomes, whose canonization as auteurs goes unquestioned.

The idea of 'small nation cinemas' enjoys an ambiguous relationship with the idea of 'nationhood' where many aspects of its industry, circulation and reception inevitably function as transnational. In her study of European film funding, for example, Anne Jäckel notes that co-productions account for the majority of current output from Portugal and that, as is indeed the case here, without co-productions 'many small countries would not have a film industry'.[4] Where these European co-productions are transnational by definition, this inevitably inflects the definition of Portuguese 'small nation' cinema as 'national'. Moreover, as Janelle Blankenship and Tobias Nagl put it, smallness 'is not simply introduced as exceptional "other" to the imagined norm (of averaged-sized nation-states); smallness is also inscribed on the temporal axis',[5] that is, as 'backwardness'. So what happens to this 'small nation' sense of otherness, as well as to the sense of 'backwardness', in an era, not to mention a funding context, that is structured by transnationalism, and that is also witnessing a supposed 'de-centering' of cinemas, within a more 'democratic' (to use Lúcia Nagib's term[6]) understanding of world cinema? Or, to put it another way, if cinemas now move much more freely in relation to both national canons and Hollywood's pervasive presence (the latter still being the case, at least in the exhibition sector, in Portugal, and across Europe more generally), then what precisely are they 'others' *to*, how is it that they are different? What spaces and temporal frames do they come to occupy?

Mette Hjort's work on small cinemas makes particular note of 'mono-personalism', as a risk peculiar to the small cinema context.[7] This is especially true in the Portuguese case, where Manoel de Oliveira's remarkable eighty-year career made him virtually synonymous with Portuguese cinema, at home and abroad. His most obvious successors in the role of Portuguese auteur abroad have been Pedro Costa and Miguel Gomes, although the Oliveira factor continues to exert an influence in so far as Portuguese film is still placed in an 'art cinema' niche at international festivals. The work of Portuguese women directors, in this context, may appear to occupy a position of 'double minority'. It is an example of both the cinema of small nations and women's cinema, in a filmmaking context which is (semi-)peripheral, at least in relation to European cinema, and in a country where the audiovisual industry is clearly dominated by men.

Understanding the transnationalization of contemporary Portuguese cinema as a process that is characteristic of the cinemas of small nations is, in fact, particularly productive when we also come to talk about cinema made by women filmmakers. This is because keywords, such as 'marginal', 'political' and 'anti-mainstream', are equally used within debates on gender, cinema and globalization. This confluence of notions of 'smallness' and 'minority' is made even clearer when we take Alison Butler's definition of women's cinema as a 'minor cinema' – an idea that she formulates inspired by Gilles Deleuze and Félix Guattari's idea of 'minor literature'. Minor cinema inherits the key features of minor literature, including a sense of displacement, dispossession and deterritorialization, as well as the notion that everything is political.[8] Portugal's (semi-)peripheral status often seems, in fact, to be articulated through gender. Many films examined in this volume draw on the politics of gender difference to highlight the paradoxes of Portuguese cinematic transnationalism: at once achieving global visibility, and (but?) using it to stress, challenge and problematize a position of periphery. However, to state that Portuguese women's cinema inevitably results from and mirrors a position of 'double minority' is clearly an assertion that needs to be qualified and confronted.

First, it is important to note that Portugal's 'peripheral' position is partial and relative. This is not only true in relation to Portugal's cinematic culture; this conceptualization of Portugal's geopolitical positioning has long been established in sociological analysis. The writings of Boaventura de Sousa Santos famously adapt and refine the world systems theory categorizations devised by Immanuel Wallerstein in the 1970s, to characterize Portugal in terms of a mediatory 'semi-periphery'.[9] Portugal enjoys, for example, the centrality associated with EU membership in relation to its former colonies in Africa, but remains in many other respects, peripheral to Europe, a feeling given new impetus and intensity since 2011 by the economic crisis. This is particularly interesting and productive when we explore the ramifications of (semi-)peripherality for the plurilocal nature of Portuguese cinema, and the mediatory functioning of gender difference in these debates. Portuguese cinema may also, for example, be considered to belong to 'European cinema', as a result of which it acquires potential value within the art cinema canon. Once contemporary Portuguese cinema is regarded in transnational terms and is co-opted into the variously overlapping spheres of European/world/art cinema, its 'place-based', and even linguistic, minority status is no longer as obvious as previously assumed.

Second, a growing body of scholarship on cinema and feminism has rejected the notions of opposition and exclusion often associated with women's cinema. Patricia White, for instance, argues that it is time to do away with both the idea of 'counter' and the idea of 'minor' (cinema). For White, women's cinema should not be taken as oppositional nor should it be seen as 'deterritorialized', as the idea of minority indicates. Rather, White takes 'as a pressing research question the way that women's work is reterritorialized through contemporary film culture'.[10] Similarly, Sue Thornham argues against the adoption of the term 'minor' on the grounds that it all too readily morphs into the 'marginal' as a means of exploring women's cinema. Instead, she draws on the theoretical writings of Elisabeth Grosz, to affirm that 'making space for (and I would add, in) women's self-representations involves "the creation of maps and models of space and time based on projections of women's experiences" (1995: 100), and this in turn implies the possibility of a different space-time framework'.[11]

In our vision of a 're-territorialized' women's cinema, the space and time frameworks Thornham evokes are key spheres to reflect on differences, similarities and negotiations between regions of 'minority' and the 'majority'. In the films by Portuguese women directors analysed in this volume, these spaces include rural areas and natural landscapes, which are often opposed to the city, former Portuguese colonies in Africa and locations from around the world, including films shot in Japan, Brazil and Peru. Beyond the textual elements of these films, *Women's Cinema in Contemporary Portugal* also fills the existing gaps in Portuguese film history, in ways which include exploring less common genres in Portugal, from science fiction to horror, and topical issues in society, such as abortion and shifting maternal roles. This cinema also ventures into new territories by establishing very close links with literature on the one hand, and using digital filmmaking and the museum gallery on the other. In addition to this, women's cinema enjoys an increasingly diversified presence within the contemporary film industry, with new funding mechanisms and channels of distribution and exhibition emerging as both gendered and peripheral, albeit in an increasingly de-centred world. These films demonstrate that small nation (semi-)peripheral cinemas, and films made by women directors in particular, not only bring into focus a different view of space (the space that they themselves come to occupy and expand) but also shed light on different conceptions of time. The temporal frames explored include (shifting) traditions, memory and the archive, post-colonialism, and the contemporary context of the crisis.

Referring to the feminist filmmakers discussed by White, Sophie Mayer argues that

> what's 'new' about the twenty-first century 'new feminist cinema' observed in White's work is its negotiation of a transgenerational feminist film history of four decades within a reflexive awareness of the interruption and re-vision of feminisms, and interconnectedly of film cultures, in the new millennium.[12]

This begs some important questions for women filmmakers in 'small' and (semi-)peripheral cinema contexts. Which prior generations of female filmmakers are Portuguese women directors aware of in such a process, even if, as is usually the case in the culture industries, contemporary Portuguese women filmmakers tend to dismiss the 'feminist' label? Which film cultures will they reflect or refract in the new millennium? This volume makes two important points in this regard. First, there aren't many female directors in the history of Portuguese cinema, and the filmmakers named here seem to follow very individual routes.

Second, and as a consequence of this, filmmakers in Portugal have had to look beyond the nation for female precedents and exemplars in the film directing world. Indeed, it is noteworthy that many of these women directors received cinema training abroad.

Regardless of the directors' declared relationship, or otherwise, to prior feminist legacies and female genealogies, our book is deliberately called 'women's cinema', rather than referring to 'women directors', and we deploy this term in the same sense as White. We focus on filmmakers and directors who are women, but this is not a traditional auteur study. Authorship is, as Catherine Grant has pointed out, a largely inherited conceptual framework, which feminist film scholars need to evaluate carefully, although most do concur at some level that issues of gendered cultural agency and power are at stake.[13] Following her review of female auteurism as a historical concept, through landmark figures such as Claire Johnston, Kaja Silverman, Judith Mayne and Susan Martin-Márquez, Grant reaffirms the need for feminist dialogue between political questions of gendered agency and the formalist analysis of cinema aesthetics. To explore *Women's Cinema in Contemporary Portugal* thus involves both examining the conditions of film production, exhibition and criticism, that frame and condition the making and reception of films in terms of gender, and, simultaneously, analysing the narratives, style and aesthetics of these films.

Our focus on women's authorial status is more about positive discrimination than about engaging in what Katarzyna Paszkiewicz describes as 'the discourse of exceptionality'.[14] For instance, in her book on female subjectivities in contemporary French and British cinema, Kate Ince revisits Grant's work to argue for the need to overcome authorship as a label for exclusion. As Ince contends,

> A decisive move to jettison the term *auteur* while encouraging and embracing 'new directions in authorial film practice' was made by Rosanna Maule in *Beyond Auteurism* (Maule 2008), where she argues, like Grant in 'Secret Agents', that it remains valid to consider single directors as case studies, because 'it is still a relevant category in the critical evaluation of films, and more importantly, it is tied to a specific mode of film production and marketing' (Maule 2008: 15). To replace the tired term *auteur cinema*, Maule suggests 'author cinema', which although inelegant, has the distinct advantage of drawing attention to the director herself, her location and her politics.[15]

Our volume has deliberately and unavoidably engaged with authorship in contemporary Portuguese cinema in the first two chapters, and we have done this in recognition of our indebtedness to the vital role that archive retrieval and recuperation play in feminist film scholarship. Hence, the volume begins with two case studies of specific women filmmakers, Noémia Delgado and Margarida Gil. However, most of our chapters discuss at least two different directors, and focus primarily on analysing the cinematic features and the subject matter they espouse, usually centred on historical or political engagement of one kind or another. Thus, our decision to talk about films shot by women should not be read as a token of resurrected auteurism, but rather as a means of giving women the attention that film history – and particularly the history of Portuguese film – has repeatedly denied them, by allowing feminist subjectivity and agency to emerge as legitimate objects of textual and contextual analysis.

Approaching film and feminism in contemporary Portugal

As we observed earlier, different national film traditions have long since asserted the presence of their female-directed cinemas in oppositional relation to hegemonic mainstreams.[16] Following White's seminal study, scholars working on film and gender have also started looking at women's filmmaking across various different parts of the globe. To quote White's inspired afterword, 'Contemporary cinema studies must now contend with a critical mass of films by women directors; doing so could change the world.'[17] In light of this, and in refusing to subscribe to the notion of a women's national Portuguese canon that is doubly minor, our volume seeks instead to address the failure to consider the work of women filmmakers in the inter- and transnationalization of contemporary Portuguese cinema.

The planning and making of this book started in 2017, when its two editors were awarded a Calouste Gulbenkian Foundation grant to develop an eighteen-month project on Portuguese women directors. The project involved three main tasks: a roundtable on the topic of women in Portuguese film as part of the international symposium 'Women in Iberian Cinema' in September 2017; a film programme that showcased the work of contemporary Portuguese women directors, and which was screened over two weekends in January 2019; and the current collection of essays, which involved a workshop with contributors in Lisbon in September 2018. The fact that this project, and this book, involved an almost two-year-long collaborative process with academics in Portugal, the United Kingdom and the United States, as well as with filmmakers, producers and others working in Portuguese cinema, has made it an ambitious endeavour, looking at Portuguese culture through its close relationship with social issues, and through a transnational lens.[18]

Recent scholarship on contemporary Portuguese film has attempted to examine its transnational relevance. Horacio Muñoz Fernández and Iván Villarmea Álvarez, for instance, describe Portugal as having ceased to be a point of interest for foreign filmmakers fascinated by the nation's history and culture, to become instead one of the most important cinephile hubs on the international scene.[19] They argue that Portuguese filmmakers such as Pedro Costa, Miguel Gomes and Susana de Sousa Dias are now major points of reference in the art-house world cinema canon, and their work has become meaningful for international audiences and critics not just because of their unique aesthetic features but also because of the ways in which they frame history and memory in a more global language than that used by previous generations of Portuguese filmmakers.

History and memory also provide the focus for a special issue of the *Journal of Romance Studies*, edited by Sally Faulkner and Mariana Liz. Questioning in particular the transitions (and continuities) between colony and postcolony, this volume makes an important contribution to the international visibility of Portuguese cinema, stemming from a symposium and film screening on the topic held in London, UK, in January 2016. It brings together five English-language pieces on works by filmmakers such as Miguel Gomes and Margarida Cardoso, but also the less well-known (in a directorial role, at least) Maria de Medeiros along with Filipa César.[20] Finally, Mariana Liz's edited collection *Portugal's Global Cinema* reflects, as its title suggests, on the shifting significance of contemporary Portuguese film as it becomes increasingly present on the international stage.[21] Tellingly, these three works taken together include only four women filmmakers, out of a total of just over twenty Portuguese directors discussed across all three volumes. This renders all the more acute the need which we address in the current collection, to continue and expand the debate on the inter- and transnationalization of Portuguese film through a specifically gendered perspective that considers films directed by women.

Critical work on Portuguese women filmmakers remains very limited in both the Anglophone and the Lusophone academic worlds. In the former context, Portuguese women's cinema continues to be filtered through an 'Iberian' or 'Ibero-American' lens that positions it as a subset of Spain and the Spanish-speaking world.[22] Work in this field includes the volume *Hispanic and Lusophone Women Filmmakers*, edited by Parvati Nair and Julián Daniel Gutiérrez-Albilla.[23] This, however, had only one chapter out of a total of nineteen dedicated to women filmmakers from Portugal, leaving a highly dynamic area of Portuguese film seriously under-represented and confirmed in its status here as a relative, and potentially retrograde, 'minority'. An important forthcoming initiative, which challenges this, is the conference volume *Women in Iberian Cinema*, edited by Elena Cordero Hoyo and Begoña Soto-Vázquez.[24] The volume focuses on seven Portuguese women filmmakers and invites a more intense and sustained comparatism between the two Iberian countries, although only one of its chapters is itself comparative. Furthermore, the editors' definition of both Spain and Portugal in terms of a fairly uniform, undifferentiated 'periphery' leads them to fix Iberian women's cinema in the 'double minority' straightjacket – a stance which the present volume sets out to contest.

There is no doubt that the career paths of women filmmakers in Portugal have suffered negative differentiation on grounds of their gender. The two previous works on women filmmakers, published in Portugal, support and develop this view in concrete terms. *Cineastas Portuguesas 1874–1956*,[25] edited by António Cunha in 2000, is a series of interviews conducted by Ilda Castro with women (mostly but not all directors) in the film industry. It discusses the various factors that militated for and against them, and highlights the importance of access to the right social and cooperative networks, personal connections, and family or marital ties, as well as the lack of gender equality in respect of male-dominated funding bodies and grant-awarding panels. Ana Catarina Pereira's pioneering book from 2016, based on her doctoral thesis, *A Mulher-Cineasta*[26] follows up on this with some valuable statistical updates and empirical evidence on the status of women fiction film directors in Portugal in 2009, including their distribution and viewing figures.[27] Both of these studies were instrumental in encouraging us to undertake further work on the growing body of cinematic output by Portugal's women directors. Pereira affords a timely reminder of the need to read and interpret women's cinema in feminist theoretical terms, while the interviews in *Cineastas Portuguesas* inspired us to carry the political impulse behind that volume forward into a contemporary, transnational film studies environment.

Beyond academia, the two initiatives organized by our Gulbenkian-funded project in 2017 and 2019, that inform the current book, indicate that not much has changed since the *Cineastas* volume of interviews. The strongest debate of the roundtable held in September 2017 – which brought together a film producer, a director, a scriptwriter, a programmer and a publicist – was centred on the issue of intersectionality, and the difficulties experienced by women not only on account of their gender but also on the grounds of race and class. Although most of the women intervening in the debate highlighted a number of problems experienced by women working in the film sector, they also refused to be seen as 'feminists'. Similarly, the workshop held in Lisbon in 2018 for contributors to this volume highlighted how difficult it is for academics to discuss feminism in relation to Portugal, given the strength of ongoing resistance, which is often structural, and is also addressed in the current book.

The second major event organized by the project was the 'Mostra: Realizadoras Portuguesas',[28] a series of screenings of films directed by women. Seven feature films and four short films were shown in a total of eight sessions, which took place over two consecutive weekends at the start of 2019. Margarida Cardoso, Margarida Gil, Catarina Mourão, Raquel Freire, Susana de Sousa Dias, Marta Mateus and Leonor Teles were present to discuss their work with the audience, in Q&A sessions led by guests including film scholars, critics, programmers and archivists. This series projected a clear message that a very substantial body of cinematic work by women now exists, spanning many genres, formats and attitudes to the representation of Portugal and women. Here too, most directors disavowed feminism and did not address it as such, although most agreed that the relationship between women and film was a subject worthy of discussion.

Maria do Mar Pereira notes that Portugal has simultaneously 'undergone accelerated modernization in many spheres', but 'continues to be understood as having a "modernization deficit"'.[29] The films we study here often, in fact, address precisely the void left behind by Portugal's accelerated modernization. This is expressed in the contemporary era as a series of paradoxes that simultaneously position Portugal, as both peripheral and central, powerful and benign (it is a former colonizer in crisis), feminist and sexist, depending on the context of analysis. Portugal experienced a similar situation to than occurring in Spain, where, as Duncan Wheeler has argued, there was an abrupt change from pre- to post-feminism.[30] The change in legal status and political rights for women in Portugal was, if anything, even more sudden than in Spain, arising as it did from the dramatic turnaround of the 25 April 1974 Revolution, the strongly left-leaning Constitution of 1976 and the ongoing imperatives of democratic modernization, rather than from any sustained history of women's movement mobilization under the *Estado Novo* (New State) regime (1933–74).

Daniela Melo has observed that compared with Spain's more or less contemporaneous but very differently orchestrated transition from dictatorship to democracy, Portugal's 'women's movements, alliances with parties, and context (revolution versus negotiation) yielded faster gains for women in Portugal'.³¹ This was certainly true in relation to legal, civil and labour rights. Legalized abortion, however, did not figure on the modernizing political agendas of the mainstream parties on the left, as women's rights continued to be conceived in traditional Marxist economic terms of labour rights and workforce integration. Accelerated or otherwise, the process of democratic modernization in Portugal appeared to leave women behind in this fundamental respect, and the decriminalization of abortion was achieved only in 2007 after a laborious forty-year journey.³² This was followed three years later in 2010 by a significant rights landmark for lesbian women and gay men in Portugal with the legalizing of same-sex marriage.³³ Where the internationally successful films of João Pedro Rodrigues have brought an important Portuguese perspective to cinema directed by and about gay men, much remains to be done to achieve parallel exposure and opportunity for Portuguese lesbian and transgender filmmakers and representations. The films and writings of Raquel Freire are pioneering in this regard and warrant much wider circulation and appreciation.

Women's Cinema in Contemporary Portugal aims to contribute to these complex, ongoing public debates on gender by analysing the work of fourteen Portuguese women film directors, focusing on their production in both feature film and documentary genres over the last half-century. We make no pretence at full coverage. There are many more women film directors in Portugal worthy of in-depth study than those discussed here. We are also highly aware of the predominantly white, heterosexual and middle-class social milieu which most of our women directors represent, and which sadly, to some degree, mirrors the contours of Portugal's current filmmaking scene. A more intersectionally diverse approach to Portugal's filmmakers and films remains an urgent project further to our current one, which we hope the future will see unfold and which growing transnationalization should certainly foster and accelerate.

We also, necessarily, work from the post-25 April period only. Cinema was first introduced in Portugal as early as 1896, but the first feature-length fiction film directed by a Portuguese woman, *Três Dias sem Deus* by Bárbara Virgínia, was only released in 1946. This has now been lost and only brief excerpts, held at ANIM – Arquivo Nacional das Imagens em Movimento, the National Film Archive at the Portuguese Cinemathèque – as well as a number of promotional images, remain. Thirty years later in 1976, the second film directed by a Portuguese woman, Margarida Cordeiro, was *Trás-os-Montes*, co-directed with her more famous husband, António Reis. In the years between 1946 and 2009, Pereira charts only forty-eight full-length fiction films made by women directors.[34] It remains extremely difficult to produce figures for the proportion or percentage of women working in the film sector in Portugal.[35]

Films by Portuguese women directors are often about history, politics and the past, and/or they stress particular aspects of time and temporality. For instance, they explore different conceptions of rhythm and duration, as is the case with *48* (Susana de Sousa Dias, 2010) and *Tempo Comum* (*Ordinary Time*, Susana Nobre, 2018). Long takes characterize the vast majority of the twenty-three films examined in this book. While it generally retains classical narrative structures, the cinema of Portuguese women directors allows itself time to breathe, attributing cinematic meaning to characters and landscapes. Travelling and panoramic shots are also common, from the inaugural shot of Noémia Delgado's *Máscaras* (*Masks*, 1976) to the portrayal of the city and its key narrative scenes in Leonor Teles's *Balada de um Batráquio* (*Batrachian's Ballad*, 2016) – the opening and closing films of this book. Encompassing rural and urban areas in Portugal, the continent and the islands, and other countries in Europe and beyond, the landscape of this cinema is also that of the archive, where time and space are deeply connected. This is the case both for literal 'archive films', such as *Kuxa Kanema: O Nascimento do Cinema* (*Kuxa Kanema: The Birth of Cinema*, Margarida Cardoso, 2003), and for films *about* the archive, such as *Yvone Kane* (Margarida Cardoso, 2014).

Finally, in *Women's Cinema in Contemporary Portugal*, sound plays a role that is every bit as active as the carefully composed image, in films such as *Transe* (*Trance*; Teresa Villaverde, 2006), *Cartas a uma Ditadura* (*Letters to a Dictator*; Inês de Medeiros, 2006) and *Correspondências* (*Correspondences*; Rita Azevedo Gomes, 2016). Spoken words are incredibly important in films that draw, in the vast majority of cases, on literature, as a source of either adaptation or inspiration. Likewise, with the exception of *Yvone Kane*, all the films analysed here include meaningful musical soundtracks. Diegetic and non-diegetic music are often used to comment on the image and, significantly, to expand it; for instance, this is true of the traditional Portuguese folk music in *Masks*, the celebrated compositions of Ornatos Violeta for *Rasganço* (*Rending*; Raquel Freire, 2001) and the fado performances in *Adriana* (Margarida Gil, 2005).

In terms of genre, our book deliberately includes full-length and short documentary films alongside fiction, because women directors have made a particularly strong mark on the documentary field. One likely reason for this is that funding is more readily available than it is for making fiction films. The broad inclusive scope of our project allows us to chart the specific cinematic visions that women brought to the re-emergence of Portuguese national cinema in the wake of the 1974 Revolution and African decolonization, as well as to later debates on national memory and archival retrieval. Contemporary Portuguese films directed by women also highlight in particularly clear ways the spaces of production and circulation that Portugal's cinema occupies in the digital era. Screened at art-house cinemas, film societies, film festivals, galleries and museums, these films have won various international awards. Exploring both the aesthetic features of this cinema and its positioning in relation to global changes in film production, distribution and exhibition, the ten chapters in the volume are divided into four sections: 'Histories', 'Feminisms', 'Archives' and 'Transnationalisms'.

Overview

The first section on 'Histories' is the only one to retain a degree of connection with 'auteurism'. In Chapter 1, Manuela Penafria discusses the work of Noémia Delgado. The filmography of Delgado (1933–2016) spans a long period, between 1965 and 1988. However, as we will see, Delgado completed only one full-length film, the documentary *Masks*, in 1976. Delgado's lack of access to funding prevented her from making the many feature films that she planned, some of which involved discernibly feminist screenplays. Penafria examines both the conditions which women filmmakers in Portugal faced in the 1970s and the image of women's cinema that prevailed in Portugal during that period.

In contrast to Noémia Delgado, who made no further full-length films after the 1970s, Margarida Gil has sustained an active filmmaking career over more than three decades, but has encountered obstacles with distribution, critical reception and impact. In Chapter 2, Ana Isabel Soares examines Gil's career in cinema and television; her analysis is focused on seven fiction films that Gil directed between 1986 and 2019: *Relação Fiel e Verdadeira* (*True and Faithful*, 1987), *Rosa Negra* (*Black Rose*, 1992), *O Anjo da Guarda* (*The Guardian Angel*, 1998), *Adriana* (2005), *Perdida Mente* (*Mind Loss*, 2010), *Paixão* (*Passion*, 2012) and *Mar* (*Sea*, 2019).

Section Two on 'Feminisms' explores the ways in which women filmmakers have engaged in overtly feminist campaigns such as those relating to abortion law reform, as well as with contemporary political concerns such as immigration, the environment and the effects of austerity economics. Teresa Villaverde, Portugal's most successful and best-known woman director, and the target of a major retrospective at the Centre Pompidou in Paris, in the summer of 2019, features in all the chapters in this section.[36] In Chapter 3, Hilary Owen discusses fiction films by Villaverde (*Os Mutantes* (*The Mutants*, 1998)), Raquel Freire (*Rending*) and Solveig Nordlund (*Aparelho Voador a Baixa Altitude* (2002)) to explore the ways in which these three directors, working in the late 1990s and early 2000s, made eclectic use of specific cinema genres and sub-genres rarely developed in Portugal to convey challenging, countercultural ideas about women, reproductive rights and biopolitics. Following a 'posthuman' theoretical stance,[37] Owen argues that all three directors deploy 'other worlds' as landscapes for a new 'posthuman' sexual aesthetic, in order to comment allegorically on the need for dialogue between feminism, socialism and materialism in the abortion debates of the late twentieth century.

Whereas in Chapter 3 Owen argues for a level of political engagement in the three films she explores by Portuguese women directors in the late 1990s and early 2000s, in Chapter 4, Mariana Liz underlines a contrasting absence of political commitment, or, more specifically, an ambiguity, in the way in which women filmmakers are intervening in important societal debates, in the second decade of the twentieth century. Liz thus takes a very different angle on the discussion of maternity as conceptualized in the work of Portuguese women directors. Her focus is on notions of home, family and parenthood in the films *Colo* (Teresa Villaverde, 2017) and *Ordinary Time*. With stories about the creation and destruction of families in contemporary Portugal, these films challenge the notion of crisis beyond financial paradigms, depicting, at the same time, a post-austerity Lisbon, which allows for an analysis of Portugal's modernity through these films' representations of urban space.

In Chapter 5, by Patrícia Vieira, urban space is contrasted with nature. Vieira explores the ways in which Portuguese women directors have used landscapes to address social issues. Returning to Noémia Delgado's *Masks* and comparing it with the landscapes of Villaverde's *Transe*, she draws on eco-feminist theories to argue that these two films symbolize the oppression of vulnerable women. As Vieira claims, female directors in Portugal have explored and subverted the traditional link between female characters and the natural world in order to criticize established gender mores and patriarchal social structures.

Section Three on 'Archives' focuses on the contribution that women film directors have made to the emergence of memory and post-memory politics in documentary, found footage and the essay film genres, which recollect the New State and its resistance, the Colonial War, and African independence. In Chapter 6, Estela Vieira addresses image, history and politics in Margarida Cardoso's *Kuxa Kanema* and *48*. As noted above, women filmmakers in Portugal have been particularly interested in documentary as a genre, and in using archival footage in their work to address and illustrate complex, open-ended political realities. This chapter analyses the ways in which the visual configuration of these films constitutes a powerful political statement in its own right that speaks not only to political history but also to a woman's role in the retelling of unresolved stories.

In Chapter 7, Alison Ribeiro de Menezes examines the use of archive in Portuguese documentaries by two women filmmakers: Inês de Medeiros's *Letters to a Dictator* and Susana de Sousa Dias's *48*. Menezes's analysis focuses on the affective strategies that are used to present subjects within the context of dictatorship memory: on the one hand, female interviewees who are presented with their own letters written to Salazar in 1958; on the other, photographs of detainees from the PIDE archive. Through an examination of montage and sound, Menezes presents us with a 'deviant' use of the archive for new purposes, alongside the framing of these sources within appeals for a new vision of the past. These two chapters are particularly important for an understanding of how this work by Portuguese women directors, even when it is apparently not adopting an overtly feminist stance, offers new, frequently gendered, perspectives on history and film which use global strategies to displace the 'marginalized' nation onto a transnational stage.

Ribeiro de Menezes's piece also functions as a useful transition between a more marked analysis of historical topics and a focused examination of film genre and form. Hence, in Chapter 8, Ana Cabral Martins discusses the developing genre of the 'essay film' by focusing on Rita Azevedo Gomes's *Correspondences*. This 2016 film was inspired by the letters exchanged between the Portuguese poets Sophia de Mello Breyner Andresen and Jorge de Sena, during Sena's exile. It is a historical document of both the dictatorship and its collective memory, as well as a unique film object with strong literary credentials. Cabral Martins's argument is that Rita Azevedo Gomes's career has, much like the essay film itself, similarly straddled an 'in-between space', working either in purely fictional territory or within a documentary-driven, more or less essayistic space, and that *Correspondences* therefore functions as a useful case study for the new territories being charted by women directors in contemporary Portugal. The film was screened at Locarno, Edinburgh and the Buenos Aires International Festival of Independent Cinema, and is also a testimony to the international appeal of innovative films from Portugal dealing with the national history of the country.

Section Four on 'Transnationalisms' explicitly draws Portuguese women's cinema into dialogue with international influences. Chapter 9, by Sally Faulkner, takes as its starting point Margarida Cardoso's acknowledgement of the Argentinian director Lucrecia Martel as an influence on her work and proceeds to analyse Cardoso's *Yvone Kane* in relation to a series of themes and techniques that Martel displays in her earliest feature films. These include the representation of the middle classes, Western ennui and guilt, a troubling and troubled childhood, and the investigation of ageing female characters. Unlike Martel, however, probably one of the best-known women filmmakers in the contemporary era – named president of the Jury of the Venice Film Festival in 2019 – Cardoso's work remains relatively obscure. Faulkner discusses matters of film production, distribution and marketing as well as the stylistic and aesthetic considerations that have conditioned the development (or otherwise) of strong auteurist 'brands' for each of these filmmakers.

Finally, Chapter 10, by Filipa Rosário, explores the career paths of four successful young women directors from Portugal, as they direct prizewinning documentary films, which are attracting attention on major festival circuits. Drawing on interviews with Joana Pimenta, Salomé Lamas, Cláudia Varejão and Leonor Teles, Rosário examines *Um Campo de Aviação* (*An Aviation Field*; Joana Pimenta, 2016), *Eldorado XXI* (Salomé Lamas, 2016), *Ama-San* (Cláudia Varejão, 2016) and *Batrachian's Ballad*. Her argument is that a new cinematic sensibility, stimulated perhaps by the Portuguese financial crisis (2010–14), has been emerging, and that this has, in turn, transformed contemporary cinema made by women in Portugal. Rosário maps out these new practices while examining the art-house production companies responsible for them, as well as charting the four directors' own perspectives on filmmaking. In a sense dialoguing directly with the book's opening chapter, on the constraints experienced by women filmmakers in 1970s Portugal, this chapter paints an image of emerging opportunities and the apparent freedom that is enjoyed by young female directors. Whereas Chapter 1 was focused on Portugal's transition to democracy, as well as on the tentative opening to a more globalized world, Chapter 10 argues that contemporary Portuguese cinema is now clearly defined by its cosmopolitan nature.

Problematizing matters of film and feminism over the last five decades, this volume charts the evolution Portuguese cinema, and Portuguese women directors in particular, has undergone in an increasingly globalized, and gendered, context. The idea of spatial and temporal re-territorialization is particularly apt for the framing of the cinema considered here because, as the foregoing chapters show, these films testify to the lack of a cinematographic centre. Hence the importance of considering other places, with their specific spatial and temporal features, in approaches to contemporary cinema directed by women. From the idea of minority, we thus move to an understanding of difference that frames it as positive, rather than marginal. And the works of our stellar cast of women directors, whom we listed at the outset, are representative of Portuguese cinema as world cinema in ways which make a positive difference.

Notes

1 Patricia White, *Women's Cinema, World Cinema: Projecting Contemporary Feminisms* (Durham: Duke University Press, 2015).
2 According to data by the European Audiovisual Observatory, Portugal is one of the eighteen nations in Europe (out of a total of thirty-eight) producing fewer than twenty-five films a year. See the 'Film production in Europe report' https://rm.coe.int/filmproductionineurope-2017-j-talavera-pdf/1680788952 (accessed 9 July 2019). According to ICA, twenty-three feature fiction films were produced in Portugal in 2018. See ICA, 'Cinema/Audiovisual from Portugal 2019', https://ica-ip.pt/fotos/editor2/catalogo2019/ICA_CATALOGO_2019.pdf (accessed 9 July 2019).
3 For a definition and problematization of the term, see Mette Hjort and Duncan Petrie (eds), *The Cinema of Small Nations* (Edinburgh: Edinburgh University Press, 2007).
4 Anne Jäckel, 'Changing the Image of Europe? The Role of European Co-Productions, Funds and Film Awards', in *The Europeanness of European Cinema: Identity, Meaning, Globalization*, eds Mary Harrod, Mariana Liz and Alissa Timoshkina (London: I.B. Tauris, 2015), 60.
5 Janelle Blankenship and Tobias Nagl, 'Introduction: Towards a Politics of Scale', in *European Visions: Small Cinemas in Transition*, eds Janelle Blankenship and Tobias Nagl (Bielefeld: Transcript Verlag, 2015), 15.
6 Lúcia Nagib, 'Towards a Positive Definition of World Cinema', in *Remapping World Cinema: Identity, Culture and Politics in Film*, eds Stephanie Dennison and Song Hwee Lim (London: Wallflower Press, 2006), 30–7.

7   Mette Hjort, 'The Risk Environment of Small-Nation Filmmaking', in *European Visions*, 49–64.
8   Alison Butler, *Women's Cinema: The Contested Screen* (London: Wallflower, 2002), 20.
9   Boaventura de Sousa Santos, 'State and Society in Portugal', in *After the Revolution: Twenty Years of Portuguese Literature, 1974–1994*, eds Helena Kaufman and Anna Klobucka (Lewisburg: Bucknell University Press, 1997), 34.
10 White, *Women's Cinema, World Cinema*, 13.
11 Sue Thornham, *Spaces of Women's Cinema: Space, Place and Gender in Contemporary Women's Filmmaking* (New York: Bloomsbury/BFI, 2019), 11.
12 Sophie Mayer, *Political Animals: The New Feminist Cinema* (London: I.B. Tauris, 2016), 6.
13 Catherine Grant, 'Secret Agents: Feminist Theories of Women's Film Authorship', *Feminist Theory* 2, no. 1 (2001), 113–30.
14 Katarzyna Paszkiewicz, *Genre, Authorship and Contemporary Women Filmmakers* (Edinburgh: Edinburgh University Press, 2018), 5.
15 Kate Ince, *The Body and the Screen: Female Subjectivities in Contemporary Women's Cinema* (New York: Bloomsbury, 2017), 39.
16 A number of research projects have emerged in recent years, namely 'Calling the Shots: Women and Contemporary Film Culture in the UK, 2000–2015', based at the University of Southampton. Beyond the Anglophone context, see for instance, in the Portuguese-language context, *Feminino e Plural: Mulheres no Cinema Brasileiro*, eds Karla Holanda and Marina Cavalcanti Tedesco (São Paulo: Editora Papirus, 2017); and on the Spanish context, which is also of interest for the case of Portugal, *Cineastas Emergentes: Mujeres en el cine del siglo XXI*, eds Annette Scholz and Marta Álvarez (Madrid: Iberoamericana, 2018).
17 White, *Women's Cinema, World Cinema*, 201.
18 Our commitment to a transnational perspective was also inspired by participation in an international conference at Wadham College, University of Oxford, in the UK, in March 2017, dedicated to 'Transnational Portuguese Women Artists and Writers'. Proceedings are forthcoming in a special number of *Portuguese Studies* 35, no. 2 (Autumn 2019), eds Cláudia Pazos Alonso and Maria Luísa Coelho.
19 Horacio Muñoz Fernández and Iván Villarmea Álvarez (eds), *Jugar con la Memoria: El cine portugués en el siglo XXI* (Shangrila/a cuarta parede: Santander, 2014).
20 Sally Faulkner and Mariana Liz (eds), 'Portuguese Film: Colony, Postcolony, Memory', Special issue of *Journal of Romance Studies* 16, no. 2 (2016), 1–120.
21 Mariana Liz (ed.), *Portugal's Global Cinema: Industry, History and Culture* (London: I.B. Tauris, 2018).
22 See also, for instance, Alberto Mira (ed.), *The Cinema of Spain and Portugal* (London: Wallflower, 2005), where again only four out of twenty-four single-film chapters are on Portuguese films. With thanks to Belén Vidal for pointing us to this example.

23 Parvati Nair and Julián Daniel Gutiérrez-Albilla (eds), *Hispanic and Lusophone Women Filmmakers: Theory, Practice and Difference* (Manchester: Manchester University Press, 2013).
24 Elena Cordero Hoyo and Begoña Soto-Vázquez (eds), *Women in Iberian Cinemas: A Feminist Approach to Spanish and Portuguese Filmic Culture* (London: Intellect, forthcoming).
25 António Cunha (ed.), *Cineastas Portuguesas 1874–1956* (Lisbon: Câmara Municipal de Lisboa, 2000).
26 Ana Catarina Pereira, *A Mulher-Cineasta: da arte pela arte a uma estética da diferenciação* (Covilhã: LABCOM.IFP, Universidade da Beira Interior, 2016).
27 Ibid., 197.
28 For more on the 'Mostra', and on the project, please see https://portuguesewomendi rectors.wordpress.com/mostra-2/ (accessed 2 July 2019).
29 Maria do Mar Pereira, 'The Importance of Being "Modern" and Foreign', *Signs* 39, no. 3 (2014), 634.
30 Duncan Wheeler, 'The (Post-)Feminist Condition: Women Filmmakers in Spain', *Feminist Media Studies* 16, no. 6 (2016), 1057–77.
31 Daniela Melo, 'Women's Movements in Portugal and Spain: Democratic Processes and Policy Outcomes', *Journal of Women, Politics and Policy* 38, no. 3 (2017), 268.
32 For an account of the complex coalition-building and 'velvet alliances' that women's groups deployed in abortion campaigning, and the role of the EU from the mid-1980s onwards, see Daniela F. Melo, 'The European Union, Executive Politics, and the Women's Movement in Portugal: The Consequences of Europeanization, 1986 to the Present', in *The Gendered Executive: A Comparative Analysis of Presidents, Prime Ministers, and Chief Executives,* eds Janet E. Martin and MaryAnne Borrelli (Philadelphia: Temple University Press, 2016), 165–84.
33 For an account of the journey towards same-sex marriage legislation, by the MP and activist who led the campaign in Portugal's parliament, see Miguel Vale de Almeida, 'Tripping over History: Same-Sex Marriage in Portugal', *Anthropology Today* 28, no. 3 (2012), 24–7.
34 Pereira, *A Mulher-Cineasta*, 183–5.
35 Rui Telmo Gomes, Teresa Duarte Martinho and Vanda Lourenço, *Carreiras Profissionais Segundo o Género na Produção de Cinema* (Lisbon: Observatório das Actividades Culturais, 2005).
36 Together with Catarina Mourão, Teresa Villaverde was the only Portuguese director examined in the July/August 2019 issue of *Cahiers du Cinéma*, devoted to the history of women filmmakers. For a list of directors analysed, and further information on the journal, see https://www.cahiersducinema.com/produit/juill et-aout-2019-n757/?fbclid=IwAR0dIJpHV1gvSzJ7eyl8R3jAA49LX8bpd_CsBosV9y kBQarFAoN9Ar41CNM (accessed 10 July 2019).
37 See for instance Elaine Graham, *Representations of the Post/Human: Monsters, Aliens and Others* (New Brunswick: Rutgers University Press, 2002).

Section One

Histories

1

Unfinished:
The cinema of Noémia Delgado

Manuela Penafria

A cinema with no films.[1] This short, seemingly flippant, statement at the start of a text on the Portuguese film director, Noémia Delgado (São Pedro da Chibia, Angola, 7 June 1933–Lisbon, 2 March 2016), is not intended to be read literally. Rather, it is a statement that sets out to locate Delgado in the history of Portuguese cinema, by highlighting how her work is characterized by the non-completion of cinema projects. More specifically, it is about proposals for films that were never completed, but which she intended to screen in film theatres. Her actual, completed filmography is sparse. *Máscaras* (*Masks*, 1976), a documentary shot in Trás-os-Montes, in the northern hinterland of Portugal (see also Patrícia Vieira in this volume), is the only film that would appear to justify Delgado's inclusion in the history of Portuguese cinema, since nearly all of her filmography was directed for television, and is therefore considered 'secondary'. The purpose of the current chapter is, nonetheless, to present and discuss Delgado's filmography, which covers the period from 1965 to 1988.

In order to do so, I have adopted what I have termed *teoria dos cineastas*, or 'filmmaker theory'. This emphasizes the filmmakers' own critical considerations and reflections as evinced in their written statements (including books, texts and manifestos), as well as in their verbal pronouncements in interviews, so as to ascertain the concept of cinema that they work with.[2] In Delgado's case, I adopt the term 'filmography' in its widest sense, as this allows me to go beyond the list of films which she worked on or actually directed, in order to include films that she wanted to direct but which, through no fault of her own, did not make it to the screen. These I will call 'film projects'. In her filmography, both finished films and film projects are read as symptomatic, reflecting a particular vision of cinema, because they do ultimately evidence a certain will to artistic creativity.

In order to convey Delgado's thought, poetics and affiliations, I will begin by discussing her actual filmography, and by highlighting the preponderance of documentary production within this. On the one hand, there is the single feature-length documentary that she made, *Masks*, which can be broadly aligned with ethnographic cinema. On the other, there exists a considerable corpus of biographical and cultural documentary, mostly short films screened on television, although Delgado also directed screen adaptations of short stories and novels written by Portuguese authors. In the second part of the chapter, using interviews given by Delgado as my primary source, as well as two interviews that Delgado conducted with other Portuguese directors, in which the issues addressed clearly reveal her own concerns as a film director, I will focus on her five film projects and her own personal concept of cinema. In that context, I highlight statements such as 'cinema is a form of dreaming', as well as her affirmation that films must be made viscerally, or as she puts it, in more explicitly female biological terms, *com o útero*, that is, 'with the womb'.

Noémia Delgado's filmography

Delgado's career in cinema began in the 1960s, at the height of *Cinema Novo*, the Portuguese New Cinema era, where she was involved in editing iconic films from the early years of this key period in Portuguese film history. She worked as an editing assistant on Paulo Rocha's films, *Os verdes anos* (1963), *Mudar de vida* (1966) and *A Pousada das Chagas* (1972). In the same role, she worked on *Pássaros de asas cortadas* (Artur Ramos, 1963), *… E era o mar* (José Fonseca e Costa, 1966), *Faça segundo a arte* (Faria de Almeida, 1965), *Moçambique 65* (Faria de Almeida, 1965) and *A pérola do Atlântico* (José Fonseca e Costa, 1968). In the early 1970s she participated in the editing process of *O passado e o presente* (*Past and Present*; Manoel de Oliveira, 1972), as well as of *Meus amigos* (António da Cunha Telles, 1974). Working across documentary and fiction genres, Delgado began her cinematic career in editing, working on the creation of image sequences, which necessarily followed a specific logic or poetics.

Delgado began working as a director making short films for the newsreel series *Cinemagazine*. She directed three black and white films in 35 mm format, which were produced by Cunha Telles Productions and dated 1965: *Amoladores*, *Fotógrafos Ambulantes* and *Escultura de João Cutileiro*. In 1972, she directed *Mafra e o Barroco Europeu*, a 35 mm format short colour film, referenced as a commission by Torralta.³ After working intensively as an editor, then, Delgado began to work as a director on short, supporting films, which were shown before the projection of the main feature. Even after she started directing in 1965, she continued to work as assistant director, for instance, on António de Macedo's *Alta Velocidade* (1967), a film about the production of car engines in Portugal. She was also an assistant director (although uncredited) on the film *Torre Bela* (Thomas Harlan, 1971), as well as editing assistant in its recut Portuguese version.

The last reference to Delgado, before she herself took up directing, is found in the credits and special thanks of the film *Deus, Pátria, Autoridade* (1975), directed by Rui Simões. This collaboration on Simões's film immediately precedes Delgado's most significant film, *Masks*, from 1976. Her collaboration with Rui Simões on an acutely political film about governmental and social evolution in Portugal, exposing the fascist regime that had just been overthrown, emerges as a very logical step to take, in light of her opposition to the New State (*Estado Novo*, 1933–74) regime. Delgado had been arrested by the New State's secret police force PIDE (*Polícia Internacional e de Defesa do Estado*) in 1965 and imprisoned for a month in Caxias because, allegedly, 'the Soviet Union had partly financed'⁴ one of her trips to Paris. The fact that her name is mentioned in the credits of *Deus, Pátria, Autoridade* is not surprising in that context, but since it was a fairly low-key collaboration, it indicates that she was probably already involved in the filming of *Masks* at the time. This effectively aligns Delgado with the vision of other Portuguese film directors of the same period, including António Reis and Margarida Cordeiro, who found in Trás-os-Montes, a space where they could celebrate freedom and search for a potentially lost national identity that could be recovered through cinema, during the Carnation Revolution of 25 April 1974 as well as immediately after it, and into the revolutionary period known as the PREC (*Processo Revolucionário em Curso*) (1974–6).

Masks (see Figure 1.1) was a pivotal experience for Delgado as a film director. It helped her to assert her own identity in relation to the predominantly male world of cinema in Portugal, and also in relation to a world where the urban experience was considered to be the norm. As Delgado has put it,

> It was my first feature film and I was working with an all-male team. Paulo Rocha had told me that I had to be better than ten men in order to make the film. At the time I was pissed off, I wasn't there to measure myself up against anyone else.⁵

Figure 1.1 A man removes his mask in Noémia Delgado's 1976 *Masks* (Cinemateca Portuguesa-Museu do Cinema).

In Trás-os-Montes, Delgado recorded the festivities known as the *Ciclo de Inverno*, or Winter Cycle. She filmed Christmas with its *Festa dos Rapazes* (Young Men's Festivity) in Varge, the Saint Stephen's festivities in Grijó de Parada, New Year's Eve in Bemposta, the Epiphany in Rio de Onor and finally Carnival in Podence. In the only city used in this film, Bragança, she shot the Ash Wednesday holiday of 1975. As Delgado puts it,

> I wanted to make a natural-looking film with minimum directorial intervention; I wanted the masks of Trás-os-Montes to be accurately represented, to lay down fundamental elements of their centuries-old tradition. After all, these rituals are how people live and breathe in Trás-os-Montes. I wanted the film to share that, but, since there is no such thing as an innocent film, there are also some reflections of my own.[6]

Confronted with a world of great visual wealth and a unique culture, the 'naturalness' and lack of intervention that Delgado refers to are evident in the observational register that emerges and sets the tone for the whole film. However, the intended accuracy of her recording does not imply there was no directorial interference.

Her intervention is, in fact, discernible on various levels. Right at the beginning, for instance, Delgado requests that the *Festa dos Rapazes* be restaged, while the recreation of this festivity in Rio de Onor is described by a voiceover. The audience is told that the festival had to be recreated because the ritual is no longer actually held since emigration has caused an exodus of the youth. Similarly, the audience is informed by a voiceover stating that the tradition, which involved Death wandering the streets of Bragança and the Devil chasing girls has now been 'completely lost', and so the images in the film are merely an attempt to recreate and explain the meaning of these characters. The constant voiceover is also the director's own voice, as she addresses the audience to tell them what the image cannot explain with regard to time and space. For instance, the audience is told, 'In Podence, unlike what happens in other villages, the masked men appear at Carnival, and the Saint Stephen's Day festivities are held on 26 and 27 December.' The use of natural sound, in line with the observational register of the film, highlights the actual physical presence and existence of a group of boys in disguise. Yet, immediately afterwards, there is a scene in which the boys are having supper, and classical music is heard in the background, overlapping with the sounds of the scene's natural environment. At another point in the film, an image of some baskets of bread is set to its own soundtrack. These choices signal the representation of a collective imaginary. The scene with the supper that would seem to call for natural environmental sound, for instance, is transformed, through music, into a timeless moment.

Deployed in the precise sense that pictorial art uses it, the term 'portrait' contributes to our understanding of *Masks*. A portrait is the representation of a distinctiveness that identifies and characterizes the person depicted. In painting, the face reveals the skill of the portrait through the expressivity and affectivity of its features. In cinema, however, which deals with moving images, identity cannot be reduced either to immobility or to a single figure. If the portrait genre precludes action and 'the only actions admissible in a portrait are those that reinforce the "selfhood" of the person portrayed',[7] in the case of *Masks*, these actions are most readily expressed through collective representations, for instance, of a group of people engaged in a single action. In all these rituals, individuality becomes subordinate or non-existent. In *Masks*, several faces make up a single community that shares the same mode of existence. In this sense, there is a particularly telling close-up in which one of the masked men, who is facing the viewer, removes his mask. The camera immediately homes in on this young man who then hides his face behind the mask again. The sound of classical music heard in the background makes this close-up shot a supreme moment of identity disclosure, in which the young man's face is compared with the mask that he is wearing. For Catarina Alves Costa,[8] *Masks* may be read as an ethnographic documentary film, along with *Vilarinho das Furnas* (1969) and *Falámos de Rio de Onor* (1974), directed by António Campos, and *Festa, trabalho e pão em Grijó de Parada* (1973), directed by Manuel Costa e Silva. Ethnographic documentary cinema sits somewhere between 'ethnographic archive film' and a kind of 'poetic cinema' calling on the 'ethnographic imagination'. Or to put it differently, on the one hand, there are ethnographic archive films that are 'directly connected with ethnography as a field of study and are characterized by their mission to record ... in which cinematography is bound by the idea of an unmediated observation of reality'.[9] On the other hand, there is the 'ethnographic imagination' that is exemplified in *Trás-os-Montes* (António Reis and Margarida Cordeiro, 1976). *Trás-os-Montes* is the kind of film which, as Costa puts it, 'visits a forgotten, archaic, romanticized and aestheticized world ... the kind of cinema that ultimately represents the rural world in a cinematographically reconstructed past'.[10]

In Delgado's view, cinema is meant to transcend reality without denying or eliminating it. In this sense, a particular imaginary vision remains consistently grounded in the reality that underpins it. For instance, Delgado makes a point of highlighting a further possible reading of the film. She recognizes that particular forms of social organization and a specific place are allocated to women, and to the way in which they participate in the rituals of Trás-os-Montes:

> Connected to the cycles of *birth, life* and *death*, all the corresponding elements are embodied in the masked men and their rituals. ... These are mysteries that exclude the presence of women, whose only role is to wash the intestines of the sacrificed animal.[11]

Although her film draws on the 1973 book *Máscaras Portuguesas* by the anthropologist Benjamim Pereira, *Masks* goes beyond the boundaries of strict ethnographic observation, without, at the same time, becoming purely imaginary either. The fact that Delgado herself draws attention to the role of women in the rituals indicates her refusal to record only the realm of the imaginary.

There are also everyday situations that the audience needs to see. *Trás-os-Montes* is based on an imaginary idea, an 'essence' that precedes the moment when the film is shot – and this 'essence' is then embodied in specific actions and cultural events. *Masks* effectively does the opposite of this, homing in on certain gestures and rituals, in order to reveal their 'essence'. The raw truth of these gestures emerges, for instance, in the killing of a goat, which is not glossed over, but brutally exposed. Delgado does not withhold, deny or conceal reality. She alternates, throughout the whole film, between the raw recording of events, explanations in voiceover and a soundtrack that lends every gesture an aura of its distant, ancestral past. What she records, as a result, is a particular mode of existence in the world.

There are two further titles in addition to *Masks* that demonstrate the director's commitment to representing popular culture. The films *Sombra, luz, ritmo* (1976) and *Ensaio no moinho* (1978) are more a series of recordings than actual finished films, as they have no opening or closing credits. In the first of these, there is a series of soundless shots, during which the camera, positioned indoors, shows an area with shadows and another area that is lit, apparently by natural light. A group of masked boys emerges from the shadows; when they become visible, we see them jumping, dancing and interacting with each other, or pitching hay with a stick. In the film *Ensaio no moinho* the location is a windmill where the rehearsals for the *Festa dos Rapazes* seem to be taking place. These are clearly unfinished films, but they are valuable as recordings, and useful for an analysis of Delgado's work. Although she does not mention *Ensaio no moinho*, Delgado does refer to *Sombra, luz e ritmo* in a 2010 interview, as a finished film in the sense that 'it was an experiment in gathering images. Not a very successful one. I should have known the men could not put those things across without being able to voice them.'[12]

After this foray into ethnographic cinema, Delgado worked exclusively for television. The remaining documentaries in her filmography are essentially short biographical films, which afford something of a contrast with *Masks*. The particular interest of these films, which were directed between 1977 and 1988 for Portuguese public television channel RTP (particularly for RTP's second channel, RTP2, which was launched in 1968 and has always been more culturally oriented), is that they reveal a different approach to documentary filmmaking. Delgado establishes a clear distinction between directing for big screen and small. Her television biographies focus clearly on ways of living in and interacting with the world rather than on the purely existential. The portrait genre, capturing the face and the essence of a person, tends to preclude 'action'[13] – but it is precisely the actions of the subjects in question that are foregrounded in these biographical films made for television.

In 1977 she directed four films, entitled *Eça de Queirós: Notas breves sobre, Camilo Castelo Branco, Camilo Pessanha: entre dois abismos* and *Almeida Garrett 1799-1854: escrever é lutar*, for the *As Palavras Herdadas* series.[14] These are short films, shot in 16 mm, colour, and dealing with canonical nineteenth-century Portuguese writers. Most of them feature a voiceover that tells us the writer's date of birth at the beginning and date of death at the end. This information demarcates their physical existence as a presence in the world that begins and ends the film. Between the first and the second of these dates, the films follow a specific trajectory. The first appearance of each writer is either a statue, as in the case of Camilo Pessanha, or a non-photographic image, such as a painting for Almeida Garret, and a caricature for Eça de Queirós. The exception is Camilo Castelo Branco, who appears in a black and white photo about which we are told: 'My biography is simply the statement that I was born and that is all. I have no biography.' Consequently, in the only case where there is a photograph, the comment we hear denies the possibility of a biography. What Delgado's approach seems to emphasize is the legacy that each writer has left behind, through his literary works and his imprint on the world. By playing down the common elements that usually characterize this type of film, such as images of the author's face, Delgado directs our attention towards their actions, in contrast to the 'portraiture' of *Masks*, which is a film about the collective personality of the people of Trás-os-Montes.

Quem foste, Alvarez? (1988), dealing with the life of the Portuguese modernist painter Dominguez Alvarez (1906–42), is a film which uses several voices. The first voice that speaks in the film uses a photograph to introduce us to the house where Alvarez was born. After a brief argument in a café about whether an artist is always appreciated more after his death, a voiceover tells us that Alvarez was 'a preeminent figure of that Expressionist generation which became synonymous with fantasy and anguish in the imaginary of 1930s modernity'. As in her other films, Delgado takes biography as necessarily referring to a person's actions in the world, manifested in this case through works of art which survive their authors. Delgado also contributed three films to the *Artistas* series: *Simone (25 anos a cantar)* (1982), *Rogério Paulo – actor, encenador português* (1982) and *Rui de Carvalho – actor* (1982). These are short 16 mm colour films dealing with figures that would be well known to Portuguese audiences. In all of these, there is a particular emphasis on actions rather than on close-ups of faces, which would tend to make physical features indicative of unique personality traits. As with her biographies of Portuguese writers, the spotlight is on their performances and on what they actually did in their lives.

In addition to these biographical works, Delgado made other films that had a cultural focus. She directed films on *Regiões Vinícolas Portuguesas* (Portuguese Wine Regions) in 1982 and 1983, and between 1985 and 1986 she directed six television programmes, entitled *Arte Nova e Deco no Norte de Portugal* for RTP. In 1986 and 1987 she also shot a television series entitled *O trabalho do ouro e da prata no Norte*. Between 1979 and 1983 Delgado directed several films for television, most of them short films based on works of literature. This brings us to an issue of fundamental importance for Portuguese cinema, that of adaptation. The first film in this collaboration with RTP, entitled *O ladrão do pão* (1979), is an adaptation of a poem of the same name by Alexandre O'Neill. Delgado also directed several adaptations for the television series *Contos Fantásticos*, including *O Visconde* (1980), adapted from *Os Canibais* by Álvaro Carvalhal, which would later inspire Manoel de Oliveira's 1988 film of the same title. Other adaptations directed by Delgado and named after literary works include *A princesinha das rosas* (1981), based on a short story by Fialho de Almeida; *Tiaga – Reincarnação deliciosa* (1981), from a short story by Aquilino Ribeiro; *O defunto* (1981), from an Eça de Queirós's short story; *O canto da sereia* (1983), from a short story by Júlio Dinis; *A noite de Walpurgis* (1983), from a short story by Hugo Rocha; and *A estranha morte do Professor Antena* (1983), with a screenplay inspired by a Mário de Sá Carneiro short story. According to Delgado, who is heard in voiceover at the beginning of each film, these motion pictures are described as 'derived from', 'inspired by' or 'freely adapted'. The director thus makes a point of highlighting her own creative intervention.

To sum up thus far, Delgado's professional activity may be framed within two main Portuguese cinema contexts. The first centres on her participation in Portuguese *Cinema Novo* or New Cinema where she performed minor roles such as editing assistant. She then directed *Masks*, which was funded by IPC-Instituto Português do Cinema (Portuguese Cinema Institute) and produced by CPC-Centro Português de Cinema (Portuguese Cinema Centre), a director's cooperative, which was, along with the Calouste Gulbenkian Foundation, responsible for most of the *Cinema Novo* film output. While other *Cinema Novo* directors completed their training abroad, this proved more difficult for Delgado. In 1965 she applied for a scholarship from the Secretariado Nacional de Informação (SNI – Information State Department) and was accepted at the London School of Film Technique, but the SNI subsequently suspended the public competition in which she had been the only candidate.[15] In 1971 she finally obtained a Calouste Gulbenkian Foundation scholarship to do an internship with Jean Rouch in Paris. However, Delgado's association with the CPC was not a happy one, and she was expelled for being interviewed by Alfredo Tropa on RTP. On this subject, the director herself claims that

> they were very angry because they didn't like Alfredo Tropa, but I never understood why they didn't get annoyed with [José] Fonseca e Costa, who was also interviewed by him. It seemed to me more like a male versus female thing and they ganged up. I went to work in Rome in 1976.[16]

At the end of the 1970s and throughout the whole of the 1980s, as noted above, Delgado embarked on the second phase of her professional career, working in television production. The public service model of television needed a cultural programme in its scheduling, and literary adaptations were a particularly important part of that, conforming to established definitions of what was deemed appropriate national cultural production. In this context, Delgado became clearly established as a director for television. Other directors of Portuguese New Cinema (such as Paulo Rocha or Fernando Lopes, whose television work is only a part of their careers) also obtained a level of funding for film production that Delgado simply did not get. As she stated, 'Films like *Alvarez* do not go to film festivals. … Making television is great, making *Alvarez* was really good, but it is time to explore other opportunities. … And that is what I want to do now, make fiction films.'[17] When she mentions wanting to make fiction features, it is clear that she wanted to make films to be released in film theatres and to stop being a director for television, a medium that was manifestly less artistically valued. The section that follows will focus on the feature films that Delgado wanted to make but could not.

Film projects: A particular conception of cinema

The reason I am choosing to highlight Delgado's film projects is that she herself was very clear about her desire to make feature-length films. Also, the dates when she submitted her proposals either preceded or coincided with her work as a television director. Therefore, it is reasonable to assume that while her television work was her day-to-day occupation, Delgado was still persistently seeking funding to make films for the big screen. Her funding applications, however, were constantly turned down. Was it the topics she proposed to cover? Was it because her proposals were not good enough? Was it because she was a woman working in a field where more directors were men? It is difficult to formulate any concrete answers to this without reference to the official Instituto de Cinema e Audiovisual (ICA – Cinema and Audiovisual Institute) files for the competitions that she applied to. Unfortunately, that research was not logistically possible. However, a deeper understanding of the film proposals themselves might shed some light on the topic. Delgado's film projects never actually started shooting, but it seems likely that she had their scripts finished or in the final planning stages. At least five known films fall into this category.

The film *Ciclo de Verão* was a follow-up to *Masks*. In *Masks* Delgado had recorded the Winter Cycle festivities, so she intended to continue this by recording the Summer Cycle festivities. The proposal did not go ahead, however. As Luísa Alvão has stated,

> Delgado already had a formal letter that confirmed the grant had been awarded to her, but the Portuguese Cinema Centre decided to allocate the funding to José Álvaro Morais who was working on a film about the painter Vieira da Silva, *Ma femme chamada bicho* (1978).[18]

A Escolha from 1973, which preceded *Ciclo de Verão*, was a fiction film with a screenplay written by Delgado. The synopsis of the script is as follows:

> The story is about a woman's experiences. We meet Judith as a young woman, married to a much older man, an intellectual, who gives her a view of the world that fits with his own age and experience. They live a simple life built around set choices and restrictions, trying not to get trapped in the kind of facile, conventional existence that destroys people's sanity. Their lives are organized around life as a couple. The birth of their son introduces an element of absurdity into this. The son acts as a third player who intervenes in their existence as a couple and changes their entire lives. The son is born, and the husband dies, so Judith has to learn about life again and how to reintegrate herself into society. The son grows up. A new generation emerges, demanding a new way of life and new values. Judith does not want to lose her son and at the same time she is trying to regain, through him, the 'lost paradise' of her own youth. Yet, times have changed and the word 'purity' has a new meaning based on different assumptions. Judith ends up alone, trapped between a world to which she does not want to adapt, and a world that does not fundamentally accept her.[19]

This film, which was clearly focused on a female world, was followed by another film that also featured a woman protagonist, *As noivas ou a lenda das mulheres de luto*. *As noivas* is a film with a

> political plot. ... The brides referred to here were women in mourning who had either lost their intended husbands in the Colonial War or were waiting for the return of men who had deserted the army. The PIDE (State Secret Police) were pursuing the young men who had escaped, to try and draft them back into the army.[20]

The film is dated 1977, so it comes after the Colonial War, which ended in 1974. It is another fiction film based on everyday reality. *As noivas* was submitted more than once for IPC funding. An article published in 1983 in *Diário de Notícias* informs us that Delgado 'is waiting for funding from the IPC for *As noivas* (which had been shortlisted back in 1977) and also for a feature film project called *Quinta Avenida*, about prostitution in Porto'.[21]

According to Delgado, *Quinta Avenida* 'is based on a true story',[22] and an application for funding was submitted to IPC's production plan in 1984.[23] The same film was also listed for the following year.[24] This suggests that this proposal, like *As noivas*, was put in at least twice, so it is clear that Delgado had high hopes for it. In an interview in 1984, she explains:

> The title is meant to be ironic. The film talks about a series of people in the context of prostitution. The lives and fates of these people are what interests me here, the kinds of choices they make, voluntarily or otherwise. Prostitution is not just a person who sells their body, is it? I didn't have to invent much for this one. You see it in the papers and in real life.[25]

Quinta Avenida was set to be filmed in Porto, and was at an advanced stage of planning, as Delgado explains in the same interview:

> I tend to have a very clear planning schedule when I am filming. But then when I actually start filming, I tend to change things a lot. It always happens to me. A shade of light, the décor, an unexpected sound or an actor's unconscious gesture, that sort of thing might give me new ideas and act as a creative stimulus. I like natural décors, but I choose the locations so I can use direct sound. And then … you know? … a film (she pauses) has to come from somewhere deep inside you, from the womb.[26]

A escolha and *As noivas* were both film proposals with a female protagonist, but Delgado herself singled out *Quinta Avenida* as a symbolic, identity-defining film, a film that came precisely 'from the womb'. It was a fiction film with a screenplay written by the director herself, and it is noteworthy for its strong commitment to portraying a specific reality, prostitution, which was still a taboo subject in the early 1980s.

Many years later, in 2010, on the subject of films she wanted to make, Delgado mentioned one further film, *O Físico Prodigioso*:

> I would very much like to have made *O Físico Prodigioso*, based on a novella by Jorge de Sena. So if anyone had doubts about the quality of the plot, I could say it was not even me that wrote it. I've kept the screenplay; the story is beautiful. I only added one thing: I gave a further twist to the ending. In Jorge de Sena's work, the main characters (a man and a woman who are in love) are hunted

down and killed. In my version, a red rose and a white rose would bloom in the place where they are buried and their spirits would live on. In my story, love would prevail. Love is immortal!²⁷

What Delgado adds to the story is her own philosophy of life as well as her personal vision of cinema as something that transcends more mundane, quotidian or fatalistic views of the world. Delgado's statement clearly reveals that she was developing both a poetics of her own and a strong, concrete understanding of cinematography.

The poetics and thought of film directors are revealed not only in their films but also in texts and other documents for oral or print circulation, as well as in their statements and interviews.²⁸ In the case of Delgado, it is crucial to explore what she actually says about her film projects because these statements show a very high level of reflective awareness about her own cinema. *A escolha*, *As noivas* and *Quinta Avenida* are clearly centred on the female gender. I would also point out that Delgado was both the director and screenwriter for these films. Female characters are made powerfully present, as are their life experiences or as Delgado herself would put it, their choices, the decisions they want to make and the decisions that are forced upon them.

The only one of these five film projects that did not have a screenplay written by Delgado was *O Físico Prodigioso*, adapted from the work by Jorge de Sena. In 1984, in the foreword to the fifth edition of *Antigas e novas andanças do demónio*, Jorge de Sena himself claimed that

> sometimes a historical pseudo-reconstruction can capture our surroundings, or make us experience their historicity, much better and more objectively than some highly rated but aesthetically half-baked version of traditional realism that can be, indeed almost always is ... a dubious way of representing reality which is, by its very nature, always a work in progress.²⁹

This statement would certainly have appealed to Delgado, who seemed to regard cinema as having an unalienable relationship with reality of a kind that did not fit with more conventional forms of realism. 'To put it simply, I would say that, for me, cinema is another way of expressing love. You give it and you receive it. It's a way of enjoying a dream, or of exorcizing "demons".'³⁰ This statement by Delgado gives us a better understanding of what she was trying to do when she changed the ending of Sena's novella. In her film version, love would have triumphed. Delgado is trying to tell the story of a love that survives death. 'Dreaming' and 'exorcizing demons' are the terms she uses to describe a cinema that may originate in 'life' situations but does not engage with them merely representationally, opting instead to transcend them by creating a narrative structure from which the imaginary emerges as something purified or aspired to.

If interviews afford a clearer understanding of Delgado's specific ontology of cinema, they also offer a further point of particular interest. Delgado sometimes used interviews with other Portuguese film directors to express her own concerns, and although we have two surviving interviews with two different directors, the questions she puts are actually very similar. The first interview is with António de Macedo, who had just finished a landmark film of Portuguese New Cinema, *Domingo à tarde* (1966).[31] Delgado asks António de Macedo if, at the beginning of his career, he 'had total freedom as a creator or were you tied by commercial demands?', referring to the short film *Verão Coincidente* (1962), adapted from a poem by Maria Teresa Horta, and *Nicotiniana* (1963), a film for the tobacco industry.

Pressing this question of possible creative constraints, Delgado clearly asks if there were any 'obstacles' to making *Domingo à tarde*. António de Macedo answers that the main obstacles were the process of adapting to the 'technicalities of the mise-en-scène', only having a 'small team' and getting the 'necessary documentation for filming'. Delgado goes on to ask if the fact that the film is based on a Fernando Namora novel, that is, a work already published, means it will be 'more easily accepted by the audience' and also 'about the characters, did you take them as the writer wrote them, or did you change them to how you wanted them to be?' She specifically emphasizes the issue of creative freedom, asking if Fernando Namora had raised any objections, before going on to ask António de Macedo 'if you could direct a film with a screenplay that you had developed yourself, which topic and characters would you choose and why?' António de Macedo's reply is science fiction, a genre he did indeed subsequently return to.

Through these questions, Delgado reveals an understanding of cinema as an autonomous work (distanced from literature in this case), and she insists on the creative freedom of the director. The António de Macedo interview also reveals her concerns about the processes of cinematic creation, production, circulation and reception. During the interview, Delgado clearly expresses her own personal opinions on the creative process and the division of labour:

> I believe that there is a tendency among young filmmakers to take on the work that is really the editor's. On one level, I do understand the need to recreate

things at the cutting table; but I do wonder if it isn't rather limiting for the film itself in the sense that, when this happens, you don't get the necessary distance between the creator and the work.[32]

To some extent, this non-separation of tasks has been a modus operandi for Portuguese cinema in general, and Delgado herself adopted it in the films she directed. However, she challenges this during the interview with António de Macedo. This might have been because up till that point, in the mid-1960s, she had been working as an editor for other film directors, and doing that job was her opportunity to assert her own artistic identity and professionalism.

On the issue of creation and production conditions, audience reception and even training, Delgado asks the following questions: 'Is there any potential in our country for a commercial cinema that would not require the director to make – thematic or formal – concessions?'; 'Won't commercial cinema alienate directors to some extent?'; 'If the audience is poorly educated, can we develop a cinematic language that actually speaks to our situation, so that the director can get a clearer view of the problems'; 'Would creating an affordable magazine run exclusively by people in the cinema world not be a good way to educate audiences properly about cinema?'[33] These questions reveal her interest in a cinema where creative freedoms are protected without downplaying or rejecting a close relationship with the audience, who should have the opportunity to access film culture, while Portuguese cinema itself should move towards developing its own identity. On this subject, Delgado clearly believes that ongoing financial support is vital. She asks, 'Is the economic solution to have a smaller working team or to insist that the relevant authorities make annual grants specifically for filmmaking?'[34] By using the verb 'to insist', it is clear Delgado herself supports the second option – and António de Macedo agrees.

In the second interview, this time with Faria de Almeida,[35] who directed dozens of documentaries, on two of which Delgado worked as a producer (*Faça segundo a arte* [1965] and *Moçambique 65* [1965]), the main theme is his most important film, *Catembe*. Shot in Lisbon and Mozambique, specifically in the colonial capital Lourenço Marques, the film dates from 1965, the same year as the interview. Delgado asks similar (or even identical) questions to those she had previously put to António de Macedo. These questions are followed by other related ones, especially as regards Faria de Almeida's creative freedom. Once again, Delgado is interested in learning about the obstacles the director faced, as she asks: 'Were there any difficulties during the shooting of this film that compromised quality?'[36]

What is notable here is that even when she is asking a question, Delgado takes a critical stance on *Catembe*:

> Why did you direct a film that could best be described as a documentary, as a critical analysis of customs, and not a story that was really rooted in the African context, with black men as the main characters? ... Obviously, – socially – Africa is a mixture of black and white and a Mozambican culture *per se* ... is only just beginning to emerge from that fusion. However, there is such a thing as a black culture that you can access through dance, music, oral literature, and even in habits and rituals that constitute their own kind of philosophy. Don't you think all these elements offer a rich field that could be reproduced in cinema? ... Is the fact that black men are for the most part near illiterate a reason not to make non-documentary films based on their human problems, their daily lives, what they think and feel in their day to day existence – about love, work; how they experience contact with the white man, etc.? I think you are more of a spectator in your film *Catembe* than a man really engaged in the problems of your country, which leads me to conclude that you identify predominantly as European. Do you think you will ever make another substantive film in Mozambique? ... If you want to make a good film in Africa, based on African problems, is it enough just to send a technically well-equipped crew out from here [Portugal] without prior knowledge of the country in question?[37]

These questions clearly contain an implied criticism, and Delgado hints at what she would have done as a director. She would have made a fiction film based on the lives of Mozambican people, using a storyline that she had developed herself, but drawing on her in-depth knowledge of the country's inhabitants and their identities, life experiences and stories. Delgado goes on to show an interest in Faria de Almeida's opinion about films adapted from literary works as opposed to screenplays written by the filmmaker, when she asks: 'Isn't the adaptation of a good book just a way to get round the lack of a good screenplay?'[38] What is evident here is Delgado's opinion that film directors ought to develop their own screenplays because, as her question implies, adaptations get made to cover the absence of screen-writing talent. As her earlier questions about *Catembe* indicate, Delgado sees a good screenplay as being inspired by the people and the situations being filmed. In fact, her views on whether to make adaptations or to use the director's own screenplay effectively disclose her own positioning in defence of auteur cinema, as inspired by the French New Wave, in which the film director is also the author of the screenplay.

In an interview for *Diário de Notícias* in 1983, Delgado claims, 'I never do things by halves',³⁹ meaning that she invests the same level of commitment in television work and filmmaking for cinema, as she asserts her professional identity and her technical and creative competence. In the same interview, she shows that she is conscious of the value of her own work:

> I have made use of all the skills at my disposal. ... If someone said: 'you are not good enough', then yes, sure, I would just go away. But no one has told me that, and I'm sufficiently self-aware to know. ... I've done all the jobs there are in cinema. On my own films, I am the assistant director, the director, the producer, the costume designer and the sound engineer. I do whatever needs to be done.⁴⁰

Delgado's frank expression of her feelings here is particularly interesting when she talks about filming *Masks*, and particularly about the issue of being recognized as the director: 'I don't know how they [the people of Trás-os-Montes] even realized that I *was* the director when I was surrounded by all those men!'⁴¹

Defining herself as a professional who knows her craft, every interview Delgado did shows that she was working in an environment that was hostile to her presence as a female film director and indeed, most of the time, she was the only woman. On the subject of the CPC, she states:

> We had a meeting on one occasion and I said: 'you think I am just an editor, but I'm not. You can edit and still do other stuff, even mop the floor if you have to!' But at the end of the meeting, they all decided they were film directors and I was just an editor. I was the only woman in the room.⁴²

This meeting might have taken place in the early 1970s, a time when Delgado was, in fact, working as an editor. In the context she was working in, it was exceedingly difficult for her to escape that role and work as a director. One obvious consequence of this is that if we do want to work on her as a director with her own filmography, it is her film projects that offer the best window onto her thoughts about cinema. Her idea of cinema as an art form that transcends reality is self-evident there. It is revealing if not really surprising that she says exactly the same about directing films for television:

> I have always felt really fascinated by stories like these [fantastic tales], even though I can't quite explain why. Or maybe it is because the imaginary somehow creeps into the real and this imaginary is there in all of us, lying dormant in our subconscious and our fears which suddenly wake up and take shapes that are strange and monstrous.⁴³

Delgado's interest in the fantastic also explains her filming of the *caretos*[44] in Trás-os-Montes, and the rituals displayed there through language and gesture.

Rather than being simply a director for television (or even in spite of it) Delgado clearly belongs to the history of Portuguese New Cinema, albeit unfortunately on account of those films that she did not make but which do obviously share the principal characteristics of New Cinema. As Leonor Areal puts it,

> The key members of that school are the directors who stayed most faithful to a particular idea of art cinema, or 'the cinema of poetry' (to quote Pasolini) and, according to João Bénard da Costa, they share one essential idea: the issue of image as the manifestation of another, metaphysical, dimension; the image as a *mode of interrogation*, a *manifestation of myth*, *an imaginary that eludes representation*.[45]

Delgado was a director whose actual completed filmography consisted almost entirely of films made for television. However, her actions as a film director show that she did want to film her own screenplays for the cinema. What Delgado left us, as a result, is a body of work that forces film studies to go beyond the study of actual, completed films. This is perhaps the greatest contribution that this chapter endeavours to make, and it is all the more important when we are working on cinema directed by women. What we are left with in the end are films that were made and others that were only thought of, films that are still waiting for the conditions that will enable them to emerge.

Acknowledgements

The writing of this text was only possible due to the generous support and patience of the staff at the RTP Archive, namely, Filomena Fernandes, Fátima Ribeiro and Rosário Tavares; as well as at ANIM, particularly Sara Moreira and Luís Gameiro. Access to documents at the Library of the Portuguese Cinemathèque and Hemeroteca Municipal de Lisboa was crucial for the success of this research. I am also grateful to Hilary Owen and Mariana Liz for their generous support.

Notes

1 The translation of this chapter into English was completed by Ana Rita Martins and Hilary Owen.

2   A definition of *teoria dos cineastas* can be found in Manuela Penafria, Eduardo Tulio Baggio, André Rui Graça and Denize Correa Araújo (eds), *Ver, Ouvir e Ler os Cineastas – Teoria dos cineastas*, vol. 1 (Covilhã: UBI, Labcom.IFP, 2016).
3   See António Cunha (ed.), *Cineastas portuguesas 1874–1956* (Lisbon: Câmara Municipal de Lisboa, 2000), 55. Torralta – Clube Internacional de Férias, S.A. was a tourist resort in Tróia, Setúbal, which was built in 1972. I was unable to find any information on the film *Mafra e o Barroco Europeu*, its whereabouts or the reasons that led to its production.
4   Luísa Alvão, 'Noémia Delgado', Special issue of *Revista Enquadramento*, Cineclube de Guimarães, no. 15 (2018), 10.
5   José Gomes Bandeira, 'Quem foste Alvarez?', in *Catálogo Festfigueira* (1990), 314.
6   Ibid.
7   Luiz Carlos Oliveira Junior, 'Retratos em movimento', *Revista Ars* 15, no. 31 (2017), 185.
8   Catarina Alves Costa, 'Camponeses do cinema', (PhD thesis, Universidade NOVA de Lisboa, 2012).
9   Ibid., 135.
10 Ibid., 27.
11 Anon, *Panorama do Cinema Português* (Lisbon: Cinemateca Portuguesa, 1980); emphasis in original.
12 In Ana Miranda (ed.), *Catálogo Olhadelas* (Porto: Confederação, 2010), 51.
13 Cf. Oliveira Junior, 'Retratos em movimento'.
14 In 1977 the short film *Costa de Prata* (*Silver Coast*) is listed in Noémia Delgado's filmography, but I could not find any detailed information about it.
15 Alvão, 'Noémia Delgado', 11.
16 Cunha, *Cineastas Portuguesas 1874–1956*, 53.
17 Bandeira, 'Quem foste Alvarez?', 314.
18 Alvão, 'Noémia Delgado', 7.
19 The film's screenplay is available at the library of the Portuguese Cinemathèque.
20 In Miranda, *Catálogo Olhadelas*, 55.
21 Alice Vieira, 'Noémia Delgado realizadora: não faço as coisas com os pés …', In *Diário de Lisboa* (3 September 1983), 18.
22 Bandeira, 'Quem foste Alvarez?', 314.
23 In 'Cinema português – cinco filmes para subsidiar', *Jornal de Letras, Artes e Ideias* (17 to 23 April 1984), 13.
24 In 'Cinema português, júris e projetos para 85', *Jornal de Letras, Artes e Ideias* (15 to 21 January 1985), 12.
25 Alves Costa, 'Para Noémia Delgado (sem subsídios) "o cinema é uma forma de sonhar"', *Jornal de Notícias* 96, no. 282 (20 March 1984), 24.

26 Ibid., 24.
27 In Miranda, *Catálogo Olhadelas*, 48.
28 As regards interviews and other written sources, I will only refer to the interviews actually conducted with Delgado. In the *Olhadelas* catalogue there is a reference to chronicles written by Noémia Delgado, in *Diário de Lisboa*, but I was unable to locate them. This newspaper is available online at: http://casacomum.org/cc/diario_de_lisboa/ but it has no search facility (accessed 3 July 2019).
29 Jorge de Sena, *Antigas e novas andanças do demónio* (Lisbon: Edições 70, 1984).
30 Costa, 'Para Noémia Delgado (sem subsídios) "o cinema é uma forma de sonhar"', 24.
31 Noémia Delgado, 'Gente de cinema em panorâmica: o realizador António de Macedo', *Jornal de Letras e Artes* (1965), 4.
32 Ibid.
33 Ibid.
34 Ibid.
35 Noémia Delgado, 'Gente de cinema em panorâmica: M. G. Faria de Almeida – realizador e produtor de cinema', *Jornal de Letras e Artes* (1965), 7.
36 Ibid.
37 Ibid.
38 Ibid.
39 Vieira, 'Noémia Delgado realizadora: não faço as coisas com os pés', 18.
40 Ibid.
41 In Miranda, *Catálogo Olhadelas*, 51; emphasis mine.
42 Ibid., 54.
43 Alves Costa, 'Dois dedos de conversa com Noémia Delgado', *Cinema Novo* (1981), 17.
44 Translator's note: The *caretos* tradition is believed to have originated in a Celtic religious ritual, and it is still practised in some parts of Portugal, namely in the north of the country. During these rituals, young men put on masks made of brass, leather or wood, and wear suits usually made of colourful woollen quilts with rattles in their belts.
45 Leonor Areal, 'Estética da escola portuguesa de cinema: contributos para uma definição', in *Cinema em Português: IV Jornadas*, ed. Frederico Lopes (Covilhã: UBI, Livros Labcom, 2012), 101; emphasis in original.

2

Four decades on screen: The fiction films of Margarida Gil

Ana Isabel Soares

A measure of invisibility has conditioned the writing of this piece.[1] My task was complicated, from the outset, by the difficulty of actually sourcing and watching the films of Margarida Gil (b. 1950). At the time of writing there were none on general release. Gil's latest film *Mar* (*Sea*) premiered on 16 May 2019. I will return to this in my conclusion. *Adriana* (2005) was screened as part of the 'Mostra: Realizadoras Portuguesas' – Portuguese Women Directors film season – which was part of the research project leading to this book, and which took place in Lisbon in January 2019. Some of Margarida Gil's films are occasionally screened at film festivals and other art cinema events in Portugal and abroad, and many of them have received major awards and favourable reviews. *Daisy – Um Filme para Fernando Pessoa* (1991) can be viewed online at the RTP (Rádio e Televisão de Portugal) website, since it was commissioned by RTP for a text written by José Sasportes. Also on the channel's website, is another RTP production, *Olho de Vidro*, written by António Sena. On the same platform there are two episodes directed by Gil of the documentary series *Conversas no Cabeleireiro*.[2]

There is also a lack of critical reading available on the films of Margarida Gil. With the exception of Ana Catarina Pereira's book on Portuguese women directors[3] and João Bénard da Costa's study on the history of Portuguese film,[4] Gil's work is not given the attention it deserves in writings about the cinema of Portugal, if, indeed, she is mentioned at all. One reason for this lack of visibility relates to the nature of Gil's own career, which was strongly influenced by the development of new audiovisual formats and means of distribution. Gil started out in television, and most of what she has done consists of work made on and for television. Not all of her films were made to be screened in cinemas. The different genres, formats and themes that make up Margarida Gil's filmography influenced both my access to her fictional works[5] and the methodology I deploy in analysing them. The films I will focus on are *Relação Fiel e Verdadeira* (*True and Faithful*, 1987),[6] *Rosa Negra* (*Black Rose*, 1992), *O Anjo da Guarda* (*The Guardian Angel*, 1998), *Adriana*, *Perdida Mente* (*Mind Loss*, 2010), *Paixão* (*Passion*, 2012) and *Sea*. Rather than seeking to identify a single, unifying system in Gil's work, or reducing it to one main idea, I have opted for a film-by-film historical analysis of these seven full-length feature films made between 1987 and 2019.

In this process, I will focus on thematic issues that are illustrated by the formal characteristics of these films. Although the main objective of this chapter is not to seek overall cohesion, my analysis of the films and my approach to the main issues they raise will nonetheless reveal some common traits and a certain thematic consistency. My analysis of the seven films will focus on how they approach the key topics that have always inspired Gil, in both her fiction and her documentary work, and also on what I would call a persistently literary paradigm, or at least a degree of proximity to works of literature. A third possible angle might have been an analysis of the creative relationship between Gil's television experience and her work on fiction films (practically all of which were conceived for cinema, even if they were funded by television) but that is beyond the scope of the current project.[7]

Early works and *True and Faithful*

Margarida Gil's work is, as I have already suggested, highly eclectic. There are various reasons for this. Having left Covilhã for Lisbon in 1968, Gil spent the early years of her life in Portugal's capital, working at Santa Casa da Misericórdia in Avenida da Liberdade. As a result, she had access to the Portuguese Cinemathèque screenings, which were held almost daily in the neighbouring Palácio Foz. Her love of film stimulated her curiosity about visual culture, and this was also allied to an interest in literature, which Gil pursued further by taking a degree in German Philology in the School of Arts and Humanities at the University of Lisbon. It was at this point that she met her future husband João César Monteiro[8] and subsequently became his partner and assistant director, as well as acting in some of his films. When she started directing, Gil worked on documentaries, reports and interviews for public television. This happened after 1975, in what was called the 'socio-political programme department' in the aftermath of the 25 April 1974 Revolution. In 1976 she was part of *Grupo Zero – Cooperativa de Produção Cinematográfica*, a filmmaking cooperative, along with João César Monteiro, Acácio de Almeida, Alberto Seixas Santos, Solveig Nordlund and Jorge Silva Melo, among others. In the meantime, Gil worked at RTP2 (the second public television channel), developing the first weekly cultural news programme on Portuguese television. She also started working with Fernando Lopes (programme director), Fernando Assis Pacheco and Eduardo Prado Coelho. She directed her first short film, entitled *Clínica Popular Comunal da Cova da Piedade* (1975), for RTP, and the film went on to win a major award at Leipzig. Gil's work in this period thus covered topics that had been central to women even before the revolution and which it was finally possible to discuss, such as the right to choose on abortion and women's social position in relation to democracy, among other subjects that she would later return to, in both documentary and fiction.

While it is evident that Gil's career started in television, she also drew on her personal cinephile interests as well as her own practical experience in the field, acquired working with Monteiro in the 1960s. During those years, Gil had the opportunity to become directly involved in a number of different aspects of the filmmaking process. She was assistant director on *Que Farei Eu com Esta Espada?* (João César Monteiro, 1975) and also played the character who held the sword in the title. She was also assistant director in Monteiro's films *Fragmentos de um Filme-Esmola – A Sagrada Família* (1975) and *Veredas* (*Trails*, 1978), in which she acted and narrated, as she also did in *O Amor das Três Romãs* the following year. She was assistant director again for *Silvestre* (João César Monteiro, 1981) and for *Os Dois Soldados* and *A Mãe*, two short films directed by João César Monteiro, shot in 1979 and adapted from the traditional Portuguese short stories collected by Carlos de Oliveira and José Gomes Ferreira in *Contos Tradicionais Portugueses*, and by José Leite de Vasconcelos in *Etnografia Portuguesa*. She was also responsible for the executive production of *À Flor do Mar* (*Hovering Over the Water*, 1986).[9] Gil's first film for cinema, *True and Faithful*, was produced by the company that she and Monteiro had founded.

The above list of films clearly indicates how Gil built up her own experience, but it also raises the question of the proximity between her work and Monteiro's. This is not surprising given what Paulo Cunha describes as the clearly identifiable 'inclusions and exclusions – common themes, aesthetic references and production methods – that are reproduced or replicated in Portuguese cinema down the generations'[10] – indicating that strong personal and professional ties connect certain film directors with one another. This is easily verified by looking at the technical credits of each film, for example, and noting the recurrence of certain names in the filming and editing crews. Margarida Gil's projects for cinema surfaced intermittently between her other jobs as a director, and often involved the television business, in one form or another. *True and Faithful*, for instance, had production support from RTP. This stands out as a significant example of the importance of public television in a period of fairly good investment in Portuguese cinema, which occurred after the 1974 Revolution and Portugal's entry into the EEC in 1986.

The plot of the film (co-authored by Monteiro and Gil) is an adaptation of Antónia Margarida Castelo Branco's sixteenth-century autobiography, which she wrote after she entered a convent to escape domestic abuse. She then became Sister Clara do Santíssimo Sacramento. Gil worked with the poet Luiza Neto Jorge on Antónia Margarida's 'true and faithful' account before she devoted her life to the monastery, covering the eight years Antónia was married to the bankrupt aristocrat Brás Teles de Meneses e Faro. During that period, the author fell victim to serious domestic abuse from her husband, which drove her first to seek sanctuary in Santos monastery and subsequently to start her novitiate in the Madre de Deus de Xabregas Convent in March 1679. Around 1983, when the book edition of the sixteenth-century manuscript was in preparation, Gil was reading the Portuguese literary newspaper *Jornal de Letras* and came across a reference by its editor, João Palma-Ferreira (who was the director of the Portuguese National Library at the time), to the work entitled *Fiel e Verdadeira Relação que Dá dos Sucessos de Sua Vida a Criatura mais Ingrata a Seu Criador por Obediência de seus Padres Espirituais*,[11] which was held by the convent. Moved by Antónia Margarida's story, Gil decided to film it and record the difficult life the author had had with the tyrant she had married.

The original author's objective was, in accordance with literary convention of that period, to emphasize the truthful nature of the account and to highlight its 'faithful' representation of the events narrated. By placing the noun (*relação*) before the two adjectives in the Portuguese title of the adaptation, *Relação Fiel e Verdadeira*, not only was Gil creating a more natural syntax but she was also placing the interpretative weight on the noun '*relação*', rather than on the truthfulness of the account. Its truthfulness was underwritten, in principle anyway, by the original source manuscript she had adapted. Nevertheless, with this seemingly minimal change to the title (like the English word 'relation', '*relação*' can mean an 'account', a 'report' and a 'relationship'), Gil gave the story a double meaning. In fact, it is not only the account that is true and faithful (the emphasis on faithfulness and truth here highlights the anachronistic circumstances of women's lives, even in the twentieth century) but also the relationship between the two main characters which, however raw and painful it may actually be, still has to be perceived as 'true and faithful' even when it is clearly not. Hence the ironic note of the title, inflecting the interpretation of the film.

The film adaptation of the manuscript by the nun from Xabregas focuses only on the days that preceded the writing of the biography (so the film significantly reduces the passages of text that it draws on) and transfers the action to post-Revolutionary Portugal, to the last quarter of the twentieth century. The reason why Antónia's father wants her to study at the convent as a child is because 'of all that business with the 25 April', as one of the housemaids puts it. It is precisely during that period of transition, from dictatorship to democracy, that Gil identifies an ongoing legacy of gender inequality and injustice, very similar to the situation in Sister Clara's historical manuscript. Her decision to denounce this shamefully unaltered state of affairs is obvious – indeed it is made even clearer by her decision to use a very old manuscript such as her source text – and this highlights a persistent trait in Gil's work, namely her attention to the abuse suffered by social groups who are arbitrarily disadvantaged. Obviously, women form a significant part of this grouping and are therefore frequently central to Gil's perspective, across the various media, genres and formats that she uses. Indeed, as Pereira puts it, *True and Faithful* 'brings out some of the filmmaker's feminist concerns'.[12]

True and Faithful is clearly inspired by women's lives and by the historical issues that have dominated those lives down the centuries, such as expulsion from the family home as a means of economic survival and having to go into the religious life as the sole alternative to marriage – these being the only two socially acceptable choices for women. Both situations entail a loss of selfhood that is specifically caused by changing one's name. A certain seductive feminine appeal is also part of the creative impulse behind the film. The gaze always rests on the woman as the shots profile the youthful beauty of the film's lead, Catarina Alves Costa. The camera seems fascinated by Antónia's markedly feminine figure (see Figure 2.1). It matters that the film is focused solely on the period before she enters the convent, when the physical expression of her femininity has not yet been suppressed. This is made even clearer when we consider that the character of Brás in the film is much more complex as we witness, for example, his sudden, frequent mood swings and changes of mind,

Figure 2.1 Catarina Alves Costa in Margarida Gil's *True and Faithful* (1987) (Cinemateca Portuguesa – Museu do Cinema).

that are more typical of a romantic hero. The spectator is periodically shown the inner conflict that Brás lives with. At the end of the film, this conflict motivates Antónia's resolve to stay in the convent. It also intensifies the maternal role that she will have to give up once her union with God is consummated. We see Brás nestling down in a waterborne barge after Antónia has definitively made up her mind not to follow him. She rocks her cradled, sleeping husband in a gesture which re-enacts her previous rocking of her dead son, and then gently pushes her husband's boat out onto the lake. The misty waters surrounding them are a symbol of farewell, cleansing and forgiveness. Only as a nun, as a bride of Christ, will Antónia be able to watch over the souls of both her son and her deviant husband who is not redeemable in this world.

This first film set the tone for the filmmaker's ethical and aesthetic stance throughout most of her subsequent work, which uses irony and overt criticism to denounce women's unjustly subordinate position (or that of other groups oppressed or marginalized by society, such as the East Timorese, or people with degenerative diseases) in the seventeenth century or in the supposedly civilized, advanced world of twentieth-century society. Yet, even before it featured on the big screen, this tone was firmly established in Gil's early documentary films made for television. In addition to the work that she did with her 'literary collaborator' on this adaptation (the poet Luiza Neto Jorge), particularly in selecting the right passages from the manuscript, it is also important to consider the potential for aesthetic awareness that Gil's experience in television brought to the development of this film. This is clear in the filming of the indoor scenes, and in the use of voice-off either as a connecting element between scenes or as a means of achieving a sense of spatial cohesion. This is evident, for example, in the dialogue between the two housemaids, which forms the backdrop to the action in one of the opening scenes of the film. Shortly after this dialogue, one of the maids, now standing in Antónia's room, looks at herself in the mirror trying on the mistresses' clothes, and Antónia comes in and starts undressing, getting ready to be bathed by the maid. A complex web of domestic relations is condensed here into a set of knowing, conspiratorial voices (from which Antónia is somehow excluded, somewhat paradoxically perhaps, when the maid tells her that she is the only one who does not know she is going to be married), underscoring the imminent loss of her family home.

This meaningful use of space in a literary adaptation is similar to the manner in which Manoel de Oliveira, for example, displays the interiority of household space in his 'frustrated loves series' (in Portuguese, *tetralogia dos amores frustrados*), as Oliveira himself called it. This set of four feature films was adapted between 1971 and 1981 from literary works and consists of *O Passado e o Presente* (*Past and Present*, 1972), *Benilde ou a Virgem Mãe* (*Benilde or The Virgin Mother*, 1975), *Amor de Perdição* (*Doomed Love*, 1977) and *Francisca* (1981). At key moments in Manoel de Oliveira's films, as with several indoor scenes in *True and Faithful*, the camera moves around the rooms, allowing the travelling shots to either reveal or conceal characters, even when their dialogue can still be heard in voice-off. The family and the love relationships that feature in the film could not be successfully portrayed without this highly intimate close-up view of domestic space, usually achieved through the movement of the camera acting as an interrogatory, external eye which has the power to disclose what society, on the outside, may not know or see. The denunciation of abuse, the theme which Margarida Gil's film selects from Sister Clara's original account, is revisited more explicitly in *Passion*, in which Gil inverts the gendered power relations (it is the woman who subjugates the man) and, as will be discussed later in this chapter, she achieves this by filming almost exclusively indoor scenes.

The scriptwriting for *True and Faithful* takes a somewhat anachronistic approach to the original seventeenth-century text, which is, as we noted above, adapted to the 1970s. However, this sense of anachronism extends well beyond the obvious fact that the film is set 300 years after Sister Clara wrote the text. Regardless of the modern elements the film includes (cars, car-radios and references to the Carnation Revolution), the conservative environment of the old Douro families indexes the survival of old school machismo, showing how distant this was from what Portuguese social renewal ought to look like at the end of the 1970s. Both Gil and Neto Jorge might also have been aware of how close the sixteenth-century nun's account is to some of Agustina Bessa-Luís's (1922–2019) representations of family in her novels, which are also set in time periods that seem somehow inured to the world of social progress or the business of resisting inequality. Literary narratives produce a kind of continuum rather in the manner of human memory, which cinema is particularly well equipped to reproduce.

In Gil's first film for the big screen – in fact, her first feature film – other significant stylistic elements sustain the plot. The soundtrack, particularly the music, is a good case in point. An aura of timelessness connects the different periods in *True and Faithful*, and there is a good example of how music supports this, when it is played over the sequence immediately after the marriage scene but before the characters go back into the house. The film focuses on the surrounding countryside while the car radio plays Leonard Cohen singing *Last Year's Man* including the line 'The wilderness is gathering all its children back again.' This suggests that the present may also be signalling to the past and the past is returning with all its 'wild children', the children of years gone by, who could also be the women of 300 years ago. It is significant that Antónia's new husband, the oppressive and violent Brás, changes the station and interrupts Cohen's song, not least because what the audience then hears is *Salome* by Richard Strauss, reinforcing the fact that Brás's rightful place is the world of profound emotional turmoil that is evoked by the Strauss opera.[13]

The 1990s: *Black Rose* and *The Guardian Angel*

Margarida Gil's second fiction feature film was directed while she was between two television projects: *Daisy*, mentioned earlier, and *A Luz Incerta* (1995). Gil's relationship with the literary production of other writers (more specifically drama in this case) never seems to have obscured her own creative vision. The documentary genre also remains at the heart of her work, and a combination of these two different sources seems to set the tone for *Black Rose*. The film was part of the Official Selection at the Locarno International Film Festival in 1992. Filmed in Covilhã, the director's hometown, *Black Rose* marked a bitter experience in her cinema career. Although it was well received at Locarno, it was never distributed commercially.[14] Gil has expressed her belief that the film 'will eventually break out of the obscurity that distribution and screening problems and general neglect have condemned it to. If it's meant to be.'[15] Yet, the fact remains that one of Gil's most interesting and complex works is still not available for distribution. The director herself considers it to be rather 'unbalanced' – although she has stressed her own liking for it and admits that 'all my films are a bit unbalanced, really'.[16] Certainly, the term 'unbalanced' does not accurately describe the composition of the film, which was very much in line with her previous works in the way in which it balances fiction and documentary, with social problems as its background.

The plot was written by Gil and focuses on a group of people travelling home to a town in the Portuguese interior. Fernanda is a high school teacher, returning after a marital breakup, to take up teaching again. António, is a local man, returning to the town which had previously drummed him out for (supposedly) setting a local factory on fire. Quim, a young infantryman and Fernanda's former student, is returning from his barracks, possibly just for a couple of days' leave. The film begins with these three characters, who had been close in a previous period in their lives, meeting up again on a train journey. *Black Rose* combines this fictional perspective with a critical overview of the problems associated with living in a town in the interior of Portugal, focusing particularly on the effects of urban decay and neglect for homes and industries. 'Black Rose' is the name of the house that belongs to the family who own a factory. They are unable to recover their business after a fire and so they are converting the building into a guesthouse for rural tourism.

We also witness the harassment of women factory workers and problems with arson attacks and arsonists. This sort of approach, in which fiction is grounded in the description and condemnation of social problems, is, of course, evident in other Portuguese filmmakers. João Canijo, for instance,[17] points an accusing finger at the social and political issues behind provincial depopulation, crime and desolation, particularly in those areas of Portugal that are also central to Margarida Gil's life and work. Canijo's films involve complex, family centred storylines, mysterious clues that hint at past secrets and journeys home that haunt the characters' lives and the places they live in. In *Black Rose*, the camera moves between panoramic views of the town, perched on the mountainside, and close-ups of the land as Gil uses a number of wide-angle shots, which hold several narrative threads in play simultaneously.

An example of this occurs, about an hour into the film, when the young Mariana walks through the streets of Covilhã with one of the film's thuggish characters, while António watches them in the distance, now with the mountain behind him, rather than the town, and he feels intrigued and a bit jealous. A further example of multiple narrative layers occurs when António unearths the box where he keeps a magic wooden doll his father had given him when he was a child so he can now pass it on to his little brother, interweaving and combining past, present and future. Here, the perspective seems to come from two focal points at once, one close to the land and the clods of earth, enclosing a past inheritance that is free of accusation or wrongdoing, and the other at a distance from the land, where an outside eye watches the action unfold from an external viewpoint. As the character of the ex-fireman 'Barriga D'Água' (masterfully played by Mário Viegas in his last big screen role) indicates, the only way António himself can survive with any sense of family connectedness is in the graveyard. As an outcast he lives in a realm that is simultaneously inside and outside the community, sharing the terrain of the community but not its actual life.

As with other films directed by Gil, which are powerfully driven by their visual aesthetics, *Black Rose* resorts to the symbology of certain visual signs, which become pictorial through their narrative force. The colour red (evoking fire, the drama of lifeblood, crime and passion) recurs at various points in the story. When Mariana is bitten by a large viper, António sucks the poison from her ankle, just below the red skirt she is wearing. The camera then turns, and in the same take from behind the tree trunk, it rests on the face of Mariana expressing pleasure. Also, when Mariana asks Fernanda why she was chosen to play Antigone in the school play, Mariana's red blouse may link her passion for António to Fernanda's own former feelings towards him. This arresting image is repeated on the rocky mountain landscape. Another example is when António gives his younger brother Armando the magic doll he had hidden away, which supposedly bleeds when anyone upsets it. António issues the somewhat disconcerting utterance, 'that was when I died', and Armando tries to clarify this asking, 'Were you killed?' The older brother evades the question and simply replies: 'I am giving it to you now, it is yours. If it starts to bleed heavily, that will mean that I am dying again.'

The blood that the wooden doll will shed effectively functions as a premonition of the second death that will befall António after he goes back to the place where he had previously been annihilated, in a symbolic sense, by the charge of arson. A gang of thugs desecrates the graveyard at night, stealing the head of a corpse, assaulting 'Barriga D'Água' and then heading past Fernanda's house where they throw the stolen head through the window, wrapped in a red cloth. The scene's appeal is visual but also verbal. The film establishes a further connection here between the popular culture of a small twentieth-century Portuguese town and classical theatre, as Mariana is shown rehearsing the Greek tragedy *Antigone* for the school play. The lines that Mariana repeats, at home and at her school rehearsals, are identical to the questions asked by the teacher Fernanda, who suspects she might know who threw the head in the red cloth and cries: 'What do you want from me? What have I done to you?' With these words, she becomes a latter-day Antigone updated to the setting of a disco in the Portuguese interior.

Margarida Gil's third feature film, *The Guardian Angel*, was co-produced for the big screen by RTP with financial support from the IPACA/ICAM[18] and the Script Fund. Gil produced the script, co-writing the dialogues with Maria Velho da Costa. The film went on to receive the Best Film Award at the Rome Film Fest that year, and also won the Silver Plaque at the Figueira da Foz International Film Festival, while Dalila Carmo as a supporting actress received a Special Mention at the Fantasporto Film Festival. The storyline introduces the principal character to us (the psychiatrist Lúcia, played by Natália Luiza) after her father has committed suicide. The disappearance of the father, who the audience will come to realize, was Lúcia's main source of emotional support, leaves the protagonist confused and disorientated. At the beginning of the film, Lúcia's father makes his last call to her, but his daughter does not answer the phone, and so he speaks to her answering machine instead and it records his voice as he tells her: 'I wish I could tell you which way to go. I wish I could show you a free country.' The film then follows Lúcia as she goes on a journey back to a place from her childhood that is situated, non-coincidentally, near a lighthouse on the coast.

It becomes clear that the characters and the action are centred on an unstable, dysfunctional and frustrating relationship between Lúcia and her mother. The mother, played by Maria do Céu Guerra, is a member of the Portuguese Parliament. She stands for everything the daughter rejects and which the father had also rejected in terms of public exposure and living up to political and social expectations. (She is campaigning for election as mayor and the film shows frequent images of the campaign posters featuring her as a high powered 'female professional'.) This has caused her to neglect her family, and even as an adult, her daughter still complains of her mother's emotional distance. In addition to the basic plot, the film contains other running themes that are an important constant in Margarida Gil's work. These include the East Timorese Independence Struggle (which we see via the photos that Lúcia's father had taken on the island of East Timor, and which she looks at again when she wants to reconnect with her dead father), and the issue of women suffering domestic violence. Marta, the housekeeper who lives in the lighthouse and is played by Laura Soveral, shows signs of domestic abuse, which becomes a topic of conversation between Lúcia's mother and herself.

Although it was not made for television, the tone of the film is reminiscent of TV production. The very contemporary figure of the mother and her job, the lighting at the political rallies, the religious procession and the marching band are all represented with the type of naturalism more usually associated with soap operas. However, this does not obscure the cinematographic elements which drive the film, ultimately reminding us that *The Guardian Angel* was made for the big screen. The tension between these two modes of representation is symbolized by the tense relationship between the mother and her daughter. The mother has no trouble with technology and easily keeps pace with the modern world. We see her rushing everywhere, even when she is playing golf. She has no time for anything except her political commitments, and she is permanently on her phone, saying exactly what she is thinking: 'Oh Timor, Timor, yes, I know it's politically incorrect [to say this], but I'm so sick of hearing about it.' The daughter, on the other hand, is committed to her work and has absolutely no interest in achieving greater visibility. As she claims, 'My politics is my work.' Lúcia's 'salvation' comes in the form of a chance reencounter with Álvaro (played by Pedro Hestnes), a dying man who is dedicating himself to music, literature and gardening.

Understanding the mother's character in this film requires us to think about the ways in which television represents the temporal logic of the everyday. Understanding the figure of the daughter, on the other hand, and the broader ramifications of her character in relation to her father and Álvaro, takes the viewer to places that are almost obsolete and invisible in the urban environment, such as the lighthouse, the sea and the waves breaking over the rocks. The character of the daughter is thus associated with the expanded cinematic time of what is left unsaid, with the expansiveness of the landscape and with an emotional complexity that the viewer can only decode and start to understand in another temporal mode altogether. The character of Dalila Carmo, the plain-speaking housekeeper (see Figure 2.2), functions as a mediatory narrative element, introducing a humorous note to the film that is more typical of soap

Figure 2.2 The housekeepers in Margarida Gil's *The Guardian Angel* (1998) (Cinemateca Portuguesa – Museu do Cinema).

opera. Although Carmo had not at that point started appearing in soaps, the housemaid character is well established in the soap genre, which usually centres on stereotypical families from a range of social backgrounds. Indeed, there is a touch of humour in many of Margarida Gil's films, which is not entirely surprising given her professional association with the comedian, Herman José, many of whose television shows she directed. In this film, however, the humour is confined to the timeless, remote location of the lighthouse, which offers a more cinematic atmosphere.

In several of Margarida Gil's fiction films, the narrative centres, with varying degrees of intensity, on the leitmotif of a strong parent–child (especially father–daughter) relationship. In *True and Faithful* that relationship is present through its absence. The absent father figure drives Antónia into marriage, while her mother succumbs to social pressure and colludes with her son-in-law to exploit her daughter, until her own property is threatened by the situation. In *Black Rose*, the tension is between father and son. António rejects his father for going along with the judgement that got him banished from the city. They are reconciled only when the father realizes the injustice that he has done. The real reason for António's return to his native region is his desire to re-establish the relationship with his father. In *The Guardian Angel*, Lúcia is in emotional turmoil after her father's suicide, and her mother is an antagonistic focus of opposition. Finally,

Mind Loss – which I will discuss later – explores how a father and daughter cope on their own with the drama of him developing dementia. The father–child relationship motif echoes the Prospero–Miranda pairing from Shakespeare's *The Tempest*. The reference to Shakespeare is both direct and obvious, and Gil herself has acknowledged the work of the Bard as a formative influence from when she was a student and she and Monteiro became regular cinemagoers. As she has put it, 'In my student days, I was passionate about Hölderlin and Shakespeare, particularly *The Tempest*. I used to pass my work to João César. … And he always wanted to do something with *The Tempest*.'[19]

The 2000s: *Adriana, Mind Loss* and *Passion*

Gil's fourth fiction film *Adriana* has something else in common with Shakespeare's play, apart from repeating the father–daughter motif. The film places the main characters on a fictional island where physical procreation is no longer possible. As in *The Tempest*, the daughter has to leave the island and travel to the mainland to ensure the continuation of her father's lineage. Adriana's father sends her away so that she can 'start a family by natural means'. In a humorous twist, however, Margarida Gil and Maria Velho da Costa, who also co-wrote the plot, remove this reason for the trip altogether. Consequently, the point at which *The Tempest* ends with the daughter leaving the island provides the starting point for a series of adventures that the young Adriana enjoys in and around Lisbon. In the end, however, she realizes that it does not matter where she is, and so Adriana returns, still totally virgin, to the island she had previously left, where a child is indeed about to be born but to someone else, not on this occasion to her.

During the time she has spent in and around the capital city, she has learnt a great deal about people and life, getting to know down to earth street-life as well as upper-class mansions. She comes to realize that perhaps having children is not something she is ready to do yet. Nor does she need to leave the island to do it. As she sets off home, she jokes, 'Goodbye, I am off to marry a sperm whale.' Traditions on the island carry on regardless, a fact that is illustrated by the peasant women who carry baskets of bread on their heads and come to welcome Adriana home. These same women had also lined the route as she was leaving, holding their loaves of bread in front of them on that occasion, with the yeast symbolizing the potential fertilization of their wombs. The island represents all that is familiar for Adriana, and the place of her childhood memories. She leaves the safety of this confined environment behind when she dives into the sea and resurfaces on the mainland. The driving force of *Adriana*'s plot centres on the opposition between fertility and sterility (both of women in particular and of nature in general), but the film humorously deconstructs that dichotomy in the figure of a transvestite called Saturnino who channels Amália Rodrigues, the famous *fado* singer who never had children. Indeed, Adriana spends her first night in Lisbon in bed with Saturnino, after she has been conned and robbed of her money and documents before she even got out of the airport.

Adriana premiered at the sixth Rome Film Fest, and Gil also won the lifetime achievement award there. The film won Best Portuguese Film at the 2005 IndieLisboa International Film Festival, the Jury's Award at the Santa Maria da Feira Portuguese-Brazilian Film Festival (also in 2005), and both the 'Cidade da Covilhã' Grand Prize and the Best Feature Film Director Award at the second Covilhã Film Festival. Ana Moreira, who played Adriana, won Best Actress at the 2006 Portuguese Golden Globes (*Globos de Ouro*), and in the same year, the film was nominated in the Best Film, Best Actor and Best Actress categories for the performances of Bruno Bravo and Isabel Ruth. Unlike *Black Rose*, Margarida Gil always refers to *Adriana* with great satisfaction. In 2000, for instance, she wrote:

> Now that I have suffered some terrible heartache in my life, I really need to do comedy. I have written comic situations and characters even in very unhappy times. I have always felt rather drawn to do low brow, popular stuff. It doesn't bother me at all. It is what I did with *Adriana* and that was beautiful.[20]

Six years after the film premiered, Gil went on to remark about comedy genres:

> It was such fun! I have always had the inclination to do comedy, and even when I have made something very dramatic, I have flirted with comedy, ever since my first film. ... I fell about laughing when I was making this film [*Adriana*] and showing people the dialogue. I loved the sheer joy of telling the story and knowing it was completely mad, highly improbable, and totally unrealistic. But I always believed in the film and it never bothered me that it was implausible. I mean, the film really *is* completely implausible. She wakes up in bed with a transvestite who is obsessed with the idea that he is Amália Rodrigues, and whose mother sells fruit at the market. It is not exactly likely.[21]

Adriana had a very different fate from *Black Rose*, which was never commercially distributed; the film was watched by 7,019 viewers in 603 sessions.[22] However, the fact that *Adriana* is humorous and makes a comic point does not mean it was hastily or carelessly put together.[23] In fact, the photography, and indeed all the visual aspects of the film, as well as its narrative coherence and character exposition, were very finely worked out, making this one of Gil's most appealing films. A similarly heart-warming storyline characterizes *Mind Loss*, which won the Best Foreign Screenplay Award at the New York International Independent Film and Video Festival.

The plot of *Mind Loss* is socially relevant and rather distressing, as it deals with a degenerative neurological disease. The film feels like a desperate alarm call, materialized in the literally audible moment when Maria do Céu Guerra's character (playing a patient who is neither helped nor reassured by the health system) lashes out at a member of the care staff. We witness not only this outburst of despair but also José Airosa's almost clownish male protagonist, gradually sinking into depression and retreating into silence, bringing out the Chaplinesque absurdity of his situation. Both the character and the story show us the tiny humble traces that silenced, abandoned people leave behind them. The film as a whole affords a graphic investigation into what remains of a person when verbal language has gone, and memory has faded. The protagonist's mind cannot tell the difference between boots and bread, so a pair of old walking boots gets baked in the oven like a loaf, reinforcing the message that he can no longer go walking. The baking of the boots also symbolizes the idea that the road once walked in the past is now the only source of nourishment. At the same time, the film points beyond its own immediate story to cross reference other key moments in art history, such as the Van Gogh painting which features a pair of worn out boots (1886), effectively highlighting the connection between the protagonist of *Mind Loss* and the painter who also suffered from degenerative mental illness.

As with *The Guardian Angel*, Gil also wrote the story for her sixth fiction film *Passion* while the dialogues were, once again, co-written with Maria Velho da Costa. However, the visual aesthetics of *Passion* are quite different from Gil's earlier work. Considerable technical advances are in evidence here. For example, the clarity of the digital image shows the photographic skills of Gil's long-time collaborator, the cinematographer Acácio de Almeida, to much better advantage. Yet the differences between the two films go beyond technical production. *Passion* is filmed in a much more restricted space, shot almost entirely in the room where Maria Salomé is holding João Lucas captive, and the number of characters in this film is greatly reduced. The film becomes an exercise in dramatic containment, as a result, and its formal characteristics compress the narrative, making the director's aesthetic choices more explicit.

The theme of *Passion* is 'the love affairs that go wrong when they morph into relations of power, when pain is mixed with pleasure, and one partner is submissive while the other is dominant'.[24] In this sense, the film is about 'acts of love that are totally loveless'. The distinction is blurred between love and captivity, and the film goes on a journey into the dark side of subjectivity and emotional relationships. Ana Brandão plays Maria Salomé, the protagonist whose very name evokes a combination of torture and sacrifice. Salomé survives the tragedy of losing her daughter when she is killed by Salomé's husband, the child's father, who subsequently commits suicide. When she gets drunk one night with a stranger (Carloto Cotta in the role of João Lucas, a name also carrying biblical overtones), Salomé takes him to a flat that is scheduled for demolition and locks him up in one of the rooms. The dense web of metaphor that emerges from the characters' names in this film establishes strong thematic links with Gil's other films, such as her focus on the father–daughter union (which proves fatal in *Passion*), the breakdown of the family unit and the despair of mental illness. Music also plays a key role here, and she focuses, once again, on a socially complex issue. *Passion* appears to reverse gender violence, but ultimately it reminds us of the kind of cruelty that any one person might inflict on another, regardless of gender. The viewer is shown the words that Maria Salomé has written on the wall of the flat, a former home now derelict: 'We must learn to love.' Love, the film suggests, is a lesson that needs to be learnt.

Conclusion: *Sea*

Love is also, in a sense, at the heart of the message Gil conveys in her most recent and highly topical fiction film, *Sea*, released in 2019. It is based upon a script that Gil wrote with Rita Benis, and it deals with the risks faced by illegal immigrants putting out to sea in the Mediterranean. As the director returns to the kind of issues that she has been interested in throughout her filmmaking career, this work exemplifies Gil's long-running preoccupation with people, and her interest in subject matter that foregrounds the fact of shared human existence. Here too, Gil opts for humour suggesting that contemporary problems can perhaps be best and most effectively explored with a degree of levity. This might also explain why she chooses one of Portugal's most acclaimed artists and curators, Pedro Cabrita Reis, to play the commander of the ship, who is an art smuggler. (Captain Ahab is what the character of Francisca calls him in one of many literary references, as she confesses that she cannot decide what to make of him.)

The film also includes a female perspective on the lives of women, again echoing Gil's other work, as Maria de Medeiros plays Francisca – a woman who works at the European Parliament and is also a mother travelling across the Mediterranean to find her son (see Figure 2.3). She is forced to broaden her own understanding of what motherhood means when helpless refugees need the shelter that 'mother' Europe is not so easily willing to offer them. The history of Portuguese art cinema is also constantly alluded to and cross referenced in Gil's film. For example, Manoel de Oliveira's 2003 film, *Um Filme Falado* (*A Talking Picture*), interrogates Europe's past and its historical legacy in the course of a Mediterranean cruise which is similar, in some respects, to the voyage portrayed in *Sea*. In this 2019 work, Gil revisits and updates Oliveira's profound reflection on Europe and its role in the contemporary world. If Europe was the womb that nurtured and fed Western values of humanity, democracy and respect for the lives of individuals, the time and the place have come to ask ourselves whether these values are still the beacons that guide our ships across the seas.

The sheer consistency of Margarida Gil's approach to making feature films, always striking the right balance between a sober, documentary, tone of sociopolitical denunciation and a lighter, more human mode of interpersonal conversation, clearly defines the path that she has followed in a career now spanning almost half a century. She has never shrunk from tackling uncomfortable issues, in a career that began before the 1974 Revolution and has

Figure 2.3 Pedro Cabrita Reis, Maria de Medeiros, Catarina Wallenstein and Nuno Lopes in Margarida Gil's *Sea* (Ar de Filmes, 2019).

continued well into the twenty-first century, in her compassionate engagement with migration and refugee politics in 2019.

Notes

1. The translation of this chapter into English was completed by Ana Rita Martins, Rhian Atkin and Hilary Owen.
2. Available at http://www.rtp.pt/programa/episodios/tv/p26930 (accessed 5 July 2019).
3. Ana Catarina Pereira, *A Mulher-Cineasta: da arte pela arte a uma estética da diferenciação* (Covilhã: LABCOM.IFP, Universidade da Beira Interior, 2016).
4. João Bénard da Costa, 'Breve história mal contada de um cinema mal visto', in *Portugal 45-95 nas Artes, nas Letras e nas Ideias*, ed. Vítor Vladimiro Ferreira (Lisbon: Centro Nacional de Cultura, 1998).
5. For the reasons mentioned earlier, I would like to thank Paulo Cunha and Margarida Gil who allowed me to watch most of the films I analyse in this chapter; I would also like to thank Gabriela Soares and Rui Duarte (of Escola Superior de Educação e Comunicação, Universidade do Algarve) for the work they did on the film files.
6. A restoration of this film was recently completed at ANIM – the National Film Archive at the Portuguese Cinemathèque.
7. A good place to start would be Gil's own statements, in different interviews, which indicate that the director has always tried to maintain a straightforward, open relationship with television, which helped her to develop her cinematography rather than impeding or limiting it. See for instance Margarida Gil, 'Conversa' (interview with Ilda Castro), in *Cineastas Portuguesas 1874–1956*, ed. António Cunha (Lisbon: Câmara Municipal de Lisboa, 2000); Margarida Gil, 'O produtor não põe um cêntimo no filme' (interview to Vanessa Sousa Dias), in *Novas & Velhas Tendências no Cinema Português Contemporâneo*, ed. João Maria Mendes (Faro: CIAC – Centro de Investigação em Artes e Comunicação, 2010); and Margarida Gil, 'Relato de Paixões', in *Cineastas Portuguesas 1874–1956*, ed. António Cunha (Lisbon: Câmara Municipal de Lisboa, 2000).
8. As Gil explains in a statement from 2004, 'That was where we first met, at the movies' ('Notre reencontre a commencé comme ça, au cinema'), in 'Entretien avec Margarida Gil', in *Pour João César Monteiro: Contre tous les feux, le feu, mon feu*, ed. Fabrice Revault Allonnes (Crisnée: Yellow Now – Cotê Cinèma, 2004), 95.
9. Monteiro's cinema has received very substantial critical attention, even to the extent that this rather obscures Margarida Gil's role in his work. It therefore remains clear that more extensive research is yet to be done on Gil's own work as a director.
10. Paulo Cunha, 'Genealogias, filiações e afinidades no cinema português', in *Filmes Falados: Cinema em Português V Jornadas*, eds Frederico Lopes and Ana Catarina Pereira (Covilhã: LabCom, Universidade da Beira Interior, 2013), 182.

11 *True and Faithful Account of the Events of Her Life told by this Creature Most Ungrateful to Her Creator in Obedience to Her Spiritual Fathers* would be the English-language translation. The manuscript has inspired a number of historical analyses in the academic world. In 2009, Nuno Júdice wrote a novel based on it, *Os Passos da Cruz*.
12 Pereira, *A Mulher-Cineasta*, 188.
13 In his MA dissertation (2018), Flávio Scotellaro Xavier Jr. provides a more detailed analysis of how music is used in *True and Faithful*; see especially 60–2. Flávio Scotellaro Xavier Jr, 'Margarida sobre Margarida: escrita e reescrita da vida de Soror Clara do Santíssimo Sacramento', MA diss., Faculdade de Letras da Universidade do Porto, 2018, https ://si garra .up.p t/flu p/en/ pub_g eral. show: file? pi_do c_id= 18111 2 (accessed 5 July 2019).
14 Gil, 'Conversa' (interview with Ilda Castro), 223. On the ways in which distribution has influenced cinema production in Portugal, see Paulo Cunha, 'Cinema de Garagem', in *Cinema em Português – VII Jornadas*, eds Frederico Lopes, Paulo Cunha and Manuela Penafria (Covilhã: LabCom, Universidade da Beira Interior, 2016). Concerning the data about 'the number of viewers and cinemas in which [female directors' works] were screened' in Portugal since the 1970s, using the data made available by ICA, see Pereira, *A Mulher-Cineasta*, 182–6.
15 Gil, 'Conversa' [interview with Ilda Castro], 206.
16 Gil, 'Relato de Paixões', 223.
17 Pereira, *A Mulher-Cineasta*, 223.
18 ICAPA is an acronym of the Portuguese Institute of Cinematographic and Audiovisual Art (Instituto Português da Arte Cinematográfica e Audiovisual) which was renamed ICAM (the Institute of Cinema and Audiovisual Media) in 1997 and is now known as ICA (Institute of Cinema and Audiovisual).
19 Gil, 'Entretien avec Margarida Gil', 96.
20 Gil, 'Conversa' [interview with Ilda Castro], 207.
21 Gil, 'O produtor não põe um cêntimo no filme' [interview to Vanessa Sousa Dias], 54; emphasis in original.
22 Pereira, *A Mulher-Cineasta*, 185.
23 The principal idea of *Adriana* echoes, but also counterpoints, the plot of Solveig Nordlund's film (*Aparelho Voador a Baixa Altitude*, 2002), an adaptation from J. G. Ballard's short story. In a post-apocalyptic future, a couple living in a community where procreation is controlled by an oppressive government decide to isolate themselves in order to give birth to a forbidden child. See Chapter 3 in this volume by Hilary Owen for a reading of the biopolitics in Nordlund's film.
24 See 'Entrevista com Margarida Gil, realizadora de "Paixão" @ Canal 180', 20 February 2012, https://www.youtube.com/watch?v=IVUvOzzCFWY (accessed 8 July 2019).

Section Two

Feminisms

3

Monsters, mutants and maternity: The politics of the posthuman in Teresa Villaverde, Raquel Freire and Solveig Nordlund

Hilary Owen

Sangue de aborto não é sangue vertido pelo rei, é sempre vertido contra vós todos.

Novas Cartas Portuguesas[1]

Blood shed during abortion is not blood shed for the King, it is always blood shed against all of you.

New Portuguese Letters[2]

If any single issue united, shaped and defined Portuguese political feminism over the last half-century, it was the decriminalization of abortion. Finally enacted into law following a referendum in 2007, this high point of success for decades of women's rights activism occurred, however, only at the cost of wiping the fingerprints of women's rights off the campaign's overt public image and strategies of appeal. As most commentators and historians concur, a number of key factors permitted the change of climate that emerged between the failed referendum campaign of 1998, and the successful one of 2007. First, very obviously, the mainstream Left parties, and particularly the Partido Socialista (PS- broadly Centre Left) government of 2005 under José Sócrates as prime minister, began to espouse the pro-choice cause with sufficient, if not total, degrees of uniformity and determination. Second, a major and well-documented discursive shift took place in the public justification for decriminalization, away from the emphasis on women's choice and rights over their own bodies, to a far greater focus on women's health, the problem of clandestine abortions, the collective and national social good, and the legal injustices and wide inconsistencies that blighted the actual process of law enforcement and prosecution in specific, well-publicized cases.³

As Manuela Tavares notes, in an interview for *Jornal i* in 2017, the tenth anniversary year of the bill, 'The right to one's own body … could not be our main line of argument. … Feminists underwent a process of evolution that involved broadening their range of alliances and ultimately winning.'⁴ In this process, the years immediately following the failed referendum of 1998 were particularly crucial, with considerable anger and disenchantment directed at the PS, especially at the then prime minister António Guterres. Manuela Tavares refers to this time as 'yet another long trek across the desert'.⁵ During this period, notable women artists, writers and figures in public life and the media played a significant role in maintaining a high profile on the debate. Paula Rego, for instance, produced her famous series of *Abortion* pastel paintings in 1998–99. By the second referendum of 2007, the campaign had the public support of canonical women writers, such as Agustina Bessa-Luís and Lídia Jorge.⁶ The current chapter is an exploration of the role played by three specific women filmmakers and the landmark films they released in the 'long desert trek' landscape, that formed the transitional limbo of 1998–2002, before the PS took up the baton to defend decriminalization under the Sócrates government in 2005.

Reproductive politics in film

Although they belong to different generations, Teresa Villaverde, Raquel Freire and Solveig Nordlund all had something specifically identifiable to say about reproductive rights and abortion during this period. Documentaries and television films made by women in Portugal had always played a significant role in debates on abortion rights and family planning.⁷ My interest in this chapter, however, is to see how women filmmakers also insinuated their views on abortion decriminalization and choice into full-length fiction cinema. Villaverde's third feature film *Os Mutantes* (*The Mutants*) was released on 27 November 1998, five months after the failed 1998 referendum on 28 June that year. Part of its central narrative concerns unwanted teenage pregnancy.⁸ Given this context, it is almost impossible to interpret the situation of Andreia in *The Mutants* independently of the debates surrounding the 1998 abortion referendum. Three years later in 2001, one of Villaverde's former production assistants, Raquel Freire, released her own first feature film, a gothic slasher movie about Coimbra University students, called *Rasganço* (*Rending*, 2001). Freire also later acted as director of campaigns in 2007 for the *Médicos pela Escolha* (Doctors for Choice) movement, making videos for them and for other pro-choice movements. And in 2002, the veteran filmmaker Solveig Nordlund, Swedish-born but long established in Portugal, released an adaptation of the English writer J. G. Ballard's science fiction story about eugenics, 'Low-Flying Aircraft', called in the film, as in the Portuguese text translation, *Aparelho Voador a Baixa Altitude*.[9]

All three of the films I will discuss here share the fact that they place at the heart of their narratives a young, pregnant woman facing a choice. All of them, on close inspection, include coded or cryptic comments about the abortion debate, although neither Villaverde nor Freire ever uses that specific word and few, if any, critics have spoken in any detail, or at all, about this aspect of their work. Nordlund repeatedly does use the 'a' word in the safer context of a counterfactual future scenario in which forced abortions are ostensibly being resisted rather than endorsed. A further, significant uniting factor is that all of them, in different ways, make substantial use of the transnationally recognizable conventions pertaining to gothic horror and science fiction genres. This in itself is worthy of attention. As Ana Catarina Pereira has noted, these are not at all conventional genre choices in Portugal's home-grown cinema industry, even less so for women directors.[10] Insofar as these predominate over, or strategically displace, social realist techniques, they maximize the directors' critical latitude and freedom of expression. By universalizing their strategies of appeal, they create 'other world' scenarios that function as landscapes for exploring the possibilities opened up by the 'posthuman' condition. Elaine Graham, drawing partly on the theoretical writings of Rosi Braidotti, gives the following timely reminders about the historical gendering of what we call monstrosity and the non-human:

> In androcentric cultures where 'human nature' is equated with characteristics privileged as male, women and monsters are 'that which is other than ... whatever the norm may be'. ... Monstrosity, femininity and deviance, as markers of alterity, therefore, are not stable categories but inversions of hegemonic norms. In showing forth abomination, monsters are the evidence of the crime, the symptom of the disease, the misbegotten exemplars of the 'faultlines' by which the normal and the pathological are established.[11]

The dialogues that these three films establish with the 'monstrous', the 'non-human' and the putatively 'posthuman' afford them a position from which to critique the exclusion of specific, alienated forms of embodiment (female, raced, gay or differently abled) by the androcentric false neutral of universal humanism, human rights and broadly socialist collectivism. Strategically deploying these definitions of monstrosity, deviance and the alien body to invert and destabilize hegemonic gender norms, they are able to lay bare the various epistemological 'faultlines' that criminalize women for abortion. In this context, the shift towards viewing the abortion question through a posthumanist lens (as a stand-in, I would argue, for a direct and overtly feminist-identified one) effectively takes the fight to the enemy. It holds the distorting mirror of monsterization up to the social hypocrisies of both Roman Catholic and Marxist androcentricity, and the forms of social embodiment that they impose. The films thus rely on genre conventions and techniques associated with the 'speculative' fiction-making of horror and science fiction to afford a powerful locus of critical distantiation and alienation.

Dysnarrating the icon

Of these three films, *The Mutants* might appear superficially to be the most amenable to social realist interpretation. Villaverde's narrative centres around three alienated adolescents, the so-called mutants of the title, in a contemporary Lisbon that is radically defamiliarized as Villaverde reveals the 'city beneath', effectively turning landmarks such as Rua Augusta, the banks of the Tagus and Rossio railway station into a new and threatening landscape. The interlocking and fragmented narratives of three adolescents loosely structure the film, following a generally downward trajectory that leaves all of them in an even worse position by the end.[12] The black Cape Verdean boy, Ricardo is ultimately kicked to death for a minor incident of burglary, and his distraught friend Pedro finds no comfort in his dysfunctional alcoholic family. But the most dramatic and controversial element of the film involves the unhappily pregnant Andreia, played by Ana Moreira in her first major role. Failing to find the child's father (who is possibly Ricardo) or to procure an abortion, she winds up giving birth in the public toilet of a petrol station and then abandoning her baby.[13]

Cristina Álvarez López and Adrian Martin have issued a timely and insightful warning against the easy referential retrieval of sociopolitical issues in Villaverde's films that would ultimately 'flatten' them into 'mirror-reflections of realities and topics *outside* cinema'.[14] Rather, as they go on to note, 'Both the cinematic style and the narrative construction of Villaverde's work violate the most typical principles of what we conventionally take to be the realism of social issue films.'[15] If there is a political edge to *The Mutants*, regarding the context of abortion and choice embedded in the final scenes of Andreia giving birth, I would argue that it arises from the way Villaverde draws on specific cultural iconographies in order to unstitch and de-auratize their symbolic mythical status. As Álvarez López and Martin have indicated, the image of the Holy Family, rendered unstable and internally fractured, proves central to most of Villaverde's work in one way or another (see also Mariana Liz in this volume).[16] In this sense, Villaverde bears out the findings of Claire Johnston's now classic essay 'Women's Cinema as Counter-Cinema'. In respect of the non-realist genre choices of women directors in early Hollywood, Johnston states:

> Because iconography offers in some ways a greater resistance to the realist characterisations, the mythic qualities of certain stereotypes become far more easily detachable and can be used as a shorthand for referring to an ideological tradition in order to provide a critique of it.[17]

It is in this relationship with Catholic myth and iconography, and its deconstruction by anti-realist techniques more akin to the gothic and horror genres, that Villaverde inscribes her most compelling engagement with the politics of Andreia's plight, as we will go on to discuss later. Priming the viewer for this climactic point in the film, however, Villaverde lays an enigmatic trail in which neither Andreia's dialogues nor her unpredictable actions offer up any immediate explanation of her situation.

While the word 'abortion' or 'termination' is never spoken aloud, it is cryptically alluded to on more than one occasion. Álvarez López and Martin have borrowed from Alain Robbe-Grillet's theories of narratology and his idea of 'dysnarration' to describe the fragmented, discontinuous narratives that characterize Villaverde's cinema, emphasizing 'the *suspension* of narrative, of its conventionally driving motor forces and mechanisms of spectator identification'.[18] One consequence of this, as they observe, is that events and their meaning are only grasped, if at all, retroactively after the fact. For example, Andreia is shown at one point, with no immediate diegetic rationale, hammering on the closed door of a flat, possibly still hunting for the child's father. However, the scene that follows raises other explanations. The woman in the flat below comes to find her and offers her a meal, asking, as she sits surrounded by Catholic iconography, 'Do you believe in God? ... He could punish you.' This short exchange retroactively raises the possibility that the previous scene had actually represented Andreia's searching out an illegal abortionist's address only to find they have moved on. This reading is subsequently reinforced when the director of Andreia's social institution is deciding where to send her next. He asks her, 'Did you do something while you were out there?' to which she replies, 'I didn't do anything while I was out there. Everything is exactly as it was.' The director cynically concludes, 'It's too late now anyway to do what you were trying to do.' The coded, public understanding of illegal and taboo terminations remains elliptically implied in these exchanges. These techniques of dysnarration implant in the film the embedded 'trace narrative' of a powerful social taboo on abortion. Only when the viewer is finally confronted with a bloodstained and screaming Andreia, who has clearly gone into labour in a public toilet, do the full consequences of her unwanted pregnancy become incontrovertible and hyper visible.

This sudden eruption of an all too visible horror (and Andreia's birth scene is far more violent and prolonged than either Ricardo's death or Pedro's sexual exploitation) acts as the negative payback for society's forced concealment of her truth. This is also, I would argue, where Villaverde's take on the potentialities of gothic horror have a clear role to play. On a superficial level, the screaming and bloodshed evidently evoke the slash and splatter sub-genres of horror as well as reconnecting to the film's opening sequence in which Andreia has already drawn her own blood by thrusting her hand through a glass window. However, the most specific carry-over from horror genre here is the way in which Villaverde negates the totalizing effects of realist suture, freezing the viewer into a suspended limbo space that is neither the proximity of identification nor the distance of reflection. As Carolin Overhoff Ferreira notes, the birth scene is shot using forty-eight images per second with the sound desynchronized from the image such that the 'physical pain is extended by the slow motion'.[19] And the slow motion effect emphasizes the exposure of the workings of suture. In its classic definition by Kaja Silverman (drawing on Jacques-Alain Miller and Jacques Lacan) the concept of suture serves to identify the relationship between lack or loss, and subjectivity in the way that spectatorship operates, such that the film's narrative sutures 'over the wound of castration'.[20] The perspective of the viewer is meant to be sutured to that of a character on screen, among other ways, by virtue of the classic shot/reverse shot process where the gaze alternates between the characters in an exchange. The viewer and the film use a range of visual, intellectual and other techniques to suture over the gaps and limitations in what the viewer is given to see, and this creates an illusion of completeness that classic, realist cinema maintains by keeping the sutures invisible.

What is very specific to the horror genre, however, is the way in which it refuses to make the operations of suture invisible. It does not endeavour to maintain the realist illusion of completeness. Thus, according to Judith Halberstam, 'Suture precisely appears as a surface effect and the [horror] film constantly attempts to call our attention to cinematic production, its failures and excesses.'[21] As Overhoff Ferreira and others have observed regarding the variable workings of suture in *The Mutants*, part of its effect derives from the fact that 'hardly ever is there a shot/reverse shot'.[22] POV shots are also very few and far between, as Overhoff Ferreira notes, with the result that 'the film's spectator/text-relationship is complex and unstable. The spectator is invited to shift between emotional involvement and distance.'[23] Deprived of all visual agency in this scene, Andreia never gazes directly back. Her eyes are either lowered (in an ironic take on the iconic modesty of the Catholic Madonna) or casting widely around her in panic for a supporting presence that is not there. The deployment of slow motion and desynchronized sound here eventually gives way to a very long extreme close-up of her still, sweat-drenched face, only partially visible, with the emphasis on her lowered eyelids (see Figures 3.1 and 3.2). The Madonna and Child iconography is further fractured here by the absence of a child. The baby itself is neither seen nor heard during the scenes in the toilet. The camera focus rests solely on Andreia. Only after the fact of the birth, when a stranger finds the baby and a group gathers round it, is the viewer effectively given the knowledge that the child has even been born alive. Andreia's own attention, meanwhile, is taken up with escaping the scene undiscovered.

Figure 3.1 Andreia about to give birth in a public toilet (Madragoa Filmes, 2001).

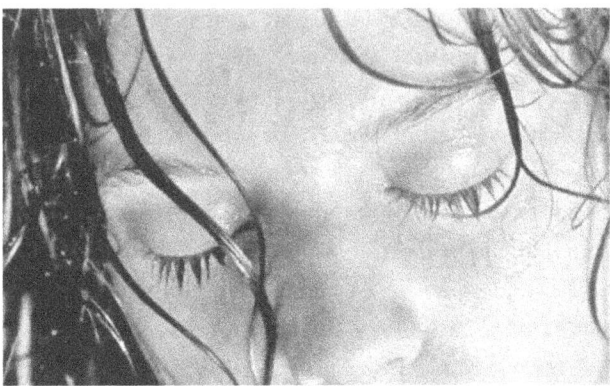

Figure 3.2 Still image of Andreia after the birth (Madragoa Filmes, 2001).

For this thoroughly desacralized maternal goddess, the only sanctuary is a public toilet. And Villaverde wastes no time in reminding us that this toilet is in Portugal. It is not happening 'somewhere else'. The 'here and now' of her situation in Portugal, in 1998, is strongly subliminally underlined in the scenes before and after this one, with Villaverde's use of background colours in the mise en scène, to evoke the predominant red and green of the Portuguese flag, which we have also repeatedly seen hanging outside specific state institutions in different places. Throughout most of the film Villaverde has constructed an alienated, dystopian vision of a Lisbon that lies just beside and beneath the familiar city landmarks. The delinquent children are termed 'mutants' because they bear a message of warning about what humanity might evolve into. This was previously powerfully evoked with Pedro's close-up gaze to camera, over the electronic voice of Arnold Schwarzenegger on a fairground game, stating in English, 'I am the future.' Yet, as the mother of a child for the next generation, it is Andreia who is most obviously and literally the 'bearer of the future'.

In the closing credits, the limitations of national progress are brought sharply into focus with the symbolic choice of a song that has strong historic overtones, the bard of the 25 April 1974 Revolution, Zeca Afonso, singing *Que Amor Não Me Engana* (Love does not deceive me) which he wrote in 1973, while imprisoned in Caxias. What ought to be a clear historical anchorage point for the film and a milestone of change since 1974 becomes, instead, in relation to Andreia's fate at least, a far more ambiguous marker of women's unfinished revolution. Indeed, by choosing a song that itself hangs somewhere between personal love balladry and political protest in Afonso's oeuvre, Villaverde encapsulates Andreia's dual lack of political voice as a victim who has been viciously *enganada* (deceived) both by love and by the historical failure of socialist politics to address her dilemma.

The Coimbra ripper

The limits and blind spots of complacent, historical socialism are even more pointedly critiqued in the second of these three films, *Rending*. This gothic slasher movie was the first feature film of Raquel Freire, released in 2001 three years after *The Mutants*. Indeed, as noted earlier, a young Raquel Freire was credited as working for Teresa Villaverde on *The Mutants*. Freire herself, a native of Porto, is well known as an LGBT activist, writer and filmmaker, and a Coimbra Law graduate, and former vice-president of the Associação Académica de Coimbra. The film draws its name from the famous *rasganço*, the final stage of Coimbra's traditional student *praxe* rituals, which entails ripping the clothing off fellow students at the end of their studies, as part of the rite of passage that signals their going out into the world as graduates.

Freire first introduces us to this hieratic world of an ongoing *rasganço* ritual from the perspective of an outsider, the mysterious Edgar. He is not part of Coimbra's intellectual oligarchy, and as such comes to embody a dark and threatening urban underclass from Lisbon.[24] In a single night he seduces three women connected with Coimbra University, the final year law student, Ana Rita; the worker at the hostel where he stays, Maria dos Anjos; and the Marquesa Dona Zita de Portugal who is a psychology professor, the daughter of a long line of Reitores, and the wife of a lecherous medical professor, Dr Filipe Portugal. In the figure of Edgar and the Coimbra students, with their vampiric *praxe* and their seeming love of biting, Freire draws together two readily recognizable horror genres: that of the vampire, particularly in its American teen college drama mode and that of the slasher or splatter movie. Indeed, Freire has referred to Luis Buñuel's *El Ángel Exterminador* (*The Exterminating Angel*, 1962), as the inspiration for the figure of Edgar, while his name was drawn from Edgar Allan Poe, evoking the great literary founder of the gothic and vampire bride narratives.[25]

Systematically excluded from student social activities and from the possibility of studying at the university, Edgar responds to his humiliation and emasculation by embarking on a serial rape and slashing spree (see Figure 3.3).[26] He targets five Coimbra women students (Laura, Leonor, Sofia, Lígia and Ofélia)

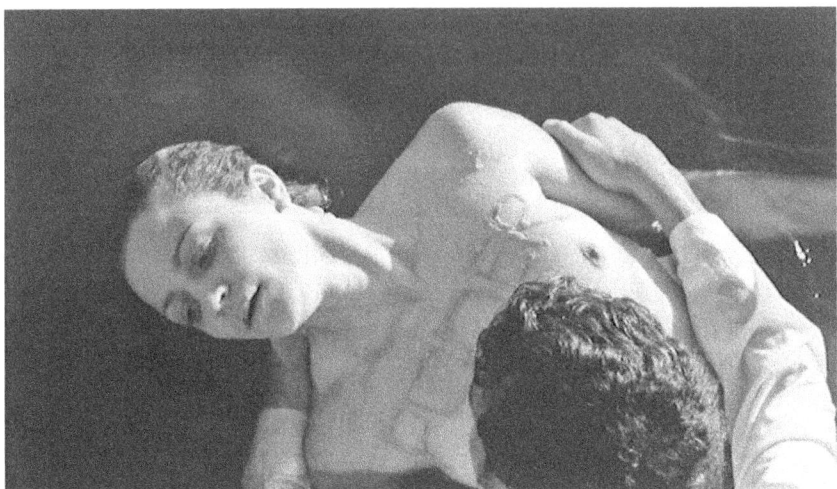

Figure 3.3 The slashed body of Ofélia being pulled from the water (Lusomundo, 2001).

and carves across their naked chests the following letters and words: AAC (Associação Académica de Coimbra) – U (*Universidade*) – *Saber* (Knowledge) – *Praxe* (Student Tradition) – *Poder* (Power). He draws his explicit inspiration from the textbook legal definitions of rape, perversion, right to life and qualified homicide, and from the lectures given by the promiscuous law professor, Carvalho e Melo. The professor significantly tells his students that Man is the foundation of the law, effectively erecting the cornerstone of universal humanism that is targeted by Edgar's crimes. As he prepares to carve his latest inscription onto the body of his fourth rape victim, Lígia, the phrase 'life is indubitably the most protected juridical good in the Portuguese Penal Code' is read out by Edgar in a voiceover to the scene. If Edgar's masculinity, as a less educated, working-class man, is undermined by his exclusion from Coimbra's male student rituals, he is, nonetheless, able to reassert it by disfiguring the bodies of the raped and mutilated women and impregnating Ana Rita as the stakes of his revenge drama.[27]

In Freire's film, the punishment of the human body is visited disproportionately on women. All of his crimes against the students target the integrity of the female body as male property, be it the rape and slashing of the Coimbra boys' girlfriends, or the sowing of deviant seed in Ana Rita by a social inferior outside the Coimbra circle. The humanist tenets of the law (which Edgar scornfully reads to himself before each attack, having ripped the pages from the Faculty's Law manuals) are shown to be powerless in the defence of the female body. Further, the *praxe rasganço* metaphor, the ripping that Edgar enacts at the heart of this film, by slashing female bodies not clothes, is literalized here to expose the filmic workings of suture.

Rending effectively unstitches the elite heterosexual 'romance' of fado courtship and Queima das Fitas in such a way as to expose its status as straight, white, bourgeois patriarchal and, in the refracted guise of Edgar, monstrous. Edgar most readily infiltrates Coimbra by dressing up and taking part in a pre-existing, fetishistic culture of sexploitation. As Halberstam observes,

> The genders that emerge triumphant at the gory conclusion of a splatter film are literally posthuman, they punish the limits of the human body and they mark identities as always stitched, sutured, bloody at the seams, and completely beyond the limits and the reaches of an impotent humanism.[28]

Edgar is never caught by the law. Rather, his body-ripping ascent to a posthuman status exposes the terms on which Coimbra's hegemonic human sexuality is granted. The literalization of the *praxe rasganço* metaphor at the heart of this film clearly unpicks heterosexual identities suggesting new polymorphous gender alignments. However, where abortion and gay marriage remain illegal, the all too real bloody punishment of human body limitations is not equally borne, or equally dealt out, by all forms of body. A gay male student falls victim to a vicious gay bashing as a gang hacks off his long hair during Queima das Fitas. And Leonor, the lesbian partner of the Associação Académica president Inês, still becomes one of Edgar's rape and slash victims alongside the four straight women. Inês's status in the Associação sets her up too as an indirect target for masculine 'honour-based' revenge.

The vulnerability of female flesh is granted specificity here through its capacity to be impregnated and forced to reproduce. When Ana Rita goes to the doctor to confirm her pregnancy, the automatic assumption is that she should not think twice about going ahead with maternity. She is a Roman Catholic, in her final year at university. As the female doctor confirms, it is what everyone, including herself, did in their student days, and the father will doubtless be reconciled with the idea in time. Yet, the woman doctor's own lack of a wedding ring suggests all did not, in her case, end as well as she claims. The doctor's optimism comes further unstuck, when Ana Rita will not confirm who the father is, hinting that he is not a Coimbra student but an outsider. When Ana Rita is subsequently taken to a medical clinic after fainting in the crowd at the Queima das Fitas, she overhears two nurses discussing the horrors of clandestine abortion attempts they have witnessed as they admit they still remember every individual case they see. One remarks, 'Those young girls that die in the hospital, almost like animals, there are no proper facilities. And as for the midwives … .' Another nurse relates her personal experience: 'In my case, the midwife grabbed hold of me, dragged me to the door of the building, and then dumped me there on the ground. If it had not been for Dr Filipe Portugal … .'

The only solution for her had been recourse to Dona Zita Portugal's doctor husband. He readily performs clandestine abortions, not least for the women he has himself impregnated, as the nurse indicates, adding hastily to keep it quiet because 'walls have ears'. The long historical existence of 'undercover' abortion is later underscored when a camera pans along and then moves in close-up to scrutinize a glass case display in the Museu de Ciências, housed in the Colégio de Jesus, filled with scientific specimen jars of deformed and pre-term foetuses (see Figure 3.4). The POV becomes implicitly Edgar's as the focus switches to show him walking along the display and examining scalpels as he caresses his own knife before his final attack. Given that exploited foetal images were a mainstay of pro-life campaign literature, Freire tellingly reframes them here through the desiring gaze of a slasher rapist. One row of jars is superimposed on another and another to convey the long continuity of a medical history that has always included contingent, scientifically 'useful', undercover abortions by the powerful.

Figure 3.4 Foetal remains on display in the Coimbra University, Museu de Ciências (Lusomundo, 2001).

Ana Rita, in contrast, seems to have little choice but to bear the child to term, and to keep silent about Edgar's lower-class paternity, where his revenge has taken the form of bastardizing and hybridizing the elite. The students' own Marxist revolutionary aesthetics are made to appear unknowingly complicit with this through Freire's ironic play with the resistance classic from 1963, *Trova do Vento que Passa* (written by Manuel Alegre, and immortalized for that generation by Adriano Correia de Oliveira). The conventional Marxist agricultural tropes of the closing verse *há sempre quem semeia, / há sempre quem diz não* (there is always someone who sows the seed / there is always some who says no) rebound disproportionately on the female body as the symbolic soil in which the revolution implants itself. The *quem semeia* who sows his seed this time is clearly Edgar, bent on class revenge.

In the closing scene of the film, after Dona Zita de Portugal has identified the killer to the police, we see Edgar bringing red and white flowers for the *rasganço* ritual of Ana Rita. Her closing *rasganço* ceremony is an ironic 'deflowering after the fact'. The violent slashings of the various rape victims pre-empt the enforced bloodshed that awaits Ana Rita too. She is exposed to the threat of public shame as Dona Zita implies that she has identified the child's socially inferior paternity, remarking, 'I hope it does not look like the father.' Where the Coimbra elites would normally reproduce among themselves, endogamously like vampires, the class struggle has become demographic, with the weaponization of rape propelling the bodies of women, and the abortion question, onto the front line, in a way that the old Marxist resistance songs of the 1960s repeatedly intoned by the students, cannot begin to engage.[29] The viewer's gaze is sutured to Edgar's masterly POV in an extreme vertical shot downwards at a trapped and abject Ana Rita, a mask of gothically cascading blood red roses, red carnation fragments and tears, as the camera then tracks from one corner to another of the upper quadrangle to signal Edgar's disappearance. The abortion and gay bashing issues ground this film in a lived, political domain where freedom of sexual fantasy and identity cannot simply be acted out by all at equal risk. For slasher movies in particular, as Judith Halberstam argues, the actual fragility of skin itself 'emblematizes the unstable boundary between representation and reality that horror plays with, thus disrupting the usually expected safe relations between them'.[30] Under the surface of Ana Rita's skin, exposed to the public with her *rasganço* at the end, is the monster demon child of the rapist Edgar that she will have to bear into the future. Attacks upon skin in slasher movies draw attention to the skin's function as pure surface, and thence to the relation of surface to depth, in this case the chaos, disruption and moral darkness that lie hidden beneath Freire's Coimbra.

The road to nowhere?

The third and last film I want to look at, from 2002, inverts the perspective of the previous two by representing a dystopian totalitarian world of forced terminations. Moving away from the posthuman monstrosity of classic gothic horror, it illuminates the question of choice in the boldly counterfactual science fiction context of a future time and place that are ostensibly not Portugal and also not the present. Set in the 'future' thirty years on from when it was written in 1976, J. G. Ballard's original story is located in the real Spanish Costa Brava seaside town of Ampuriabrava, cast here as a decadent and decaying resort, at the end of time and space. As many critics have observed, one of the most strikingly successful aspects of Nordlund's visual design was her use of the purpose-built, but soon to be abandoned, 1950s Portuguese seaside resort of Tróia (near Setúbal).[31] In Nordlund's film it is a liminal 'nowhere land' by the sea, with a hotel inhabited by a cast of elderly international grotesques, creating a kind of globalized pre-apocalypse.[32]

The main topic discussed in the resort at the 'end of the universe' is that populations are declining to the point of countries becoming non-viable. As we are told, 'Sweden is no longer operational.' Babies are constantly being born with physical abnormalities (such as exposed optic nerves and deformed genitalia) and then designated as 'zotes'. They are thus routinely aborted in increasingly huge numbers, causing population replacement to fall dangerously below viability. In the original Ballard work, a heavily pregnant Judith and her husband come to Ampuriabrava, where they are hoping after six previous abortions to finally produce a normal child under the tutelage of the mysterious Dr Gould who has the medical care of Judith. Gould, however, also undertakes mysterious, unexplained journeys in an old turbo propeller crop sprayer plane, the low-flying aircraft of the title.

The couple's experience of fleeing to the hotel is framed by a climate of fear, clandestinity and militarized police persecution all too recognizable from the ongoing abortion struggles of the early 2000s. Just as Freire borrowed and repurposed classic pro-life icons such as foetuses in jars, Nordlund's film makes constant use of postered slogans such as 'We believe in the Future' and 'This is us' alongside idealistically Aryan-looking babies. The film narrative superficially endorses resistance to forced termination as a form of eugenics, affording Nordlund a far greater latitude to use the 'abortion' word openly, than seems to have been possible for either Villaverde or Freire. However, the issue of a woman's right to make her own reproductive choices remains at the ideological heart of the film in such a way that the abortion debate continues to be held in view, albeit counterfactually. And many of the film's dominant images effectively play in both directions. At one point in the film version, Judite has a nightmare about an agonizing, blood-soaked birth strapped onto a doctor's couch, an image of extreme institutional control. An earlier sequence in the film shows a nameless pregnant woman on the run from three armed policemen and a helicopter. This violent policing of pregnancy across a national border powerfully evokes Portugal's options for obtaining an abortion at that time, either travelling abroad undetected or resorting to the backstreet.

In 2004, only two years after this film was made, Paulo Portas, as Portuguese defence minister, ordered the navy to fire on the Dutch abortion clinic boat, 'Women on Waves' when it entered Portuguese waters. This begs the question of how recognizable the Portuguese referents were in this film, amidst this clearly transnationalized allegory of apocalypse from an English source. Certainly, J. G. Ballard's original name for Dr Gould is retained in English, and other European languages figure, but the predominant language used is Portuguese. Furthermore, the central husband and wife characters have Portuguese-spelled first names, Judite and André, the latter a change from his name Richard in the Ballard original.

The film adaptation remains truthful to Ballard's central premise of the Forrester couple finally realizing that the aborted zote babies represent in fact the next phase of human evolution. However, where Ballard focuses primarily on the decisive agency of the two men, Forrester and Gould, Nordlund's adaptation gives Judite the dominant perspective and makes birth a woman's choice. She also makes Judite aware of the zotes' evolutionary significance through her interaction with another woman, Carmen, who turns out to be Gould's daughter, a zote kept secretly alive. Carmen appears as an exotically beautiful nocturnal ghost who wanders the hotel in dark glasses, her presence marked by strange, electronic music, green signs and blue lighting. She can only discern objects and directions with the help of luminous green painted traces left for her to follow on walls and open spaces. Her influence on Judite grows as if Carmen were somehow controlling Judite's unborn child. Beset by unexplained physical symptoms, Judite increasingly fears the child is a monster. As Judite is drawn wordlessly into Carmen's sphere of influence, she overcomes her husband's pessimism and ensures that her zote child, Elias, is given over to Carmen's care, as the only person equipped to ensure he can live in the new world of the future. As Gould tells them, zotes can only live together in groups, and he is using his turbo prop plane to paint the world in the green luminous colour they can see and navigate by so that they can replace the current human race on the edge of extinction.

From being a monstrous non-human destined for extermination, the child becomes a posthuman guarantor of survival through the fact of his connectedness with other beings who relate similarly to the material and technological world. Parenting a living child in this context is posited as being necessarily both social and natal, in a move which cleverly sidesteps and decentres the bio-essentializing of women, at the same time as it still acknowledges the specificity of women's role in giving birth. In this context, perhaps Elias is in fact destined to be, following Rosi Braidotti's description of Dolly the cloned sheep, 'the first of a new gender, … beyond the dichotomies of the patriarchal kinship system'.[33]

This is certainly hinted at in the scene where Judite and André discuss the child's name, whiling away their time in the partly ruined chapel. They decide, at André's prompting, on his grandfather's name, Elias, the Old Testament prophet. Yet, as they do so the camera pans to the space where the image of a divine figure or prophet of the future ought once to have been in the chapel's altarpiece (see Figure 3.5). The patriarchal Christian backcloth to André's traditional patrilinear name choice has been lost, or even consciously excised. There is only an outline, an ending, a vanishing point, a space to be rewritten, or repainted, in the future. Judite meanwhile states that she knows without seeing a scan that her child is a boy, already acquiring the mysterious visionary powers possessed by Carmen. Where the shift in the planet's future is to nurture rather than natalism, there is a corresponding shift of alignment in the relations of 'new humans' such as Carmen and Elias with technology, science and the material world. In this respect, both Nordlund and Ballard pin their techno-utopian vision of planetary survival in the face of environmental and demographic destruction, on an idea that closely resembles the quintessentially posthuman figure of the cyborg.

The concept of the cyborg was famously coined for feminist theory in the 1980s by Donna Haraway.[34] Haraway's cyborg metaphor for postmodern,

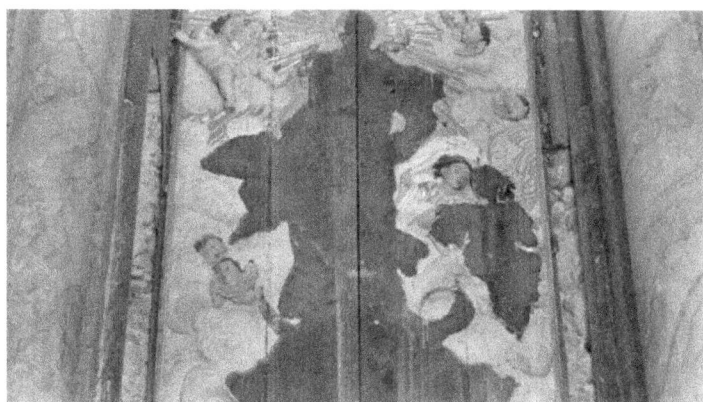

Figure 3.5 The altarpiece in the abandoned chapel (Filmes do Tejo/Costa do Castelo, 2002).

feminist subjectivity refers to 'a cybernetic organism, a hybrid of machine and organism, a creature of social reality as well as a creature of fiction'.[35] Read in this cyborgian context, Nordlund's Carmen accurately transposes the passage in Ballard's original where, as Gould tells us, Carmen 'has a huge collection of watches with luminous dials, hundreds of them, that she's been filching for years from shops. She's got them all working together but to different times, it's some sort of gigantic computer. God only knows what overlit world nature is preparing her for, but I suppose we won't be around to see it.'[36] Indeed, Carmen never appears independently of her supporting technologies, her dark glasses, her three watches, her guiding ciphers. When the couple eventually hand their child over to her, Judite tells her husband, 'Our world has ended, in fact.' The potential emotional charge of Judite handing her child to Carmen is not presented here in terms of loss. The film has progressively overlapped and merged the figures of Carmen and Judite into the same aesthetic universe during their wordless encounters, gesturing towards new forms of bodily interface for the future, and deconstructing the identification of maternity as monolith. As Carmen takes the child out into a fading of light, we see André remove his watch on which the alarm has just sounded for the end of known civilization, placing it precisely next to the luminous map of signs that belongs to Carmen.

In the final sequence, the departing red sports car bearing André and Judite sets off on a road that stretches ahead like a runway, while Gould's low-flying aircraft dips over it, tracing rivers and valleys in the green luminescent paint to guarantee planetary survival, as implied by the final extreme long-distance

Figure 3.6 Carmen's green, fluorescent zote alphabet (Filmes do Tejo/Costa do Castelo, 2002).

shot turning its perspective over the earth into that of a globe where green ciphers flash like signs on a digital screen (see Figure 3.6). These signals, in a language no longer common to mere humanity, dominate the utopian closing sequence. Gould's name, of course, contains the letters that spell 'God'. Yet he remains a resolutely post-divine human, in his posthuman quest. In this sense, the 'flying aircraft' itself, put to a new purpose, becomes the indispensable mechanical 'parent' of the future. And the bio-essentialism that underpins both the binary terms in the nature/nurture debate is deconstructively displaced by new posthumanist images of technological interface and interdependency. As Haraway reminds us, 'No objects, spaces or bodies are sacred in themselves; any component can be interfaced with any other if the proper code, can be constructed for processing signals in common language.'[37]

Conclusion

The posthuman vision in Nordlund's film lies in shifting social beliefs and possibilities in order to accommodate newly evolved bodily experiences, such as Carmen's and the child's altered vision, in a radical redisposing of bodies and sensory capacities, affective ties, social relations and the interface with the material and technological worlds and environment.[38] This social vision of a changed posthumanity (i.e. no longer monstrous) does not deny women's role in birthing, but it refuses a natalist ontology of human survival that is wholly reducible to it.[39] It de-instrumentalizes and de-centres the biologically sexed female-assigned body. As such, it affords a valuable and pragmatic, counterfactual proposal in the quest to carry the abortion struggle beyond a manicheistic discourse, pitching women's rights against the rights of the unborn child.

If anything is shared by these three films beyond their focus on abortion issues, and their astute deployment of speculative/fantasy genres and techniques, it is this emphasis on a collectivized social responsibility for the reproductive politics of the nation. *The Mutants* asks how it can be good for the nation as a whole for terrified girls to give solitary birth in petrol stations, generating the next cycle of abandoned, institutionalized children. *Rending* questions the moral and social value of a deceived woman giving birth to a child engendered by a psychotic rapist slasher, instrumentalizing the wombs of women to avenge class discrimination. Nordlund's film shifts the discursive frame of abortion debate away from bio-essentialist natalism towards a putatively collectivized social parenting as part of a necessary interface with new technologies and environments. If Haraway's posthuman cyborg in the mid-1980s was seeking to be 'faithful to feminism, socialism, and materialism', women film makers in late 1990s Portugal similarly used gothic monstrosity, the cyborgian image and the posthuman to render existing forms of humanist hegemony radically alien and anachronistic, both out of time and out of place.[40] Making a timely cinema of intervention out of these non-traditionally Portuguese film genres, they hold the pathologizing and criminalizing of the female body to the light and to account, as a means of exposing the mythical and historical faultlines that underpin these discourses, too long unexamined by anti-abortion campaigners both left and right of the political spectrum, during the 1980s and 1990s. In this sense, I would contend that the green luminous signs painted across the universe by Nordlund's Gould, the blood stains left on the toilet wall in *The Mutants*, and the bloody gothic splatter trail in *Rending*, function metonymically as the fingerprints of an embodied feminist politics being subtly reimprinted on abortion and reproductive rights debates, even as pro-choice feminist alliances were being contingently required to measure their distance from it in the early 2000s.

Notes

1 Maria Isabel Barreno, Maria Teresa Horta and Maria Velho da Costa, *Novas Cartas Portuguesas*, ed. Ana Luísa Amaral (Lisbon: Dom Quixote, 2010), 123.
2 Maria Isabel Barreno, Maria Teresa Horta and Maria Velho da Costa, *New Portuguese Letters* (London: Readers International, 1994), 135. Pro-choice arguments were first

comprehensively articulated in 1975 with the publication of *Aborto, direito ao nosso corpo* [Abortion, the Right to Our Bodies] (Lisbon: Futura, 1975) by Maria Teresa Horta, Célia Metrass and Helena Sá de Medeiros. Portugal's foundational second-wave feminist text, *Novas Cartas Portuguesas*, had also exposed the horrors and fatalities caused by backstreet abortion, as far back as 1972. A useful chronology of Portugal's struggle for decriminalization of abortion, from 1974 to 2007, was produced by Manuela Tavares of UMAR at http://www.umarfeminismos.org/images/stories/pdf/cronologialuta.pdf (accessed 1 July 2019).

3 See Rosa Monteiro, 'A descriminalização do aborto em Portugal: Estado, movimentos de mulheres e partidos políticos', *Análise Social* 204, no. 47 (2012): 586–605. See also Alison E. Woodward, Mercè Renom and Jean-Michel Bonvin (eds), *Transforming Gendered Well-Being in Europe: The Impact of Social Movements* (Farnham and Burlington: Ashgate, 2011), 195.

4 Marta F. Reis, 'Manuela Tavares sobre a despenalização do aborto: "Para nós, Guterres ficou sempre marcado": Interview with Manuela Tavares', *Jornal i*, 10 February 2017, https://ionline.sapo.pt/548255 (accessed 12 August 2017). See also Manuela Tavares, 'Feminismos em Portugal (1947–2007)' (PhD diss., Universidade Aberta, 2008); Manuela Tavares, *Movimentos de Mulheres em Portugal: Décadas de 70 e 80* (Lisbon: Livros Horizonte, 2000); Paul Christopher Manuel and Maury N. Tollefsen, 'Roman Catholicism, Secularization and the Recovery of Traditional Communal Values: The 1998 and 2007 Referenda on Abortion in Portugal', *Southern European Society and Politics* 13, no. 1 (2008): 117–29. See also Maria José Magalhães, *Movimento Feminista e Educação, Portugal décadas de 70 e 80* (Oeiras: Celta, 1998).

5 Reis, 'Manuela Tavares sobre a despenalização do aborto'.

6 Sofia Branco, 'Agustina e Lídia Jorge apoiam movimento pela despenalização. Médicos pela Escolha prosseguem formações sobre o aborto', *Público*, 13 November 2006. https://www.publico.pt/2006/11/13/politica/noticia/agustina-e-lidia-jorge-apoiam-movimento-pela-despenalizacao-1276400 (accessed 12 August 2017). On Rego's abortion pastels, see Maria Manuel Lisboa, 'An Interesting Condition: The Abortion Pastels of Paula Rego', *Luso-Brazilian Review* 39, no. 2 (December 1992): 125–49.

7 The best-known landmark of this kind, because of its dramatic consequences for the directors, was a two-part television documentary made by Maria Antónia Palla, Antónia de Sousa and the Cinequipa cooperative for the RTP1 *Nome Mulher* series in 1976 about the work of a clandestine clinic in Lisbon. It was called *O aborto não é um crime* [Abortion is not a Crime] and famously led to the arrest and prosecution of Maria Antónia Palla, who was eventually tried and acquitted in 1979. Both parts of the original programme are viewable on the RTP archive pages at: https://arquivo

s.rtp.pt/conteudos/o-aborto-nao-e-um-crime-parte-i/ and https://arquivos.rtp.pt/conteudos/o-aborto-nao-e-um-crime-parte-ii/ (accessed 1 July 2019).
The solidarity campaigns surrounding Palla's case provided an important public catalyst and a unifying cause for various disparate lobbying groups. Many women film makers from this 1970s and 1980s generation had involvement of one kind or another in the political struggles over abortion and family planning rights. Monique Rutler worked in the Cinequipa cooperative that made *O aborto não é um crime*. After the 1974 revolution, Noémia Delgado (see Chapters 1 and 6 in this volume) was involved in the housing occupations of the LUAR movement which also arranged medical support and abortion access for the poor, and she knew Maria Teresa Horta in that context. Margarida Gil (see Chapter 2 of this volume) made a short documentary called *Clínica Comunal Popular de Cova da Piedade* [The People's Clinic of Cova da Piedade] in 1975 about a family planning clinic established in the context of housing occupations. See António Cunha (ed.), *Cineastas Portuguesas 1874–1956* (Lisbon: Câmara Municipal de Lisboa, 2000).

8 See Ana Catarina Pereira, *A Mulher-Cineasta: Da arte pela arte à uma estética da diferenciação* (Covilhã: LABCOM.IFP, Universidade da Beira Interior, 2016). Pereira sees Villaverde significantly as 'the least invisible of the women directors studied', 189.

9 J. G. Ballard, *Low-Flying Aircraft* (London: Flamingo, 1992 [1976]). Solveig Nordlund would go on to collaborate with Margarida Gil to make a five-part television series in 2010 *Conversas no Cabeleireiro* interviewing five prominent women, of whom one was the obstetrician responsible for introducing family planning in Portugal.

10 Pereira, *A Mulher-Cineasta*, 295.

11 Elaine Graham, *Representations of the Post/Human: Monsters, Aliens and Others in Popular Culture* (New Brunswick: Rutgers University Press, 2002), 52–3. The 2018 film, *The Devil's Doorway*, directed by the Irish film maker Aislinn Clarke, occupies very similar territory in this respect. Released in the immediate context of the 2018 abortion referendum in the Republic of Ireland, Clarke's film also uses the horror genre to critique the Catholic Church's abuse of unmarried pregnant women in the Magdalene Laundries.

12 Villaverde gives a helpful retrospective account of the film's origins and her specific social concerns about Portuguese children in care, in an interview in 2012. Her plan had been to make a documentary about children in state institutions, but she did not get funding for it, so she opted to pursue the same idea through a fiction feature. See Ela Bittencourt, '"One day, the swan sang this with its wings": An interview with Teresa Villaverde', *Senses of Cinema* 65 (December 2012). http://sensesofcinema.com/2012/feature-articles/one-day-the-swan-sang-this-with-its-wings-an-interview-with-teresa-villaverde/ (accessed 7 July 2015).

13 Ana Moreira (Andreia) is, significantly, the only one of the young actors in the film who did not come from a real Portuguese social institution. See Bittencourt, 'One day, the swan sang this with its wings'.
14 Cristina Álvarez López and Adrian Martin, 'Broken Links', in *Portugal's Global Cinema: Industry, History and Culture*, ed. Mariana Liz (London: I.B. Tauris, 2018), 155; emphasis in original.
15 Ibid., 156.
16 Ibid., 154.
17 Claire Johnston, 'Women's Cinema as Counter-Cinema', in *Feminist Film Theory: A Reader*, ed. Sue Thornham (Edinburgh: Edinburgh University Press, 1999), 33.
18 Álvarez López and Martin, 'Broken Links', 156; emphasis in original.
19 Caroline Overhoff Ferreira, *Identity and Difference: Postcoloniality and Transnationality in Lusophone Films* (Münster: LIT Verlag 2012), 123.
20 Kaja Silverman, *The Subject of Semiotics* (New York: Oxford University Press, 1984). See also Judith Halberstam, *Skin Shows: Gothic Horror and the Technology of Monsters* (Durham: Duke University Press, 1995), 153.
21 Halberstam, *Skin Shows*, 153.
22 Ferreira, *Identity and Difference*, 121.
23 Ibid., 125. Portuguese film critic Jorge Leitão Ramos reads the children in *The Mutants* biologically rather than socially as literal genetic mutants, describing them as 'people from here, yet different, with some genetic mishap, some alteration that makes them different'. Jorge Leitão Ramos, *Dicionário do Cinema Português 1989–2003* (Lisbon: Caminho, 2005), 408.
24 Mark Steven, 'Dark, Satanic', *Sight and Sound* 27, no. 10 (October 2017): 21. As Steven notes, 'Splatter films often inhabit a world in which the working poor are made to face off against an economic elite.'
25 I am very grateful to Raquel Freire, for a series of highly enlightening conversations about her film, particularly our discussions of Edgar in relation to Edgar Allan Poe and the cinema of Luis Buñuel.
26 The vampire figure in literature and film is often, of course, feminized or queered as part of a demonization that denies it a legitimate social masculinity, and has also been variously historically bound up with anti-Semitism, class paranoia and homophobia. See Barbara Creed, *The Monstrous-Feminine: Film, Feminism, Psychoanalysis* (London and New York: Routledge, 1993).
27 Halberstam's readings of classic Hollywood Horror have described the splatter or slasher film as 'precisely the location of the dismantling and reconstruction of bodily identities and also of spectatorial positions, gazes and desires'. See Halberstam, *Skin Shows*, 138.
28 Ibid., 144.

29 In a scene where Edgar's own naked body lies alongside Zita's, Jorge Leitão Ramos has noted a certain 'sexual indefinition' and a 'projection of the feminine' in the framing of Edgar. See Ramos, *Dicionário*, 515.
30 Halberstam, *Skin Shows*, 155.
31 There is no English subtitled version which sadly restricts its circulation to a non-Portuguese-speaking audience.
32 An important cross reference for this film is Margarida Gil's 2004 feature *Adriana*, a speculative fantasy fiction about fertility and women's relationship to reproductive politics (see Chapter 2 in the current volume). The screenplay was co-written by Margarida Gil and Maria Velho da Costa and sets out the issues in a more playful, ironic mode than *Aparelho Voador*.
33 Rosi Braidotti, *The Posthuman* (London: Polity Press, 2013), 74.
34 Milly Williamson's readings of the television show *Buffy the Vampire Slayer* place the vampire not only in an ambiguous position at the limits of the human but also in the dark underbelly of what she calls, the 'optimistic cyborg metaphor'. See Milly Williamson, *The Lure of the Vampire: Gender, Fiction and Fandom from Bram Stoker to Buffy* (New York: Wallflower Press, 2005), 168. See Donna Haraway, 'A Cyborg Manifesto: Science, Technology and Socialist-Feminism in the Late Twentieth-Century', in *The Cybercultures Reader*, eds David Bell and Barbara M. Kennedy (London and New York: Routledge, 2000), 291–324.
35 Haraway, 'Cyborg Manifesto', 291.
36 Ballard, *Low-Flying Aircraft*, 105.
37 Haraway, 'Cyborg Manifesto', 302.
38 Faced with this in the 1980s, Haraway throws out the interesting contention that 'the boundary between science fiction and social reality is an optical illusion. Contemporary science fiction is full of cyborgs – creatures simultaneously animal and machine, who populate worlds ambiguously natural and crafted', Haraway, 'Cyborg Manifesto', 291.
39 Pereira, *A Mulher-Cineasta*, 297.
40 Haraway, 'Cyborg Manifesto', 291.

4

Urban homes and urban families: Teresa Villaverde's *Colo* and Susana Nobre's *Ordinary Time*

Mariana Liz

This chapter examines two Portuguese films about family, directed by women: *Colo* (Teresa Villaverde, 2017) and *Tempo Comum* (*Ordinary Time*; Susana Nobre, 2018).[1] These are Villaverde's seventh feature film, after a series of critically acclaimed productions, and Nobre's first venture into fiction, after having directed a couple of short films and feature-length documentary films. Taken together, *Colo* and *Ordinary Time* allow for an extensive analysis of 'women's films'.[2] In addition to being made by women filmmakers, they are both films about women. The two films have in common a focus on the urban and a thematic engagement with the idea of the family, as well as with the experience of maternity.

Colo and *Ordinary Time* are both about families in contemporary Lisbon. *Colo* is set a few years before the date of its release: the film takes place during the Euro-zone debt crisis, and the period of implementation of a series of austerity policies in Portugal. Even though the word 'crisis' is not once uttered in the film, *Colo* is the story of a family in which the father loses his job and the mother has to take on extra work. It is also the chronicle of their teenage daughter's reaction to this situation and the way in which the financial pressure put on the family impacts the relationship between its members. *Ordinary Time*, whose narrative is contemporary to the film's release, is about a particular stage in a family: the very beginning. Nobre's film records the first few weeks of a mother and a father with their first baby, born in 2017, observing with some distance the challenges associated with parenthood, as well as its many joys.

My analysis is centred on conceptions of family and maternity, as they are disclosed through representations of urban space on the one hand, and through issues of physicality, embodiment and conventional gender roles, on the other. While in many ways, and particularly through their focus on urban space, these films place Lisbon, Portugal and Portuguese cinema in a cosmopolitan, international and forward-looking sphere, at the same time, and predominantly through the vision they put forward of maternity, they reveal a small, constrained and conservative side of Lisbon, Portugal and Portuguese society. Hence, the chapter is concerned not just with the status of *Colo* and *Ordinary Time* as women's films but also with the ways in which these films employ what Lucy Fischer describes as the 'feminist address'.[3] Following Fischer, it asks what gender relations these films represent and what visions of femininity and masculinity are put forward; who is being targeted by these films, and invoked as an audience; and whether cinematic style and discourse place viewers in a particular gendered position. The combined analysis of *Colo* and *Ordinary Time* offers an understanding of how space and time are articulated through gender in contemporary film. Adopting a feminist address that is far from unidirectional, and at times openly ambivalent, these films show that the small nation women's cinema currently produced in Portugal and screened abroad highlights ongoing tensions between backwardness and modernity – and that these are crucial to the understanding of contemporary Portuguese culture.

Contemporary Lisbon: A city of contrasts

The analysis of the cinematic construction and representation of urban space has developed significantly in the last few decades. The expanding 'cinema and the city' field has grown so much since the late 1990s that by 2012 Charlotte Brunsdon questioned whether the topic was not already exhausted.[4] Many scholars of film and cultural geography proved Brunsdon wrong by continuing to examine film and urban space in conjunction as the two entities – and scholarly fields – mutated too. Johan Andersson and Lawrence Webb, for instance, have argued for the importance of reinventing 'cinema and the city' at a time when cinema is transformed with the advent of digital technologies and new modes of engagement, and the power of the city is questioned by continuous globalization forces.[5] This chapter intervenes in ongoing debates within cinema and the city scholarship by examining the transnational Portuguese cinema of the contemporary era and discussing Lisbon as an often ignored case study, and one that is undergoing important transformations.

The films analysed in this chapter highlight new models of production and film financing, as well as new developments in international film circuits. As a Portuguese and French co-production, *Colo* was essentially funded by Villaverde herself, through her production company Alce Filmes. Villaverde wrote and directed the film, acting also as its executive producer. While the film premiered at the Berlin Film Festival in February 2017, its distribution in Portugal was also managed and coordinated by the filmmaker. International promotion was then handed to Portugal Film, a film promotion agency created in 2015, aiming to make Portuguese cinema more visible abroad. Portugal Film works closely with distribution companies, film festivals and local exhibition networks at a global level, and has been responsible for the international dissemination of films such as Catarina Mourão's *A Toca do Lobo* (*The Wolf's Lair*, 2015), Leonor Teles's *Balada de um Batráquio* (*Batrachian's Ballad*, 2016) and Susana de Sousa Dias's *Luz Obscura* (*Obscure Light*, 2017).

Similarly, *Ordinary Time* premiered at the International Film Festival of Rotterdam in January 2018. The film was produced by Terratreme, in a Portuguese and French co-production with Cinéma Defacto. Founded in 2008, Terratreme is a production company managed by a number of young Portuguese filmmakers. Looking for new ways to fund and distribute Portuguese films, Terratreme has been responsible for some of the most widely disseminated titles emerging from Portugal in recent years, including *Linha vermelha* (*Red Line*; José Filipe Costa, 2011), *Ama-San* (Cláudia Varejão, 2016) and *A Fábrica de Nada* (*The Nothing Factory*; Pedro Pinho, 2017). *Colo* and *Ordinary Time* are illustrative examples of the new strategies being deployed by Portuguese filmmakers in the twenty-first century, on the one hand, to retain a greater degree of control over the production, distribution and promotion of their films and, on the other, to ensure they reach a wide audience, within and beyond the country (see also Filipa Rosário in this volume).

Just as cinema practices are transformed in today's Portugal, contemporary Lisbon is also undergoing a series of changes that make it a particularly interesting case study for scholars researching housing and planning, tourism and gentrification, Europe and globalization, among other topics. While research into these issues has been expanding, not much has been written about the relationship between contemporary Lisbon and film. This is despite the fact that, over the last few decades, Lisbon has been shot by high-profile international directors such as Alain Tanner (*Dans la ville blanche* [*In the White City*], 1983) and Wim Wenders (*Lisbon Story*, 1994), having also featured in big-budget productions such as *Night Train to Lisbon* (Bille August, 2013). Although there are marked differences in these films' style and narrative, the foreign gaze of these filmmakers tends to emphasize touristic views of the city, privileging, for instance, Lisbon's historic centre and the banks of the river Tagus as cinematographic locations, and insisting on blue skies and sunny views of the city, generally accompanied by traditional fado music.

In contemporary Portuguese cinema, Lisbon appears as a more complex city, even though historic neighbourhoods are now filmed as often as peripheral or marginal locations, which were common in Portugal's filmmaking of the 1990s.[6] In the films examined in this chapter, the city emerges as a sign of the cosmopolitan nature of these families, standing also as a proxy for their high education levels, easy mobility and wide access to a variety of resources, as well as information. On the one hand, these films showcase the huge economic progress of Portugal, displaying, as a consequence, the late modernity of its capital, Lisbon. On the other, they are set during or immediately after the financial crisis that hit southern European nations particularly hard, and therefore highlight the arrested development of the country and its urban spaces. For this reason, the Lisbon screened in *Colo* and *Ordinary Time* is one of sharp contrasts.

Colo was shot and is set in Olivais, a working-class neighbourhood not far from Lisbon airport. Essentially a residential area, the neighbourhood is depicted as enclosed between two contrasting ideas. On the one hand, Olivais is not just next to the airport (in itself a symbol of modernity and cosmopolitanism), but it is also in walking-distance from Parque das Nações, one of Lisbon's most newly developed areas, entirely rebuilt for the World Exhibition 'Expo' in 1998. On the other, the neighbourhood is essentially composed of a series of buildings, and shown here as 'dormitory' area, where space is restricted and time is insignificant. As the film is set during the financial crisis, the glimpse of modernity provided by shots of the airport and Parque das Nações functions more as a reminder of what progress was meant to have become. Although not quite a suburb, there is no particularly defining character to Olivais. All we see in *Colo* are high-rise buildings and mostly empty streets, often shot from high angles as the characters look down from the windows in their upper-floor flat. The film's mise en scène emphasizes the distance between the home and the city, and therefore the isolation of the neighbourhood, as well as the loneliness of the characters apparently trapped inside.

Ordinary Time, by contrast, is set in Lisbon's historic centre, in Bairro das Colónias in Anjos. Although the film leaves out the now widely circulated narrative about the pressures of gentrification and the growth of tourism in Lisbon,[7] it is important to keep this narrative in mind. Due to the rise of visitors to the city and the widespread dissemination of short-term rental accommodation, the people currently living in neighbourhoods such as Bairro das Colónias are, in their vast majority, foreigners and/or 'gentrifiers'. The protagonists of *Ordinary Time* are upper-middle-class 'hipsters',[8] and as argued below, this has implications for how space, time and gender are articulated in the film. Lisbon appears in *Ordinary Time* as a bustling capital, as shots of city centre rooftops at night are accompanied by the sound of sirens and cars. By contrast, the flat where the film's protagonists live seems quiet and detached, self-contained in its smallness, as well as in the white and pastel colours that characterize it and emerge in opposition to the more colourful, vibrant city outside.

One of the strongest distinctions these films offer in terms of visions of urban space is between the outside, ample, seemingly free space and the restricting interior. In both cases, the mise en scène is structured to give us a sense of limits and constraints. Characters are often framed by obstacles, such as trees, walls and (rarely) other people, which push them to the corners of the frame. In *Ordinary Time*, for instance, this is presented as one of the downsides of living in the city centre. With the exception of the film's opening two minutes, in which classical music signals the birth of the baby, there is almost no music in *Ordinary Time*. The film's silent or hushed shots tend to be long in duration, and the camera is fixed, with shallow focus. The film's sound, mise en scène and camera work reinforce the austerity of the plot, as well as the symmetry and geometry of doors, stairs and windows in the flat, reminding the viewer that these characters must navigate very carefully not just the experience of first-time parenthood but also the small spaces of an old city centre flat.

Similarly, in *Colo*'s initial sequence, we see Marta (the couple's teenage daughter) outside. This is a very wide shot, which shows us a view of Lisbon as planes fly by, and Marta experiencing the loudness of the airport, as well as the strong wind. Seconds later, she is in her flat, in her room. After briefly lying in bed, she gets up to open a cage; she holds her pet bird in her hand, and blows onto its head, as if wanting to provide a similar experience of feeling the wind on her face (see Figure 4.1). This contrast between being stuck and experiencing freedom is reinforced by a travelling shot, following her wandering through a narrow corridor, calling 'dad!', 'mom!', only to realize she is home alone. In the following shot, the father comes home. 'I went out for a walk,' he says – and at different points in the film, all the characters will be seen exercising their need

Urban Homes and Urban Families   93

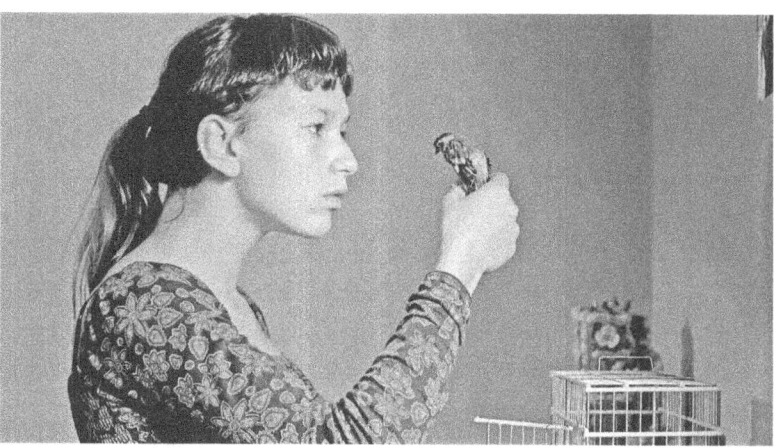

Figure 4.1 Marta holding her pet bird in *Colo* (Portugal Film, 2017).

to go out, leave the flat and take advantage of the wider spaces that characterize the urban sphere.

If, inside the house, the camera is forced to navigate tight spaces, outside shots are wide, reducing the characters to their smallness in the density of the city. Depicted in this way, the space the characters inhabit looks less like a city or a flat, and more like a prison. In one important scene towards the start of the film, the father is on the roof of the building, and makes a phone call to learn that he has not been shortlisted for another job interview. As in the opening scene of the film, with Marta in the wind, natural elements are highlighted by the editing, and seem to weigh down on the father. In this case, however, it is not the darkness of the night but the extreme brightness of the sun that makes him uncomfortable. Against a clear blue sky, white walls frame him, and aggressively reflect the strong daylight, as the camera travels to the right and back to the left, capturing the father's profile, and seemingly watching a wild animal pacing in a cage. Unemployment is another form of entrapment depicted in the film. From this rooftop, we see Parque das Nações – the modern Lisbon – once again. As hinted earlier, this is a negative mirage of the city's modernity that highlights Portugal's backwardness, particularly within the European context.

Colo's ambience is one of pastel colours and dark environments. A large number of scenes take place indoors, and many of these on cloudy days or at night, with the film presenting a faded or fading vision of the family, the city and the country, very much in line with the emotional and financial austerity the characters experience. With the exception of the scene on the roof of the building, in which the brutality of the sunlight stresses the pain experienced by the father, the film is essentially characterized by washed-out, incomplete dialogues, as characters whisper, often, and literally, by candlelight, once money runs out to pay for electricity bills.

Urban space is doubly disparaged in these films: it is simultaneously propitious for confinement (as characters move inside) and depicted as too wide and even dangerous (when they are outside). It follows, then, that characters look for ways of escaping this environment, and temporarily leave the city. In *Colo*, the daughter and a friend, subsequently followed by the father, undertake journeys in pursuit of freedom. These are journeys of excess where tension is released, and that are almost surreal in narrative and aesthetic terms. In the first of these other spaces (and other times) appearing in the film, the two teenagers miss the last bus home and end up following the course of the river Tagus until dawn – appropriately discussing the pregnancy of one of the girls, and what possible steps to take. In the second of these journeys, the father hijacks a friend's car, and coerces his friend to drive him to the beach. The friend eventually leaves, but the father spends the night at the beach, and we see him jumping naked into the sea, first thing in the morning.

Water is an important element in *Colo*, and a recurrent trope in Villaverde's cinema. It signifies both cleansing and (re)birth, particularly as characters bathe in it, as the father does in the scene at the beach. As Villaverde herself has mentioned, the presence of water signifies a return to the maternal womb, which is significant in a film called *Colo*.[9] *Colo*, which does not have an international, English-language, title, but whose title could be translated as 'cradling' (*dar ou levar ao colo*), is a film about hugging, caring and protecting. Here, water is what allows characters to start over, to have a moment of reflection and often heightened emotion, and to then return to their lives. The father, for instance, after his ocean dive at a moment of crisis and uncertainty, and after recovering from his time away from home, re-emerges within the film's narrative with a new purpose in life: to care for someone else, even if not an actual member of his family.

Although the plot lines of father and daughter increasingly diverge as the film moves on, for Marta an attachment to the river is similarly not only a constant throughout the film but also a source of comfort, if not orientation, once her family falls apart. Hence, in the film's final scene she encloses herself in another possible home, locks herself inside the fisherman's hut and closes the windows to be in darkness – this time, not blocking out the bustling city, but rather seeking proximity to the calming water. In *Colo*, the music is mostly diegetic. However, the film's final scene tracks Marta and the fisherman hut, with classical music. Open-ended, the film draws on the eerie tones of Shostakovich's Violin Concerto no. 1 to highlight the drama of its resolution. This final enigmatic scene seems to signify, if not the end of the family, the beginning of a new one, in which Marta is alone, and fulfils, at the same time, the roles of caring and cared-for individual.

Similar scenes of escape emerge in *Ordinary Time*, where the city apparently contrasts with the countryside in the Alentejo. Marta, the mother in Nobre's film, talks to an old woman in the Alentejo about her easy life in the city, at least in contrast to the hardships of the old days in rural Portugal. However, with the exception of the actual space they have, inside and outside their urban and rural homes, the family's visit to the Alentejo does not offer a massive contrast with the urban environment they inhabit. The modernity (and consequent ease) attributed to urban space is at odds with the conservatism that characterizes these hipster characters. For the upper middle classes living in Lisbon's historic centre, life is a conflation of old and new that can be experienced anywhere. This is best exemplified by their predilection for old songs, which they listen to on vinyl – in Lisbon, as in the Alentejo, in the city as in the countryside, since commodities affordable to these characters travel with them across space and time.

In *Colo*, as in *Ordinary Time*, Lisbon is the city where homes are built, where families spend their days and where mothers develop their identities. As Doreen Massey reminds us, 'That place called home is frequently personified by, and partakes of the same characteristics as those assigned to, Woman/Mother/lover.'[10] As she goes on to argue, 'The construction of "home" as a woman's place has … carried through into those views of place itself as a source of stability, reliability and authenticity. Such views of place, which reverberate with nostalgia for something lost, are coded female.'[11] Whereas the urban space represented in these films appears not to be feminine because of its harshness and apparent rationality, as well as its lack of connection to nature – an exception being, perhaps, the bird taken care of by Marta, in *Colo* – the urban is actually very feminine because of its focus on the home, and on the importance this has for female characters in particular. The view of the home as a place of solace is, according to Massey, 'a view of place which searches after a non-existent lost authenticity, which lends itself to reactionary politics, and which is utterly bound up with a particular cultural reading of something called Woman'.[12]

Although these two films put forward a critical vision of Lisbon as a geographical and financial space, the association they suggest between women and the home, and the way in which both are depicted, is far less progressive.

As Linda McDowell has put it, feminist geography aims 'to examine the extent to which women and men experience spaces and places differently and to show how these differences themselves are part of the social constitution of gender as well as that of place'.[13] Hence, the home is an important object of analysis not just as a location within the urban sphere of contemporary Portugal but also insofar as it can be seen as a proxy for gender relations. These films represent a city in transformation as a space for families, who also suffer from wider changes in society. The visions of femininity and masculinity put forward are conflicted, or similarly in transition. Gender relations articulate a number of conservative visions of place (home) and space (the city), as well as of the roles that are commonly perceived to be the right ones for mothers and fathers. The discussion of the films' 'feminist address', to use Fischer's terms, is continued below, as I confront these films' apparent spatial modernity with their more limited conception of gender roles and motherhood.

The construction of family and the experience of motherhood

For Cristina Álvarez López and Adrian Martin, 'Family is at once the most cherished and the most fragile structure in the cinema of Teresa Villaverde.'[14] As Álvarez López and Martin argue, all of Villaverde's films have eventually focused on 'the disintegration of the family'[15] (see also Hilary Owen in this volume). This is also the case of *Colo*, whose finale sees mother, father and daughter being displaced to three different homes. *Colo*'s narrative displays the range of emotional and financial challenges involved in taking care of someone or something else – as in the case of Marta's bird. This is a film about the maternal gesture and its limits.

In *Colo*, as in *Ordinary Time*, both men and women experience the role of carers. As Lucy Fisher has argued, conceptions of male mothering, and what she identifies as 'postmaternity', are common in contemporary cinema. As she puts it, 'While, superficially, this trope seems to express a benign male nurturant impulse, it arises at the *expense* of woman.'[16] Similarly, in the two films discussed here, women assume this role more often than men; they experience caring as a burden, especially when this is combined with their other tasks and responsibilities, within and beyond the family sphere. Throughout Villaverde's film, the mother is in charge. She constantly gives directions to the father, including about the way in which he should deal with their daughter. She has to make decisions about bills, dinner and where they will live, as well as about her working hours and well-being. Although the father prepares breakfast and dinner for his wife, this happens not out of choice, but because he is trapped at home. The father's being there stems not from the fact that he is a homemaker, but rather from his inability to play the role of the family provider. He is only available because he is unemployed, and the film's main plot line is precisely centred on how much this exhausts the mother.

A key sequence, towards the end of the film, illustrates this tension in stylistic and aesthetic terms. When the mother, played by Beatriz Batarda, says they are moving to her mother's house, she begs the father not to cry, anticipating his reaction. They are in their bedroom, and the framing presents the mother as bigger than the father. The open door points towards her, and she is clearly the dominant figure, as she is closer to the viewer, and occupies more space in the frame. This conversation is followed by the father telling his daughter's friend that he wants to take care of, and indeed act, as the father to her child. As he leaves the bedroom from the left of the frame, in the following shot, we see the father entering the kitchen from the right. Marta's friend is sitting on the counter, in the left-hand corner. The camera is next to her, and it is she who looks bigger now. He needs to get very close to her to affirm his space and position. Unable to care for his daughter, and seemingly for his wife, he longs for a second chance, but his attempt at parenthood, as the precise camera work reminds us, comes from a position of weakness. In addition, a low angle pictures this ominous conversation, reminding the viewer that there is something not quite right about this dialogue and this relationship. Moments later, the camera is level when the mother is saying goodbye to the daughter. Mother and daughter are equals, but oblique angles appear in the scenes in which the father is driving the narrative forward.

In *Colo*, the anxiety of the outside world overflows into the family home, contained and contaminated by the pressures of the urban sphere. Even though it is true that, when they are not home, the characters drift, home is more of a prison than a place to look for solace or for references that somehow anchor them. Hence, at the end of *Colo*, characters are displaced to other 'homes' – the father to his mother-in-law, with a surrogate daughter; the mother to her friend, where she ends up cooking dinner; Marta to the fisherman's hut, where she hides in isolation. The notion of home as a prison is similarly visible in *Ordinary Time*. For instance, we never see the mother out of the house in Lisbon. The only time we see her going for a stroll with the baby is in the rural setting of the Alentejo. By contrast, the father goes out all the time and everywhere, and the two characters even have a fight about this towards the end of the film. This is a very well-attested experience of motherhood, since, as Anália Torres reminds us, 'For women parenthood often implies being pulled inside the household and postponing their work while men, on the contrary, tend to be pushed outside.'[17]

Ordinary Time was born out of the director's personal experience of maternity. In an interview about the screening of the film at the Rotterdam Film Festival, Nobre talks about the experience of maternity as one of reclusion, characterized by countless visitors narrating their own experiences of parenthood, and, in between the silences, filling the gaps of these intimate days.[18] The film's original title refers to the phrase 'Common Time' meaning, in Christian tradition, the moments of 'ordinary' liturgy, beyond the readings attributed to important dates, such as Christmas and Easter. Hence, the film imbues the space of the home with a very specific tempo. The film's narrative is characterized by the slow passage of time, a series of quiet moments, where not much seems to happen, as well as, precisely because of the absence of marked episodes (and a very realistic lack of sleep), the disorientation between night and day.

The temporal experience of parenting is thus anchored in the physicality of the female body. Whereas bodily expressions of solitude and alienation were expressed in *Colo* through Marta's self-harm episodes, *Ordinary Time* highlights the pressure that cradling a baby imprints on the body, picturing a more physical side of maternity. Nobre's film opens with an image of the body of the mother, lying down and breathing slowly, still pregnant (see Figure 4.2). This shot is immediately followed by that of the newborn baby. Directly after, the film cuts to the mother, who we assume is being driven home from the hospital, in the back seat, looking at the baby in the car, and then outside the window, as if contemplating the life that is about to start. Throughout the film, there are a series of scenes about breastfeeding, including one displaying the technicalities involved in pumping milk. Topics of discussion include how to prevent mastitis and how often the baby feeds, with the maternal body emerging as fulfilling a very specific function.

The film's attention to the body adds another level to the distinction between how women and men experience parenthood, as well as to how mother and father are affected. While realistic, this is taken for granted: the time and the physicality of motherhood are necessarily different from the experience of fatherhood, but this is merely presented as a given. As E. Ann Kaplan has argued, in recent

Figure 4.2 The pregnant mother at the start of *Ordinary Time* (Terratreme, 2018).

decades, feminism has been co-opted by capitalist discourse, and its oppositional character needs to be rethought.[19] It is as if now that it is widely accepted that women are free to make a choice about motherhood, and that fathers are more present in parenting than before, the constraints and inequalities still embedded in it can no longer be challenged. *Colo* and, more obviously, *Ordinary Time* seem also to wonder what, as gender-conscious films, they might actually be 'against'. Yet, as Kaplan writes, 'It is precisely in such moments that we have to struggle to keep oppositional positions alive.'[20]

As McDowell has put it, 'The older associations between home, domesticity, and femininity are being challenged by active labor market policies that insist that the key social responsibility of the ungendered individual at the centre of neo-liberal policies is labor market participation.'[21] In *Ordinary Time*, the mother is seen doing quite a lot of domestic work, including folding socks and cleaning the bathroom. In one scene, we see her exhausted on the sofa. As both mother and baby fall asleep, her top is covered in milk stains, and when she wakes up, she immediately gets up to breastfeed. In another scene, she keeps an eye on the baby while working on a translation – presumably, her regular job, and therefore, having gone back to work, while on leave. As the baby cries and she asks the father for help, he replies: 'But I have just sat down.'

Early on in the film, the father leaves the house to go to work and, when asked, says he does not know when he will be back. The film highlights not just a tension between the figure of the mother and the father, and what is expected from each of them, but also a contrast between maternity and work, and between maternity and autonomy, here seemingly incompatible. For Torres,

> Portuguese women are ... caught by the motherhood penalty ... mothers are committed with the normative expectation to engage in intensive mothering, with children above all other activities; but at the same time they must perform accordingly to labour market normative demands about the ideal worker, who would sacrifice all other concerns for work.[22]

A similar discussion emerges in Kaplan's work on the representation of motherhood, as she talks about women who are performing two roles (as mothers and workers), but none of them 'right'.[23]

In *Ordinary Time* the father is present, for instance, by bathing the baby, and holding her, at night, in bed (see Figure 4.3). The film's director has been adamant in interviews that this is a story about how emotionally present fathers can be for a newborn.[24] However, *Ordinary Time* is mostly about the mother, and a mother who seems to be doing more than her share, in terms of paid and unpaid work, and in terms of her emotional, physical and functional presence. In fact, recent scholarship on the topic shows that mothers not only continue to do a great deal of unpaid and often under-valued work but also are increasingly asked (or feel the need) to do more and more. Research on the issue offers 'compelling evidence to support their claim that mothers are uniquely and unfairly positioned to absorb the damage from neoliberal policies'.[25] Uncertainty, combined with precarity,

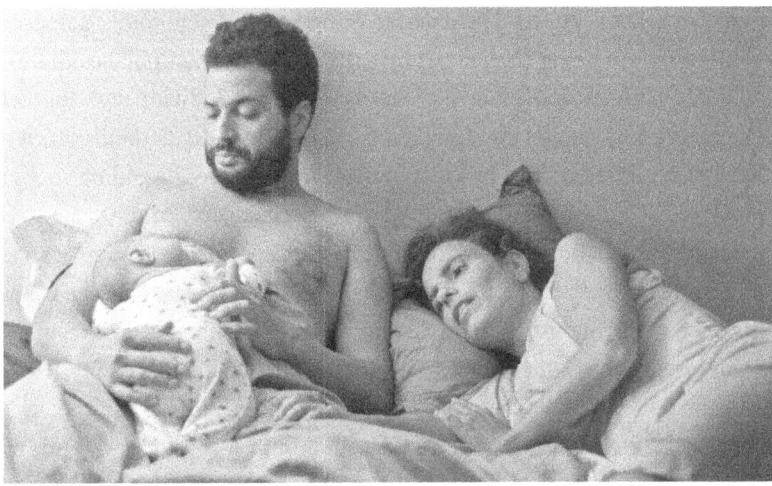

Figure 4.3 The father holds the baby in *Ordinary Time* (Terratreme, 2018).

prompts mothers to do more – particularly when mothering is under-supported and under-funded, as is the case with austerity, and even post-crisis Portugal.

In this same interview about *Ordinary Time*, Nobre claims she had no intention of including a particularly gendered conflict in the film. According to the director, the narrative was meant to be sequential: 'In the end I made a film, which is not a feminist film, but a film about women today, and how they can be mothers in an urban context'.[26] She also concedes fathers are allowed more free time, but argues that the film shows just how much fathers – at least this father – are incredibly present in affective terms, even if not as present in what she calls 'practical life'.[27] For a film that is positioned as realistic, filming the family almost like a documentary, and focusing on the rhythms of, to use the director's own terms, 'practical life' (which are those seen as unexceptional, or, to refer back to the film's title, 'ordinary'), gender issues are not absent, but they are presented somewhat conservatively, including by omission. Conflict on how much mother and father look after the baby, for instance, arises. However, as argued below, this is dismissed in the editing, as the scene that follows is another scene of the family's routine, in which the mother is at home with the baby, and the father is out with a friend.

What we see in these films are hesitant representations of men. Not perfect, but not anti-heroes either, as was traditionally the case in classic melodrama,[28] the fathers are not only seen making mistakes throughout but are also offered redemption in the final scenes of *Colo* and *Ordinary Time*. Even though *Colo* is clearly a film about women – Marta, a daughter, and her (pregnant) friend, an exhausted mother, and a confused grandmother – Villaverde claims the film's protagonist is the father.[29] In *Colo*, despite the fact that this is framed as an ominous ending, the father is somehow allowed to carry on with his life, but a strange, morally wrong, life, and with the 'wrong' characters, by moving into the house of his mother-in-law, with a surrogate daughter, who the owner thinks is her granddaughter. Similarly, towards the end of *Ordinary Time*, the father talks to his friend about his decreased libido since the birth of his daughter. The previous scene sees Marta being angry with him for not doing enough to help with the baby; the following scene shows us a friend explaining to the mother how to pump breast milk. Framed like this, the conversation between the two men seems to present the father as the victim of a life that has certainly changed, but for everyone, if not more dramatically for Marta. The onus is still on women to be the heroes – and it is in this sense that the films' placement of the viewer is dubious and its 'feminist address' is problematized.

Space and gender in Portugal's interrupted modernity

As Virgínia Ferreira notes, writing in 1998, 'The position of women in Portugal today is marked by this context of juridical equality imposed from the top down, of a weak individualization of lifestyles, and of pronounced social and economic elitism.'[30] In line with the ambivalent conceptions and practices of gender equality, as well as with cultural forms of engagement with this notion, still experienced in contemporary Portugal, the feminist address of these films remains somewhat disappointing. Whereas, for instance, Villaverde makes a clear political statement by exploring austerity and its aftermath through a focus on the family, and hence in a different way to her male counterparts, including Miguel Gomes, Marco Martins and Pedro Pinho,[31] neither *Colo* nor *Ordinary Time* is, unlike the films discussed by Hilary Owen in this volume, overtly resistant or critical. Both *Colo* and *Ordinary Time* demonstrate a lack of direct political engagement. What these films seem to show is that privileged, highbrow women filmmakers are unwilling to engage in a debate, at least in meaningful terms, which is crucial for contemporary Portuguese culture and society. *Colo* and *Ordinary Time* raise a number of issues to do with family life in austerity-stricken Portugal, as well as with gender equality in contemporary urban settings. However, they are timid in their conclusions, leaving viewers with a sense that while this is a discussion worth having, the films do not quite yet know in what terms this should be happening.

Colo and *Ordinary Time* do not hide the difficulties involved in motherhood, in the creation and support of a family, especially in urban contexts and post-crisis Portugal. The mother taking on two jobs in *Colo* and the mother doing paid and unpaid work through the early stages of motherhood in *Ordinary Time* are tokens, in these films, of what it means to be a mother in contemporary Portugal. These are also symbols of the late but accelerated modernity that characterizes urban centres in Portugal, and particularly, contemporary Lisbon, as issues such as living space and mobility, the difficulties in the formation of neighbourhood communities and the inefficiencies of public transport are also represented on screen. But by presenting this extraordinary burden on mothers as normal, and by choosing not to challenge these views, neither *Colo* nor *Ordinary Time* can be read as very political films, at least as regards gender issues – an argument that is corroborated in statements by both directors in recently published interviews.

The unwillingness, and moreover, refusal to engage with, gender issues, or to be seen as a feminist, is, as Ferreira points out, partly explained by the almost five decades of the New State dictatorship that politically, institutionally and culturally framed women as inferior citizens and as human beings.[32] As she puts it, even after the fall of the regime in 1974, 'The only feminist ideology that has become widespread is a diffuse or official type of feminism. There is no public debate; and when discussions do arise, most of the participants emphasize, "I am not a feminist, but ... ."'[33] The cultural and political effects of very long dictatorial regimes, in Portugal, as in Spain, also contribute to a perceived conservatism in matters of gender – even if, as mentioned above, this is now starting to change. In Spain, as Duncan Wheeler proposes, feminist concerns have recently started to emerge in middlebrow melodramas produced in the last few decades.[34] In Portugal, however, it is as if, weary of the negative connotations of gender differentiation, women directors do their best to be seen as equal to their male counterparts – not through equality, but by toning down their voices, even when it comes to subjects which, although hedged round by obvious feelings of ambivalence, they are still more willing to approach than male filmmakers.

As Ginette Vincendeau wrote in 1986, in her work on French female directors, 'There is something both depressing and challenging about your object of study denying its own existence.'[35] Similarly, it is very disappointing that Portuguese women directors reject their role as conscious political agents. However, there are two important caveats to attach to this argument. The first is that, discouraging as these quotes might be, they are aligned with the reality of Portuguese society. For instance, as Torres notes, 'Whereas equality between men and women concerning paid work seems an acquired value, and even if there is great agreement concerning the need for an increased role of men in care and domestic responsibilities, the caring role of mothers in the family continues to be considered central.'[36] Portugal and Spain are the European countries where women perform the greatest amount of unpaid work in the domestic setting.[37] This is to do both with a persistence of old conceptions of the family and with the structural lack of support and new social policies for this area. Unlike in many other European countries, in Portugal, when women return to work, it tends to be to full-time work. Grandparents, on the other hand, are often far away (for reasons such as emigration) or still working (especially since the austerity years), and cannot be seen as a replacement for paid childcare, which tends to be very expensive.

On a more positive note, the second important caveat is that, to return to Vincendeau's quote, we should be more challenged than depressed by these comments. Just as these films highlight a tension between backwardness and modernity in their representation of urban space, so do they also bring to the fore old and new conceptions of gender. While it is important to read interviews with Portuguese women filmmakers as part of a context that is corroborated by social sciences research, these more contextual points must be paired with film analysis. And in the close readings of these films, what we observe are productive tensions at best, overt hesitations at worst.

The tension between backwardness and modernity, and its articulation in terms of space and gender, is clearly visible in these films. Both *Colo* and *Ordinary Time* hint at a characterization of Portugal that suggests the nation is experiencing a suspended or interrupted modernity. This is visible in the representations and symbolic constructions of urban space – Lisbon is full of promise, but also full of contradictions. It is also seen in gender relations, and particularly, conceptions of maternity – these too, are defined by a series of oppositions, and are full of paradoxes. In either case, the presence of tensions indicates that changes have been taking place and will continue to do so. It is not just space but also gender, that is a useful category of analysis in the study of the country's (late) modernity, including for what can, in my view, and despite the ambivalent stance of these films, be framed as a more optimistic reading of contemporary cinema, as well as contemporary Portugal.

Notes

1   This research was kindly supported by FCT grant SFRH/BPD/115319/2016.
2   Lucy Fischer, 'Feminist Forms of Address', in *The Routledge Companion to Cinema and Gender*, eds Kristin Lené Hole, Dijana Jelača, E. Ann Kaplan and Patrice Petro (London and New York: Routledge, 2018), 37.
3   Ibid.
4   Charlotte Brunsdon, 'The Attractions of the Cinematic City', *Screen* 53, no. 3 (2012), 209.
5   Johan Andersson and Lawrence Webb, 'Introduction', in *Global Cinematic Cities: New Landscapes of Film and Media*, eds Johan Andersson and Lawrence Webb (London and New York: Wallflower, 2016), 1.
6   Tiago Baptista, 'Nationally Correct', *P: Portuguese Cultural Studies* 3 (2010), 14.
7   See for instance Luís Mendes, 'What Can Be Done to Resist or Mitigate Tourism Gentrification in Lisbon?', in *City Making & Tourism Gentrification*, eds Marc Glaudemans and Igor Marko (Tilburg: Stadslab, 2016), 35.

8   For a discussion on current understandings of the hipster, see for instance Ico Maly and Piia Varis, 'The 21st-Century Hipster', *European Journal of Cultural Studies* 19, no. 6 (2016): 637–53.
9   'Interview with Teresa Villaverde: Director' (2017) *Cineuropa*, http://cineuropa.org/en/video/323517/ (accessed 10 October 2019).
10 Doreen Massey, *Space, Place and Gender* (Minneapolis: University of Minnesota Press, 1994), 10.
11 Ibid., 180.
12 Ibid., 11.
13 Linda McDowell, *Gender, Identity and Place: Understanding Feminist Geographies* (Minneapolis: University of Minnesota Press, 1999), 12.
14 Cristina Álvarez López and Adrian Martin, 'Broken Links', in *Portugal's Global Cinema: Industry, History and Culture*, ed. Mariana Liz (London: I.B. Tauris, 2018), 151.
15 Ibid., 152.
16 Lucy Fisher, *Cinematernity: Film, Motherhood, Genre* (Princeton, NJ: Princeton University Press, 1996), 175; emphasis in original.
17 Anália Torres, 'Women, Gender, and Work', *International Journal of Sociology* 38, no. 4 (2008), 11.
18 In Hugo Gomes, 'Susana Nobre: "Um realizador não se faz de um filme"', *c7nema*, 27 April 2018, http://www.c7nema.net/entrevista/item/48038-susana-nobre-um-realizador-nao-se-faz-de-um-filme.html (accessed 10 October 2019).
19 E. Ann Kaplan, *Motherhood and Representation: The Mother in Popular Culture and Melodrama* (London and New York: Routledge, 1992), 215.
20 Ibid., 216.
21 Linda McDowell, 'Spaces of the Home', *Home Cultures* 4, no. 2 (2007), 130.
22 Anália Torres, Bernardo Coelho and Miguel Cabrita, 'Bridge over Troubled Waters', *European Societies* 15, no. 4 (2013), 543.
23 Kaplan, *Motherhood and Representation*, 189.
24 In Gomes, 'Susana Nobre: "Um realizador não se faz de um filme"'.
25 Kara Van Cleaf, 'Mothering through Precarity', *Feminist Media Studies* 18, no. 3 (2018), 509.
26 In Gomes, 'Susana Nobre: "Um realizador não se faz de um filme"'. In Portuguese in the original: 'No fim há um filme, não feminista, mas sobre as mulheres de hoje, e como é que elas são mães numa cidade.'
27 In Gomes, 'Susana Nobre: "Um realizador não se faz de um filme"'.
28 See for instance Thomas Schatz, *Hollywood Genres: Formulas, Filmmaking and The Studio System* (New York: Random House, 1981).
29 'Interview with Teresa Villaverde: Director'.
30 Virgínia Ferreira, 'Engendering Portugal', in *Modern Portugal*, ed. António Costa Pinto (Palo Alto: The Society for the Promotion of Science and Scholarship, 1998), 163.

31 Portuguese films about the Euro-zone debt crisis and the austerity imposed in Portugal include Miguel Gomes's trilogy *As Mil e Uma Noites/Arabian Nights* (2015), Marco Martins's *São Jorge/Saint George* (2017) and Pedro Pinho's *A Fábrica de Nada/The Nothing Factory* (2017).
32 Ferreira, 'Engendering Portugal', 163.
33 Ibid., 186.
34 Duncan Wheeler, 'The (Post-)Feminist Condition', *Feminist Media Studies* 16, no. 6 (2016), 1058.
35 Ginette Vincendeau, 'Women's Cinema, Film Theory and Feminism in France', *Screen* 28, no. 4 (1986), 4.
36 Anália Torres, Bernardo Coelho and Miguel Cabrita, 'Bridge over Troubled Waters', 542.
37 Anália Torres (ed.), *Igualdade de Género Ao Longo Da Vida* (Lisbon: Fundação Francisco Manuel dos Santos, 2018).

5

Natural women? Nature and femininity in Noémia Delgado's *Masks* and Teresa Villaverde's *Trance*

Patrícia Vieira

The portrayal of women in relation to the natural world, which crops up repeatedly in the Portuguese film tradition, affords a productive point of entry to the analysis of Portuguese cinema directed by women.[1] In this chapter, I triangulate the already complex relationship between women and the moving image with the environment, and argue that the films of Noémia Delgado and Teresa Villaverde discussed here resort to depictions of nature in order to comment upon gender issues, going back to, and reflecting upon, the broader tradition of linking women and the natural world in Western culture.

Women, film and the environment

In order to examine the relationship between Portuguese cinema made by women and the environment, we must briefly survey the connection between cinema and the environment, on the one hand, and women and the environment, on the other. Leaving aside the large ecological footprint of the film industry – after oil refining, movie-making is the worst environmental offender in the city of Los Angeles[2] – which depends, like any other human activity, on concrete materials and natural resources, cinema as an artistic and cultural production cannot but engage with the natural world.[3] Unlike literature, which is able to avoid describing the landscape, cinema has from its inception relied heavily on depictions of nature that are necessarily captured by the lens.[4] Even in films that take place in urban environments, or in those that focus on human-driven plots, natural elements end up creeping into the shots and colouring the action.

Given this centrality of the natural world in cinema, it is not surprising that the field of cinematic eco-criticism has grown steadily over the past few years. Several studies have focused on films that overtly thematize environmental issues, such as climate disaster films and other natural dystopias, films that call for environmental activism, nature documentaries and so on.[5] Paula Willoquet-Maricondi has established a distinction between 'environmentalist' films, that is, those that foreground environmental topics as elements of the plot (for instance, Steven Soderbergh's *Erin Brockovich* [2000]), and eco-cinema, which would include only those films that have an overt activist intent (such as Nadia and Leila Conners's *The 11th Hour* [2007]).[6] For Willoquet-Maricondi, eco-cinema may adopt a variety of approaches to draw viewers' attention to the environment:

> A lyrical and contemplative style may foster an appreciation for ecosystems and all of nature's constituents – air, water, earth, and organisms. Alternatively, ecocinema may deploy an overtly activist approach to inspire our care, inform, educate, and motivate us to act on the knowledge they provide.[7]

Willoquet-Maricondi, then, draws the line between films that explore – and often exploit – environmental issues, leaving the status quo unquestioned and sometimes even bolstering the very consumerist ideology that causes environmental problems,[8] and those films that, in one way or another, promote an eco-centred agenda.

Willoquet-Maricondi's distinction seems to be an offshoot of Scott MacDonald's argument that 'eco-cinema' – the term was coined by MacDonald in 2004[9] – hinges upon a retraining of perception fostered by long duration shots and other techniques used in avant-garde and independent films. While MacDonald and Willoquet-Maricondi agree that the label 'eco-cinema' does not apply to films that simply discuss environmental questions, MacDonald places more emphasis on filming technique as the hallmark of this kind of movie. For him:

> The fundamental job of an eco-cinema is not to produce pro-environmental narratives shot in a conventional Hollywood manner (that is, in a manner that implicitly promotes consumption) or even in a conventional documentary manner (although, of course, documentaries can alert us to environmental issues).[10]

He believes that the 'job of an eco-cinema is to provide new kinds of film experience that demonstrate an alternative to conventional media-spectatorship and help to nurture a more environmentally progressive mindset'.[11] 'Is it not possible', asks MacDonald, that such experiences in eco-cinema might prompt viewers to 'guide inevitable environmental change in directions that nurture a more healthy planet?'[12] The Portuguese films directed by women analysed in the following pages do not adopt an overtly eco-centred agenda. They do, however, in line with MacDonald's theorization of eco-cinema, use a range of filming techniques to draw attention to the environment and to the link between the oppression of women and the domination of nature.

MacDonald's optimistic take on the social impact of what he calls eco-cinema is disputed by other critics, sceptical of a linear connection between avant-garde filmmaking and environmental activism. As David Ingram points out, the audience for the films MacDonald has in mind is self-selecting, so that these movies might end up preaching to the converted.[13] Furthermore, there is a conceptual leap between innovative filming techniques, no matter how aesthetically successful they may be, behaviour change and sociopolitical praxis. For Ingram, there might not be the need for the category 'eco-cinema' at all, given that 'films may promote cognitive and emotional learning about environmental issues even when they are not considered ecologically or politically "correct" by some ecocritics'.[14] In the same vein, Pietari Kääpä points out that 'if the definition of an ecological film involves texts which reflect the existence of humans in the wider ecosphere, it is very difficult to delineate a non-ecological type of cinema'.[15]

Since cinema necessarily engages with the natural world, any film can, in theory, be approached from an eco-cinematic point of view. I concur with scholars such as Steven Rust and Salma Monani, who believe that all films subject to 'productive ecocritical exploration and careful analysis can unearth engaging and intriguing perspectives on cinema's various relationships with the world around us'.[16] Eco-cinema studies, then, should not be limited to films with either an overt or implicit ecological message. Rather, it is a mode of analysing and interpreting cinema that focuses on the ways in which films depict various aspects of the environment. While cinema, like any other human endeavour, cannot escape the clutches of anthropocentrism, the camera has a certain amount of autonomy, as Dziga Vertov showed us as far back as the 1920s. It might therefore afford a glimpse into the non-human world or, at the very least, allow us to consider our human perspective anew, enriched by an attentive reflection on our environment.[17]

If the link between cinema and the environment has been the object of critical attention mostly in the last couple of decades, scholars with an interest in eco-feminism have long pointed out the persistent association of women and their bodies with nature, landscapes and the environment as a means to underline their physical existence as opposed to their rational selves.[18] Caroline Merchant, for instance, shows how the state of nature before organized society was regarded as a feminized space of anomie, a raw material that had to be moulded by male rationality.[19] Building on this insight, Val Plumwood argues that the inclusion of women in the sphere of nature has been a powerful tool for their oppression, given that everything bodily and linked to the natural world – emotions, passion and so on – has been devalued when compared to reason.[20] For Plumwood, one of the most common ways to debase women and nature is the backgrounding of both,[21] a strategy that has left its traces in the very notion of the environment as a background for human action in literary works and also in cinema. Plumwood suggests that the ties binding women and nature should not simply be dismissed as a relic of the past in order for women to become 'fully human', that is, more like men. Women (and the environment, for that matter) should avoid conforming to the master model, which has always been a male one,[22] and question instead the gendered divisions between body and reason and humanity's domination of nature.[23] The two films I analyse in this chapter question the ideological foundations of a male-controlled society that oppresses women and exploits nature. Men behave in a disorderly, transgressive manner in one film and in an outright brutal fashion in the other, undoing what Plumwood describes as the master model of men's rationality that has been deployed to justify male domination.

'Eco-feminism', a term first used in 1974 by the French writer Françoise d'Eaubonne, recognizes sexism and the exploitation of the environment as parallel forms of oppression and aims to reveal the ways 'in which the logic of domination has functioned historically within patriarchy to sustain and justify the twin dominations of women and nature'.[24] Furthermore, it highlights how ideas of nature and the naturalization of socio-economic, racial, gender and other inequalities have been deployed as a powerful tool for social and political control.[25] Feminist film scholars, specifically, have researched how cinema often conveys the latent male desire for mastery over both women and nature. Pat Bereton's analysis of natural disaster films, for example, shows how nature can be presented as a threat to human existence, in which case survival means re-inhabiting safe and familiar spaces and re-positioning women in traditional roles.[26] In a similar vein, E. Ann Kaplan's study of what she defines as 'pre-trauma' disaster films, that is, those which represent impending ecological catastrophes, found that these films 'unconsciously focus on *male* fantasies about a catastrophic future, as against those *females* might envision'.²⁷ Kaplan adds that the plot of many of these films revolves around a white male saving a woman or a child, who tends to be portrayed as a victim.²⁸ Such research on the relation between women, film and the environment has not, thus far, focused specifically on women's cinema, a blind spot I begin to address in this chapter.

A key issue when discussing the centrality of the natural world and its connection to women in cinema, and of particular relevance for my analysis of Delgado and Villaverde's work, is the distinction between setting and landscape. According to Martin Lefebvre, setting 'refers to spatial features that are necessary for all event-driven films – whether fiction or documentary. ... This space is constructed by the spectator from audiovisual cues ... and ... is the place where the action or events occur.'²⁹ For the most part, natural spaces tend to function as a setting in mainstream cinema, where the golden rule is that 'everything must be subordinate to the narrative'.³⁰ Still, Lefebvre posits the existence of two modes of spectatorial activity, a spectacular and a narrative mode: 'Spectators watch the film at some points in the narrative mode and at others in the spectacular mode, allowing them both to follow the story and, whenever necessary, to contemplate the filmic spectacle.'³¹ It is the spectatorial mode that gives way to the emergence of landscape in film.

For Lefebvre, 'the contemplation of filmic *spectacle* depends on an "autonomizing" gaze ... *which enables the notion of filmic landscape in narrative fiction (and event-based documentary) film; it makes possible the transition from setting to landscape*.'³² Cinematic landscape, then, manifests itself when the viewers' attention is drawn away from a film's action and onto the natural (and we might add urban) environment where it takes place. While Lefebvre does not focus specifically on the case of cinema that is not driven by a plot, we might speculate that in these films the spectatorial mode is more prevalent and that such movies tend to focus on portrayals of the landscape, as opposed to merely using the environment as a setting. The films by Portuguese women directors autonomize the natural world as a landscape, turning it into one of the elements of the plot that is depicted in tandem with the portrayal of female characters. This juxtaposition of the environment and the female characters functions as a commentary upon the age-old association of women and nature identified by Merchant and Plumwood, among others, weaving a subtle critique of the subordination of both in a male-dominated society.

In the rest of this chapter, I undertake an eco-cinematic analysis of two films by Portuguese women directors: Noémia Delgado's documentary *Máscaras* (*Masks*,

1976) (see also Manuela Penafria in this volume) and Teresa Villaverde's *Transe* (*Trance*, 2006). Both of these films address the relationship between humans and the natural environment and, more specifically, the different ways in which women have been associated with nature in key moments of Portugal's recent history. Delgado's film was shot in remote villages in the immediate aftermath of the Carnation Revolution, a time when Portuguese society was undergoing a rapid process of urbanization that meant the ties binding people to the land were also changing drastically. The film documents traditions linked to natural cycles and the restricted role of women in these rituals, as well as the loss of some of these customs in the wake of modernization. Villaverde's *Trance* deals with another decisive stage in Portugal's recent past, namely the catapulting of the country into a globalized world thanks to the opening of the borders separating it from the rest of Europe with the Schengen agreement. The film portrays a transnational Europe where both nature and women have become disposable, with forcefully displaced people no longer able to forge meaningful connections to the environment. In both cases, the directors highlight parallels between the depiction of women and the portrayal of the environment as a means to address commonplace approaches to nature, as well as to gender inequalities.

My guiding questions in the analysis of these films are therefore as follows: Given the persistent cultural association of women and nature, how do Delgado's and Villaverde's films represent both women and the natural world? In which ways do these films challenge or subvert prevailing attitudes towards the natural world and towards women? How does the depiction of the environment and of women differ in these films and how do these divergences reflect evolving views of women and nature in Portugal?

Masks – patriarchy and tradition in rural Portugal

Delgado's feature-length documentary *Masks* deals with the celebration of rites connected to the winter solstice in Trás-os-Montes, a mountainous region in north-eastern Portugal. Even though these ceremonies are solely for young men, who don masks and engage in a series of traditional rituals that signify their passage into adulthood, Delgado's film highlights the position of women in the villages, in connection with the stunning natural environment of the area. *Masks* begins with a travelling shot of the mountains to the soundtrack of a female voice from the region, which establishes from the outset the link between nature – here presented as landscape and not mere setting – and femininity.³³ After the initial travelling shot, we see a man ploughing a field with a pair of oxen. The subtext of these two images is simple: women are associated with the natural world as it is, while men are responsible for its transformation. This dichotomy crops up again and again in the movie. When the first village to appear in the movie is introduced, we again see a man absorbed in agricultural tasks: this time sowing a field. And the film is interspersed with shots of women engaged in daily activities – carrying a child, washing clothes, preparing food – together with other travelling shots of nature (see Figure 5.1). By linking women and the natural world, the director both portrays the status quo and comments upon the patriarchal culture that the film subtly condemns.

Delgado paints panoramic portraits of nature, such as the initial travelling shot or wide-angle shots of the mountains and fields, but she also pays close attention to natural details like trees, birds, farm animals and so on. This ecologically attuned mode of filmmaking *avant-la-lettre*, similar to the style adopted in Portuguese directors António Reis and Margarida Cordeiro's films, evokes what MacDonald defined as eco-cinema, in that it focuses the viewers' attention on the natural world in its variegated forms. The crosscutting between images of nature and sequences depicting the social mores of the various villages emphasizes the indebtedness of village life and the rituals depicted in the film to natural cycles. Similarly, close-ups of women, which mirror those of animals and plants, underline the abiding presence of a part of the population that is excluded from the male-driven action.

Figure 5.1 Women and landscape: Noémia Delgado's 1976 *Masks* (Cinemateca Portuguesa-Museu do Cinema).

In a telling scene from *Masks*, an adolescent girl carrying a young white goat passes by a group of young male revellers. She seems ashamed of being there, afraid of what the men might say or do to her, and only relaxes once she gets out of their way. In another scene, a group of women encounter the partying men at dawn and, again, look embarrassed at finding themselves in a male-dominated space. The solstice rites involve transgressive behaviour on the part of the young men, who are allowed, for instance, to enter all the houses in the villages, 'steal' food from them – a piece of bread, ham, chorizo and so on – and behave in a loud and rowdy fashion that would not be permissible for women.[34] In a village where the rites take place during Carnival, the young men dress up as devils and chase after girls and women, as the voice-off in the film explains.[35] In another village we actually see two men dressed up as devils pretending to lash women away from the streets in a parable of male power. The young men's often sexually explicit body language, together with the fact that they celebrate their passage into adulthood, accompanied with heavy drinking, suggests that the women they encounter are, at least potentially, at risk of sexual harassment and violence. The men's attire, imitating demons, implies that, while men are permitted a modicum of misdemeanour, women need to protect themselves against falling into sinful conduct. The film makes it clear that, in this region, outdoor spaces are male-controlled and women venture into them at their own risk.

If existence in the mountainous area where *Masks* was filmed is predicated on a battle against a harsh natural environment, the film suggests that the social mores of the region also depend upon a systematic domination of women. In the village of Santo Estevão, the solstice rites involve a public outdoor meal that takes place near the church, at the heart of town. The main table is occupied by the symbolic representatives of the population: the priest, the oldest man, the poorest man and other influential males from the community. As Delgado states in an interview, 'They [the women] could not participate. A woman never appears at the men's table. Those who wear the masks are men. Women are completely forbidden to participate, they cannot be master of ceremonies, they can be nothing.'[36] The absence of women from the table of village representatives and from the ceremonies as a whole is indicative of their sidelining when it comes to the public sphere, to decision-making and to positions of power within village society.

The link between the drive to rule over nature and over women is nowhere clearer than in the sequences depicting men fighting against and slaughtering animals. In the village of Santo Estevão, the rituals include a fight between the revellers and the village bulls; the first one to hit the floor with his back loses the competition. Later, two young men, naked from the waist up, imitate the fight with the bulls, using the same movements until one of them falls on his back, to the relish of a male-only audience. The metaphorical correlation between male virility and bulls is widely known and crystalizes in cultural events such as bullfighting. The celebration of male initiation rites in Santo Estevão therefore follows in a long tradition that relates male behaviour to the comportment of certain animals deemed to be particularly strong. Male strength and aggressiveness are here naturalized and used to justify male privilege.

Beyond fighting, the rituals in several villages involve the slaughtering, dismembering and eating of an animal by the partying group of young men. The voice-off explains that the slaughtering of a calf is an 'essential part of the celebration'. The documentary accompanies every detail of this process, from a close-up of the animal's throat being cut open, through its bleeding, quartering and cooking, to the final close-up of its bloody head and bloodshot eyes, in an image that evokes the famous scene from Luis Buñuel's *Un Chien Andalou* (1929), where a woman's eye (in actuality a cow's eye) is slit open. In a village from the district of Mogadouro, the men slice open a goat's throat in order to bleed it to death, and the film captures the sound of the animal's horrifying death throes, while in yet another village the documentary stops for a long close-up of a slaughtered animal's snout. Besides the obvious connotations of male bonding that killing and partaking of a meal of animal flesh entail, this all-male rite evokes other gender-related asymmetries. The extreme close-ups of the dying or dead animal snouts neatly mirror those of women's faces interspersed throughout the more action-packed sequences of the male rites unfolding on screen. While extreme close-ups are usually of women's faces or of animal snouts in the film, men tend to be portrayed in motion, while performing the various parts of the ceremonies. In this sequence, the calves and goats are powerless in the face of the groups of men and, in light of the link established in the film between women and the animals, their bleeding cannot help but bring to mind the blood of menstruation.

The subtext of these scenes is that the passage of men into adulthood involves learning how to exercise mastery over nature and over the female population of the villages. By persistently focusing on the natural world and on women, however, *Masks* signals that existence in the region and the male rites depicted in the documentary are directly dependent upon nature and could not take place without female presence. In a telling comment on the role of women in the area, Delgado states that 'the only thing they do is to cook the calf or buck that is sacrificed'.[37] Relegated to the margins of the ceremonies, women's work behind the scenes and the animals they prepare for a meal are what makes the celebrations possible. Women and nature are backgrounded and subordinated in a context where both are in fact crucial to daily life.

While not overtly a feminist film nor one that advocates for environmental activism, Delgado's documentary does draw attention to the persistent association of women and nature in a patriarchal cultural setting. By bringing to light the cultural mechanisms justifying the oppression of women and elements of the natural world, the film leads viewers to question the sense of entitlement displayed by males throughout the celebrations. Filmed in the immediate aftermath of the Carnation Revolution that ended a decades-long dictatorship in the country – in the poems read by revellers from one of the villages as part of the solstice rituals, there are references to the Revolution, the only time these momentous political events are mentioned in the film – *Masks* is both a nostalgic homage to a worldview about to disappear with the profound social changes underway at the time and an indictment of that very mindset. Delgado herself reflects upon the challenges she faced as a filmmaker during this period: 'I was a woman, very much alone, in the midst of so many men,'[38] a position that colours her filmmaking perspective. Ostensibly about male rites of passage, the film, directed by a woman, problematizes the very traditions it depicts, predicated on gender imbalances and on a view of men as masters of nature.

Trance – women and nature in a globalized Europe

Teresa Villaverde's film *Trance* takes viewers to another historical moment, a time when the borders separating Portugal from the rest of Europe have opened up in the aftermath of the country joining the EU (then EEC) in 1986. Far from the closed rural setting and age-old traditions depicted in *Masks*, Villaverde's film is about a globalized world, where everything is transient and people are on the move in search of better living conditions. The film narrates the life of a young woman from Saint Petersburg, Sonia (Ana Moreira), who leaves her hometown for Germany, where she finds work in a car dealership. Living in the country illegally, Sonia is kidnapped and sold into prostitution in Italy and, towards the end of the film, in Portugal. Although it is a fictional film, *Trance* depicts the fate of thousands of women and girls from Eastern Europe, forced into sex work in the more affluent Western countries by traffickers who keep them in virtual slavery.[39]

Masks was embedded in the culture and environment of northern Portugal, in agricultural societies where life was dictated by natural cycles and predicated on the struggle against and the taming of natural elements. This symbiotic relationship with the natural world is all but absent from *Trance*, a film about uprootedness and constant displacements that preclude any meaningful connection to nature. Still, Villaverde's film, like Delgado's, establishes a parallel between women and the natural world, although it offers a different perspective on this correlation. Delgado's film draws attention to the connection between women and the environment as a way to highlight the features of a patriarchal worldview that hinged upon the domination of both. Villaverde's film, conversely, underlines the similarities between an indifferent, detached relationship with the natural world and an equally callous approach to women as disposable beings. The film comments upon the negative repercussions of transnationalism and global capitalism, regimes under which human and non-human beings are valued only insofar as they can easily be converted into money.

The beginning of *Trance* already alludes to natural elements, as the credits appear on a grey screen to the sound of wind and of people walking, both of the latter portending the constant movement that is to be the hallmark of the film. Sonia's time in her hometown is marked by images of the Neva River, again pointing towards the movement to come, and long sequences portraying an icy landscape, at times shot from above. The aerial images of the frozen, white environment could be interpreted as a visual descriptor of Sonia's own life in Russia, petrified in an emotional and economic deadlock for which migration is the only way out. Viewers can both see and hear the sheets of ice opening fissures and breaking, in the same way as the protagonist's life will come undone abroad. In between the sequences depicting the snowy expanses outside Saint Petersburg, we hear a dialogue between a child – presumably Sonia's son – and an adult. The boy asks, 'Is a planet to be destroyed? Whenever we want?' and a man's voice answers, 'Yes'. 'Always?' asks the boy, and again the answer is 'Yes'. This environmentally attuned dialogue foreshadows the destruction of Sonia's own world by her enslavement as a sex worker but, more broadly, it hints at the rampant environmental degradation brought about by the globalized world represented in the film.

Sonia's trip from Russia to Germany is accompanied by images of green spaces seen first from a train, then a bus and finally a boat. These travelling shots of greenery show that the natural world itself is in transit, a far cry from the view of nature as a stable given we find in *Masks*, where its regular cycles determine human activities. Scholars such as Kääpä have argued for the advantages of transnational cinema in raising ecological awareness, in that it oscillates 'between the specificities of place and the ambiguities of the planetary', thereby overcoming 'some of the limitations of the binary between globalized and national forms of eco-cinema'.[40] Kääpä's argument chimes in with Ursula Heise's view that, in addition to an attunement to local space, ecological thought needs to cultivate an awareness of planetary environmental challenges in order to be effective. While some transnational films depicting a variety of spaces may directly foster ecological awareness, *Trance* contributes to this goal only circuitously by underscoring an increasing human alienation from our surroundings in a globalized setting. The film depicts the natural environment as a site of passage connecting one place to another, the implication being that transnationalism often results in a sense of detachment and loss. The lived experience of nature within close-knit communities such as those depicted in *Masks* all but disappears in *Trance*, but the promise of freedom that this liberation from natural and social bonds might have brought for women fails to materialize for the protagonist of Villaverde's film. Sonia faces a hostile foreign nature that is as indifferent as her captors in the face of her plight. As human ties crumble in a globalized world, so does the relationship between humans and their environment. The result is an even worse form of female domination than the one portrayed in *Masks*, in that women such as Sonia become objects to be used for male pleasure and discarded when they are no longer of service.

Sonia experiences only fleeting connections to the outside world, such as when she feeds breadcrumbs to the ducks in a lake during a brief stop in her bus trip on the way to Germany. Her abduction and enslavement as a sex worker mean that she is mostly kept indoors, locked in cars, rooms and industrial containers, so that she will not escape from her kidnappers (see Figure 5.2). Still, *Trance* eschews any facile connection linking closed spaces with imprisonment, and nature and the open air with freedom. For instance, shortly after her kidnapping, Sonia escapes into a forest. She is wearing a green pullover that seems to suggest her kinship with the green trees and bushes and, therefore, to underline the commonplace association of women and nature (see Figure 5.3). A tree that comes crashing down, probably felled for timber, and gunshots, presumably from hunters, further establish a parallel between the protagonist's bleak situation and the natural environment. While the forest is treated as a

Figure 5.2 A container in Teresa Villaverde's *Trance* (Atalanta Filmes, 2007).

Figure 5.3 Sonia in the forest in Teresa Villaverde's *Trance* (Atalanta Filmes, 2007).

resource, where logging and hunting take place, Sonia will be equally abused by her captors. But perhaps because she is in a foreign land, the protagonist fails to find any common ground with the natural world around her and cannot find solace in a place that is alien to her. She wanders through the forest unable to find nourishment or shelter; the camera's blurred images of the tree canopy in a POV shot signify her increasing disorientation. Her emaciated body is lying next to a tree when her captor picks her up and takes her back to his car to continue their journey.

In another sequence, her abductor throws Sonia into a bathtub full of water and leaves her in the cold and damp bathroom until she begs for her clothes. And later on she is once more tortured with water running through her naked body. Again, the film systematically undoes the long-established association of women and water, which becomes here a means of punishing the protagonist. The scenes of Sonia's torture and degradation using water contrast with her longing for the snow of her native Russia towards the end of the film, when she is already in Portugal. *Trance* mixes shots of Sonia's voyage with memories and the fantasy world in which she becomes more and more entrapped as a means to escape the unbearable reality of her circumstances. Having crossed the whole of Europe, from its north-easternmost region to the southwest, she dreams of snow and cold in the Portuguese heat. These images of snow point to the protagonist's desire to go back to a familiar environment that has been forever lost with emigration and her ensuing kidnapping. She yearns for a time and place where she experienced a sense of belonging, a time and place that, as the film suggests, may never have existed, even in one's homeland, in the context of globalized world.

Perhaps the most shocking sequence of *Trance* is Sonia's subjection to rape by a dog, as retribution for her last attempt to escape her captors, towards the end of the film. The disjointed images of her naked body, her deafening cries and the dog's loud bark and rapid breathing make for the most horrifying moments of the film. The protagonist's estrangement from the natural world, from plants and animals, has been fully accomplished, as they end up contributing to her downfall. Women, like natural elements such as the dog in this sequence, have become mere goods to be used at will. Alternatively, as Ana Filipa Prata points out, borrowing Giorgio Agamben's formulation, they are turned into 'naked life',[41] devoid of the protections afforded by custom and habit in traditional societies and guaranteed by law in modern nation states. Viewers only see parts of Sonia and the dog in this sequence, pointing to their fragmentation as bodies, pieces of flesh to be freely exchanged for money in a world that exploits those who are most helpless.

In both Delgado's and Villaverde's films the fate of women is tied to that of the environment. Carefully avoiding a redemptive narrative that would hark back to an idealized union between female characters and nature, both directors tacitly acknowledge the interrelation between the social position of women and attitudes towards the natural world in their films. In *Masks*, the association of women and nature points towards the domination of both in a patriarchal society. Filmed in the immediate aftermath of the 25 April 1974 Revolution that put an end to more than four decades of the New State dictatorship, the film comments upon the social subordination of women in Portuguese villages, a situation that reflects the broader male-dominated ideology prevalent during the New State. The documentary shows how men were perceived as the active parties in the transformation and taming of the natural world and in the ritual ceremonies depicted in the film, with women being relegated to the margins and functioning, like nature, as mere background to the action. Delgado emphasizes the subordinate position of women, at the same time as she shows that their work actually underpinned all daily activities, thereby implicitly criticizing their sidelining in the celebrations and in public life.

Trance depicts a world out of joint, where human connections with one another and with their surroundings have been severed by economic hardship, migration and enslavement. While the age-old association between nature and women variously analysed by eco-feminists is shown in Villaverde's film to be an artificial construct, constant displacements preclude the forging of a new, more meaningful relationship between the female protagonist and the environment. The estrangement of humans from nature in a transnational Europe, where people are constantly on the move, goes hand in hand with the exploitation of women, who become nothing more than commodities. Filmed on the cusp of profound changes in Portugal, *Masks* decried an ossified, patriarchal social structure that was about to crumble even as the documentary was being made. *Trance*, in turn, reveals the underside of some of these social transformations that allowed for both the natural world and certain humans, such as economically vulnerable women, to be regarded as expendable. Contemporary globalized society is shown to be built upon these human and non-human beings whose bodies are used, abused and then disposed of when no longer needed.

Notes

1 The research for this article was funded by a grant from the Portuguese Foundation for Science and Technology (FCT), Project IF/00606/2015.
2 For more information on the environmental impact of filmmaking, see Nadia Bozak's book *The Cinematic Footprint*, which aims to understand 'how an awareness

of movie making as an industry, one that is as plugged into "nature" and the resources it yields as any other, reconfigures our interpretive and practical approach to the cinematic image throughout film history'. Nadia Bozak, *The Cinematic Footprint: Lights, Camera, Natural Resources* (New Brunswick, NJ and London: Rutgers University Press, 2012), 1.

3 As Scott MacDonald points out, 'The filmstrip, at least on one level, encapsulates the way in which modern life and the natural world are imbricated: the light-sensitive silver salts that create a visible image when exposed to light are suspended in a thin layer of gelatin, one of the chief ingredients of which is collagen. Collagen is produced by boiling the bones and tissues of animals. Celluloid, the base on which the emulsion is layered, is made from cellulose. That is, the "life" we see moving on the screen is a kind of re-animation of plant and animal life within the mechanical/chemical apparatus of traditional cinema.' Scott MacDonald, 'The Ecocinema Experience', in *Ecocinema Theory and Practice*, ed. Stephen Rust, Salma Monani and Sean Cubitt (New York and London: Routledge, 2013), 18.

4 Martin Lefebvre reminds us that 'one of the first wonders the cinema offered its viewers was that of images of the natural world in movement. Early spectators enjoyed the sights of crashing waves and tree leaves rustling in the wind.' Martin Lefebvre, 'Between Setting and Landscape in the Cinema', in *Landscape and Film*, ed. Martin Lefebvre (New York and London: Routledge, 2006), xi.

5 See E. Ann Kaplan, 'Visualizing Climate Trauma: The Cultural Work of Films Anticipating the Future', in *The Routledge Companion to Cinema and Gender*, ed. Kristin Lené Hole, Dijana Jelača, E. Ann Kaplan and Patrice Petro (London and New York: Routledge, 2017), 407–16; Pat Bereton, *Environmental Ethics and Film* (London and New York: Routledge, 2016); Ellen E. Moore, *Landscape and the Environment in Hollywood Film: the Green Machine* (New York: Palgrave Macmillan, 2017); and Stephen Rust and Salma Monani, 'Introduction – Cuts to Dissolves: Defining and Situating Ecocinema Studies', in Rust, Monani and Cubitt, *Ecocinema Theory and Practice*, 1–13.

6 In Willoquet-Maricondi's words: 'An important distinction I wish to establish between "environmentalist" films and ecocinema is the latter's consciousness-raising and activist intentions, as well as responsibility to heighten awareness about contemporary issues and practices affecting planetary health. Ecocinema overtly strives to inspire personal and political action on the part of viewers, stimulating our thinking so as to bring about concrete changes in the choices we make, daily and in the long run, as individuals and as societies, locally and globally.' Paula Willoquet-Maricondi, 'Shifting Paradigms: From Environmentalist Film to Ecocinema', in *Framing the World: Explorations in Ecocriticism and Film*, ed. Paula Willoquet-Maricondi (Charlottesville and London: University of Virginia Press, 2010), 45.

7   Willoquet-Maricondi, 'Shifting Paradigms', 45.
8   Adrian Ivakhiv, 'Green Film Criticism and Its Futures', *Interdisciplinary Studies in Literature and Environment* 15, no. 2 (Summer 2008): 4–5. As Ellen Moore suggests, Hollywood's commodified environmentalism displays 'a constant point of tension between what we know to be true (overconsumption is harming the planet) and the never ending imperative from the culture industry (don't stop consuming)'. Moore, *Landscape and the Environment in Hollywood Film*, 20.
9   Scott MacDonald, 'Toward an Eco-Cinema', *Interdisciplinary Studies in Literature and Environment* 11, no. 2 (2004): 107–32.
10 MacDonald, 'The Ecocinema Experience', 20.
11 Ibid.
12 Ibid., 41.
13 David Ingram, 'The Aesthetics and Ethics of Eco-Film Criticism', in Rust, Monani and Cubitt, *Ecocinema Theory and Practice*, 48.
14 Ibid., 59.
15 Pietari Kääpä, 'Transnational Approaches to Ecocinema: Charting an Expansive Field', in *Transnational Ecocinema: Film Cuture in an Era of Ecological Transformation*, eds Pietari Kääpä and Tommy Gustafsson (Bristol, UK and Chicago, US: University of Chicago Press, 2013), 27.
16 Rust and Monani, 'Introduction – Cuts to Dissolves', 3.
17 As Rust and Monani state, 'Cinema and ecocinema studies enable us to recognize ways of seeing the world other than through the narrow perspective of the anthropocentric gaze that situates individual human desires at the centre of the moral universe.' Ibid., 11.
18 The word 'nature' comes from the Latin word *natura*, which goes back to the verb 'to be born', thus connecting all things natural to the act of birth, as opposed to creation by humans through craftsmanship, for example. The word 'environment' is much more recent and denotes everything that is around us, which can include both natural and urban environments. I will skirt the debate about the advantages and disadvantages of each of these terms for eco-criticism. For the purposes of this chapter, the two words will be used interchangeably, unless otherwise indicated.
19 Carolyn Merchant, *The Death of Nature: Women, Ecology and the Scientific Revolution* (New York: HarperOne, 1989), xxiii.
20 Val Plumwood, *Feminism and the Mastery of Nature* (London and New York: Routledge, 1997), 20.
21 Ibid., 21.
22 Ibid., 23.
23 Ibid., 24.
24 Bereton, *Environmental Ethics and Film*, 22, 82-3. As Noël Sturgeon explains, 'Basically, ecofeminism claims that the oppression, inequality, and exploitation

of certain groups (people of colour, women, poor people, LGBT people, Global South people, animals) are theoretically and structurally related to the degradation and overexploitation of the environment. Theoretically and ideologically, they are related because Western ideological frameworks operate dualistically, separating culture and nature, men and women, white people and people of colour, humans and animals, mind and body, rationality and emotion, straight people and queer people. Furthermore, eco-feminists argue, these dualisms are value-hierarchical, with the first term in the previous list assumed to be superior to the second.' Noël Sturgeon, *Environmentalism in Popular Culture: Gender, Race, Sexuality and the Politics of the Natural* (Tucson: University of Arizona Press, 2009), 9.

25 Ibid., 12. Sturgeon adds: 'Those who are made to seem closer to nature (while inferior to those who are thought of as "civilized") have often also been given the burden of symbolically representing the tragic aspects of development, as inhabitants of a lost, imaginary Eden.' Ibid., 13.

26 Bereton, *Environmental Ethics and Film*, 85.

27 Kaplan, 'Visualizing Climate Trauma', 411; emphasis in original.

28 Ibid.

29 Lefebvre, 'Between Setting and Landscape in the Cinema', 21.

30 Ibid., 24, 28.

31 Ibid., 29. Lefebvre adds: 'The spectacle halts the progression of narrative for the spectator. … When I contemplate a piece of film, I stop following the story for a moment, even if the narrative does not completely disappear from my consciousness.' Ibid., 29.

32 Ibid; emphasis in original.

33 In an interview, Noémia Delgado explains that the voice we hear is 'the voice of a woman singing, a peasant woman from Trás-os-Montes'. Ilda Castro, 'Entrevista com Noémia Delgado', in *Cineastas Portuguesas 1874–1956*, ed. António Cunha (Lisbon: Câmara Municipal de Lisboa, 2000), 43.

34 Delgado explains that, once they donned their masks, men were 'completely changed'. 'It was not easy at all to film them,' she comments, because 'they were gripped by madness'. Castro, 'Entrevista com Noémia Delgado', 45.

35 The voice-off is that of Portuguese poet Alexandre O'Neill, who was Delgado's husband at the time.

36 Castro, 'Entrevista com Noémia Delgado', 42.

37 Ibid.

38 Ibid., 56.

39 Ginette Verstraete discusses 'the alarming increase in the forced sex trafficking of women and children in Europe today – Amnesty International (AI) talks of 500,000 women having entered Europe this way in the last years'. Ginette

Verstraete, 'Women's Resistance Strategies in a High-Tech Multicultural Europe', in *Transnational Feminism in Film and Media*, eds Katarzyna Marciniak, Anikó Imre and Áine O'Healy (New York: Palgrave Macmillan, 2007), 116.

40 Kääpä, 'Transnational Approaches to Ecocinema', 37.

41 Ana Filipa Prata, 'Transdifference and Abjection in Maria Velho da Costa's *Myra* and Teresa Villaverde's *Transe*', *Portuguese Studies* 33, no. 2 (2017), 215.

Section Three

Archives

6

Image, historical memory, politics: Margarida Cardoso's *Kuxa Kanema* and Susana de Sousa Dias's *48*

Estela Vieira

Despite their different cultural and historical contexts, Margarida Cardoso's *Kuxa Kanema: o nascimento do cinema* (*Kuxa Kanema: The Birth of Cinema*, 2003) and Susana de Sousa Dias's *48* (2010) are films with significant formal affinities. They are both first and foremost films about the image and about filmmaking; their content is literally visual material, photographs in the case of Sousa Dias's work, and filmstrip or film footage in the case of Cardoso's. Unconventional documentary films, *Kuxa Kanema* and *48* rely largely on archival images to reflect upon the relationship between image, archive, filmmaking, historical memory, and political import. Meta-cinematographic, they conceptualize the moving image and the relationship between visual and historical narratives. Like many contemporary artists, Cardoso and Sousa Dias are concerned with unveiling suppressed experiences, undoing dominant narratives, and raising consciousness; that is, they are devoted to making historical or political documentaries that call for the spectators' engagement with the content of their stories. But these two Portuguese women directors also have an important aesthetic aim, which I would argue is ubiquitous throughout their work. Both filmmakers aim to find novel cinematic forms and narratives that help audiences understand how a political past and its traumatic memory is still extant in the present – even if this is marked by absence. Their work is concerned with capturing a 'what if', a potentiality and an ambiguity possible with film, and in this way, they are largely asking viewers to reflect on the form of their filmmaking.

Documenting the past and uncovering injustices and political conflict is a central premise of Cardoso's and Sousa Dias's work. Yet relying on documentary imagery for their films is effectively a creative choice and aesthetic tool. The directors wish to engage viewers in unique ways, trouble conceptualizations of film and reconsider imagery's implications. Their 'found footage', to use Jaimie Baron's notion of the emergent and diverse types of indexical audiovisual documents or evidence about the past appropriated in films, is used strategically to reflect on the stakes of filmmaking in our contemporary milieu. Baron argues that the archive ought to be understood as an experience of reception, which is what she calls the 'archive effect', or a relationship between viewers and the film that re-theorizes associations between film and archive as a source of historical knowledge.[1] Cardoso and Sousa Dias likewise aim to rethink the medium in relation to history, politics, and gender, and create visual expressions that shake viewers' historical consciousness and compel them to reconsider cinematic conventions. This chapter will analyse the ways in which the visual configuration of these two films constitutes a powerful political statement that speaks not only to political history but also to a woman's role in retelling unresolved stories. Cardoso and Sousa Dias not only re-examine this cinematic genre and the objectives of contemporary filmmaking but, as I also hope to show, the aesthetic intentions of their documentary productions are as much a form of memory politics as they are a form of feminist politics.

Documentary or feminist filmmaking?

According to Bill Nichols, documentaries are made with different assumptions: 'They involve a different relationship between filmmaker and subject, and they prompt different sorts of expectations from audiences.'[2] However, as he admits, these differences guarantee no absolute separation between fiction and non-fiction films. Patricia Aufderheide writes that while 'documentaries are *about* real life; they are not real life. They are not even windows onto real life. They are portraits of real life.'[3] Most scholars of film, and of documentary filmmaking in particular, agree that it is virtually impossible to distinguish or define categorically what documentary is or how it differs from fictional cinema. Still, there are theoretical ways of engaging, and thus conceptualizing documentary filmmaking, and as we will see Cardoso's and Sousa Dias's work strives to do this. Paula Rabinowitz explores in her study of American political documentaries the evolving intersections between history, documentary, and cinema, while highlighting the intricate role gender plays in this manifold theoretical history.[4] Women filmmakers have been particularly interested in documentary as a genre, and in using archival footage in their work to illustrate complex and open-ended political realities while addressing gender roles and identities. But as Diane Waldman and Janet Walker remind us, it is only recently 'that documentary theorists and historians have begun to engage seriously with feminist film theory and to write women back into documentary history'.[5] While historically, feminist film criticism has tended to avoid documentary or focused solely on explicitly feminist documentaries, clearly feminist thinking can be applicable to documentary filmmaking in general. Thus, choosing to work in the genre is useful for women not only to extend the possibilities of documentary and critique its more classical conventions but also to rethink a woman's role in a cinematographic tradition and in the industry more broadly.

In her book on Portuguese filmmaker António Campos (1922–99), *O paradigma do documentário* (The documentary paradigm), from 2009, Manuela Penafria, wishing to break down the strict categories between documentary and fiction film and show that Campos was much more than 'an ethnographic documentary filmmaker', argues that his filmography makes an important contribution to our discussion of a Portuguese cinematography.[6] Penafria claims that it is indeed possible to pinpoint a tradition, or an aesthetic of filmmaking in Portugal inherently intertwined with documentary. This would be film conceptualized as 'anticinema' – a word Campos used on several occasions to characterize his own work – as experimentation, as working on the margins of dominant trends and almost exclusively on one's own, as filming intended primarily for the viewer made by directors that hide themselves and their camera.[7] Thus, when a Portuguese filmmaker chooses to make a documentary film, one should not consider this as a choice to work in what typically might have been considered a minor genre, but as a creative choice building on a tradition; a choice to make a film that represents an alternative or radical path, one that goes against the grain, but that builds on major national precedents. In addition, two of the country's first women filmmakers, Noémia Delgado (1933–2016) and Margarida Cordeiro (1938–), who made films with her husband António Reis, were along with Campos, in the vanguard of this important non-fiction, ethnographic, poetic filmmaking (see also Manuela Penafria in this volume). This innovative, path-breaking documentary work, an integral part of the Portuguese New Cinema project,[8] has proven decisive to the identity of contemporary Portuguese cinema and, as the work of Delgado and Cordeiro shows, had a strong female precedent.

It is in this framework that I want to understand the work of Margarida Cardoso and Susana de Sousa Dias: to conceptualize their films not as fiction films but nevertheless as creative films, as a mode of being in the panorama of contemporary filmmaking and in the panorama of a Portuguese cinematographic tradition. I read their films as interrogations that ask what is conceivable politically, culturally, ideologically, or aesthetically in contemporary filmmaking. What are the potentialities of cinema today, and is it perhaps the task of a woman filmmaker to reflect on the inherent ambiguities of the image, and to propose the possibilities of film in our current cultural context?

Furthermore, though the films are not exclusively about gender issues, I also want to argue that they put forth a feminist politics. Ana Catarina Pereira claims female-directed cinema in Portugal suffers from a 'double invisibility'.[9] Few would disagree with the fact that Portuguese women's filmmaking is very little recognized within Portuguese cinema, itself insufficiently known whether inside the country or among an international viewership, despite this small-nation cinema's increasing prominence. The two films adopt strategies that respond to this double invisibility. The directors seemingly hide their own image-making behind the archival material, and as I will subsequently show, they give a form to their invisibility, making us aware of their presence in the modes of their filmmaking. This is why the story or the narrative in the documentaries is twofold. On the one hand, it tells a political narrative, and on the other, it is a story about making a film, a story that asks about the significance and the possibilities for a Portuguese woman to make a political film. In blurring categories between fiction, image, and political reality, the films force us to rethink filmmaking as a feminist intervention within a national and global context.

Margarida Cardoso's *Kuxa Kanema*: The birth of a film

After completing a degree in image and audiovisual communication, Margarida Cardoso, who was born in 1963 and lived in Mozambique until the age of twelve, started in the field as a cinematographer for a series of films made for Portuguese public television (RTP), *Histórias de mulheres* (*Stories of Women*, 1983). She was also production assistant on several films including João Botelho's *Um adeus português* (*A Portuguese Farewell*, 1985) – one of the earliest Portuguese fiction films about the Colonial War – before working consistently in the 1990s as a scriptwriter, production assistant, and assistant director on over forty films.[10] Her own work focuses on Lusophone colonial and post-colonial themes and contexts, including her well-regarded documentaries, *Natal 71* (*Christmas 71*,

1999) – which relies on archival footage from the last years of Portuguese colonial rule in Africa – and *Kuxa Kanema*, as well as her two fiction films, *A costa dos murmúrios* (*The Murmuring Coast*, 2004) – based on Portuguese writer Lídia Jorge's renowned novel, and *Yvone Kane* (2014) – a loose fictional adaptation of the biography of the real-life Angolan guerrilla fighter, Sita Valles (see also Sally Faulkner in this volume).

Kuxa Kanema documents the founding of Mozambique's *Instituto Nacional de Cinema* (National Institute of Cinema) or INC immediately following the country's long-fought-for independence from Portugal in 1975. The INC became in the 1970s and 1980s one of the most important centres for film production in Sub-Saharan Africa bringing together filmmakers, technicians, and other devotees from Europe and the Americas dedicated to film and socialist revolutionary causes. Some of the INC's productions were collective projects, or co-productions, teaming third cinema filmmakers from Cuba and other Latin American countries with Mozambicans. A number of these producers and directors are interviewed in the documentary, including Mozambican-born Brazilian filmmaker, Ruy Guerra, who also served for a time as the institute's director. Victoria Pasley describes these important transatlantic exchanges in her study of *Kuxa Kanema*, which she calls 'a testimony to the birth and achievement of Mozambique's cinema and its final demise'.[11] Besides a series of state-funded films and documentaries, the institute also produced a weekly newsreel called *Kuxa Kanema*, and its goal, as stated by a voiceover at the beginning of the film, was to capture the image of the people on screen and deliver that image back to the populace, the majority of whom still remained largely unexposed to the moving image. Beyond educating Mozambicans about the various government programmes, and transmitting the values of the social revolution, the institute would also aim 'to forge national unity across ethnic and linguistic diversity'.[12]

Parallel to the story of the rise and fall of the INC is the history of the formation of the socialist country itself. The institute is thus a metaphor for the People's Republic of Mozambique as we see the hopes and prospects of the country governed by the *Frente de Libertação de Moçambique* (Front for the Liberation of Mozambique), or FRELIMO, begin to fade, and the political conflicts and the internal war intensify. In the aftermath of the 25 April 1974 Carnation Revolution, which finally ended the Wars of Independence giving national autonomy to the former Portuguese African colonies, Mozambique suffered military attacks backed by the white-minority regimes of neighbouring South Africa and Rhodesia. A violent 'civil war' ensued against another political faction, *Resistência Nacional Moçambicana* (National Mozambican Resistance), or RENAMO, that would officially end in 1992 with peace accords. But a hopeful era characterized the first years of the FRELIMO government which saw expanded education and health and social services, and the engagement of an enfranchised and expectant population. The film showcases the hopefulness, optimism, and confidence that existed initially before the decay and demise of both the institute and the political situation. The film is thus about the possibility or the becoming of a social state reflected in the potential of the image.

It uses footage shot in the 1970s and 1980s by the institute, and intermingles these sequences with interviews of former directors, screenwriters, sound engineers, and other technicians and workers of the INC. The interviews were conducted in the 1990s when Cardoso spent months going through the abandoned and disordered material which she found in the headquarters of the institute after it was ruined by a severe fire. Not exactly a well-cared for official archive, the material is nonetheless state-owned. The film in fact gives the footage the archival status it lacked. The documentary puts the images and footage into a novel context, different from the initial intention or setting, giving these visuals a new framework, a new opportunity. It is as if the documentary were bringing together all the films that could have been; a series of possible trailers for countless films never completed. Thus, it is about potential as much as it is about loss. Cardoso's documentary, besides being a story about the connection or the relationship between filmmaking and political ideology, also testifies to the autonomy and endurance of the visual. In addition, it questions how audiences and filmmakers are implicated in relating political conflict and narrating the making and unmaking of national communities.

Kuxa Kanema, which literally means in the local Bantu languages the subtitle of the film, 'The Birth of Cinema', was, as noted above, the weekly newsreel used by FRELIMO to promote its educational and ideological campaigns. However, 'The Birth of Cinema' also echoes an infamous title, D. W. Griffith's 1915 silent landmark of American film history, *The Birth of a Nation*. The apt, ironic and ambiguous reference, whether conscious or not, is striking. *Kuxa Kanema* narrates the birth of a film industry and the founding of a new socialist nation, one determined to be free of racial prejudices and race-inflected economic and political inequality. Griffith's work is a founding work of cinematic realism with its innovative and groundbreaking techniques, while telling the distorted historical narrative of a racist nation. This allusion is one example of the ambiguities the film addresses throughout, some explicitly others more subtly.

While the film honours and documents the influential power of images, it also questions their authority and critiques the abuse of the visual potential and the political manipulation often associated with image making. The interviewees make clear that once the political situation intensifies the INC becomes merely a propagandistic arm of the party to indoctrinate Mozambicans and assure FRELIMO's political survival.

The structure and tone of the film recreates this ambiguity between film's boundless promise and its perilous potential. Besides talking about the sense of hopefulness that they felt, the interviewees or workers of the INC often discuss the limited resources, the failures or the amateurish quality of the work and the inevitable ideological and creative breakdown. These monologues, however, are often contradicted by the visual presentation of the archival material. Beautiful images accompanied by poignant sound, including stirring music and strong voices, interrupt these negative comments. The interpolated footage shows literacy campaigns, examples of peasant empowerment, community building, and communally mobilized labour building schools and other public infrastructure. There are several examples of these transitions when the words of the interviewees are muffled and overpowered by dynamic chants, music and visuals; the archival imagery thus prevails over the more conventional form of the documentary: the interview. For example, when film director Camilo de Sousa speaks nostalgically of the forlorn hope of creating a country that would be different from others, he says, 'We were going to domesticate the elephants to help build roads, we were going to change the world.' As he speaks these words, the scene shifts to a moving, fervent moment showing the singing and dancing of a group of people praising the revolution. There is a way in which the archival material is impressed on the viewer and seems more powerful than the documentary itself. Besides echoing incongruities between aspirations and the ensuing reality, the older footage takes over, muting the voice of the interviewee with its dominant sound and fast-paced movement, creating a visual energy and drive that seems to be inherent to the moving image, or so the film suggests. The power of imagery, however, is also made clear in the use of static visuals. Every so often the director interpolates meaningful stills of the footage and superimposes these over an interviewee's voice. Thus, the images or the films within the film have a ubiquitous uncanny presence. For example, the screenwriter Luís Patraquim is always shown with some of the work he helped create in the background on a screen (see Figure 6.1). The force of these omnipresent visuals, sounds, and movement gives the narrative of loss and decline a different picture, suggesting

Figure 6.1 Luís Patraquim viewing Mozambican newsreel footage (First Run/Icarus Films, 2003).

a sense of hope, potential, a 'what if'. Viewers thus perceive the endless and enduring presence and possibility of these historical and visual documents.

How the dual narrative, the political narrative and the story of filmmaking, relate to Cardoso's memory and feminist politics becomes apparent if we focus on the opening and closing scenes. One of the first examples of footage the film shows is the voice and image of its charismatic protagonist, Samora Machel, Mozambique's revolutionary leader and first president. This is followed by the quick movement of the materiality of film, a quick-paced flipping of the 35 mm filmstrip showing Machel (see Figure 6.2), which in turn is interrupted by the female voiceover we hear throughout the film (spoken by Portuguese actress Mónica Calle – supporting actress in Cardoso's *The Murmuring Coast*). She introduces the historical background for establishing the INC and its objectives. She says, 'The image has a power, and the new president, Samora Machel, is conscious of that.' In addition, right after the images of Machel, the hands – which we can safely assume to be the filmmaker's – hold another strip showing a black Mozambican woman working in the field.

This parallel between Machel's cinematic purpose for film and the institute is supplanted by female presences, the voiceover, the subsequent footage of the peasant woman and the body or hands of the director. This reinforces the analogy that I find more significant than the one established in the film between the formation of INC and that of Mozambique's nascent socialist state, and this is the simile that links *Kuxa Kanema*, Cardoso's documentary or her

Figure 6.2 Samora Machel on film reel (First Run/Icarus Films, 2003).

filmmaking, with *Kuxa Kanema*, the concept of educating and transforming society and communities through film and images. Phil Hall writes in praise of the film, which he claims is 'among the very best films ever made about filmmaking … Machel's failure is Cardoso's triumph'.[13] In other words, Machel and Cardoso have a similar understanding of film's possibilities; they are both conscious of the power of the image, but only Cardoso is able to engage creatively and critique that potential.

The final scene reinforces this correlation further. After the voiceover reminds us that television now dominates the airwaves in Mozambique, that the 1992 peace accords did not revive the institute and that the INC has not made a film in years, it tellingly closes with a shot of Machel chanting, '*a luta continua, a luta continua*' ('the fight continues, the fight continues'), followed by, 'thank you, friends'. His and the film's last words are also the director's sign off. Both Machel and Cardoso thank viewers for watching and listening to their appeal for political action. In a sense his call to arms is also the film's consciousness of the power of the image reminding us self-reflectively of the importance cinema can have in the building and forging of a society and its political memory. And while Cardoso sympathizes politically with at least some of Machel's socialist ideals, the director is anything but Manichean. In fact, the film constantly examines the ambiguous power of the image. *Kuxa Kanema* is openly critical of the racist and aggressive states and policies that inflamed the war against FRELIMO destroying the government and massacring innocent people, but it is also a compelling critique of how the state-run policies were ideologically manipulative. As Robert Stock has shown, *Kuxa Kanema* belongs to a category of contemporary Mozambican films that begin to question 'an idealized national history written by FRELIMO' and confront internal issues while negotiating the country's colonial and post-colonial past.[14]

These parallels between political and cinematographic contexts allow Cardoso to reflect on the connection between documentary filmmaking and historical memory. The film reproduces echoes from the archival material in the scenes representing the 'now' exemplified in the depictions of the decaying empty building and surroundings. For example, soon after replaying some of the footage capturing a devastating massacre of Mozambicans committed by Rhodesian military forces, Cardoso interviews and films an important sound technician for the INC, Gabriel Mondlane. The bloodstains of the slaughter victims documented in the archival material (see Figure 6.3) resonate with the water damage on the floor of the institute as well as with the filmstrip Mondlane is holding in his hands (Figure 6.4). Mondlane is handling the 35 mm film as Cardoso's camera films him. The scene creates a shadow, a visual, filmic memory of the violent history. This crossing-over seems to suggest that filmmaking, or retelling or reflecting on political narratives, is a connected and collective process that requires not only different people working together and varied perspectives but also a joint historical consciousness and awareness of how the storytelling process implicates viewers, filmmakers, and technicians alike.

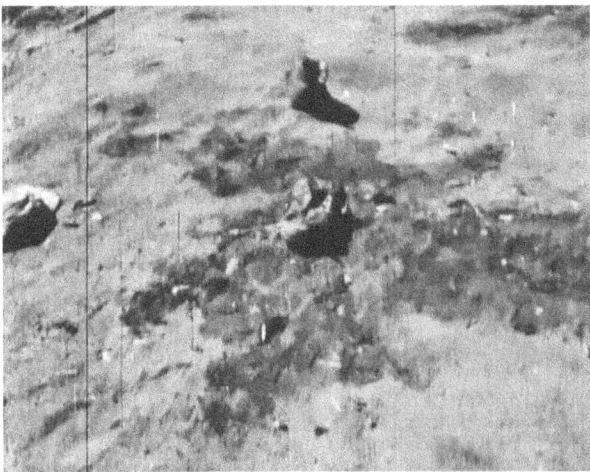

Figure 6.3 Bloodstained ground (First Run/Icarus Films, 2003).

Figure 6.4 Gabriel Mondlane in the dilapidated Instituto Nacional de Cinema building (First Run/Icarus Films, 2003).

This is also why the documentary is preoccupied throughout with framing the cinematographic. There are many images of cameras, screens, reels, sound recording equipment, filmstrip. The shot often shows the archival footage on screens large and small. In fact, screening is recurrently thematized. One of the interviewees is filmed sitting in the cinema. Footage captures the mobile projection units, many of which were donated by the Soviet Union, and used to bring the INC's work to rural communities. Isabel Noronha, Cardoso's last and only female interviewee, sits in front of a large round glass window reminding us of a camera lens (see Figure 6.5). By revealing its apparatus and tools, the self-reflective documentary intensifies the sense of visual potentiality so important in the film.

Cardoso brings *Kuxa Kanema* to a close with a woman, the director and producer Isabel Noronha, who speaks of the brutality of the war that ensued, explaining how impossible it was to capture with the camera the horrors witnessed by crews sent out into attacked areas: 'It was such a terrible situation and so humanitarianly violent, that you did not even think that what you were seeing was real, therefore, it was almost as if what we were seeing was the film and not reality, because otherwise it was intolerable.' Speaking of the disconnects and links between reality and fiction, and about filming this reality or unreality, relates to the work of Cardoso's documentary as well. Noronha's voice also resonates with the director's own. These female voices, Noronha's, Cardoso's implicit voice and the female voiceover throughout the film, remind viewers

Figure 6.5 Isabel Noronha (First Run/Icarus Films, 2003).

of the complexities of witnessing or documenting, in cinematographic terms, political conflict or historical reality. Similarly, Cardoso is also questioning in her film what is real, historical, fictional, and political. It seems more important, the film is suggesting, to interrogate, doubt, and show that visual representations have evolving and conflicting meanings, and that viewers ought to be cognizant of this ambiguity, and of the possibilities and limits of images and film.

As Eric Allina-Pisano points out, the story narrated in the film 'is not only that of the Mozambican state but also that of Cold War politics and of the processes of globalization that have intensified in the last decade'.[15] Thus, while it is about a political past that never came to be, the film is also suggesting that the current political present is a historical consequence. Robert Stock has shown in his reading of the INC's first full-length documentary, *Estas são as armas* (*These Are the Guns*, 1978) directed by Brazilian Murilo Mendes who collaborated with Luís Bernardo Honwana, that it was common to use colonial archival images, such as colonial newsreels and official Portuguese military footage, reframing them to promote an anti-colonial, anti-imperialist rhetoric.[16] While *These Are the Guns* is less subtle than the work of Cardoso or the work of Sousa Dias, all of these political films, whether fictional or not, articulate a specific post-colonial memory politics by resituating archival footage or imagery. Yet, the female-conceptualized documentaries not only offer historical critiques but also theorize formally the aesthetic and political potential and complexities of bringing together historical memory, filmmaking, and archival material. *Kuxa Kanema*'s female voices (the director's, the voiceover's, Noronha's) question the ambiguities, limitations and potentialities of image making.

Moving images in Susana de Sousa Dias's 48

Just as Cardoso found in the burnt-out building that housed the Mozambican film institute what would become the source material for *Kuxa Kanema*, Sousa Dias's cinematographic work was forever changed after her contact with photographic evidence and film footage gathered in the archives of the headquarters of the former Portuguese military and secret police force PIDE/DGS (*Polícia Internacional e de Defesa do Estado/Direção Geral de Segurança*; International and State Defence Police/General Security Directorate). While Cardoso lived in Mozambique until the age of twelve, Sousa Dias was twelve at the time of the Carnation Revolution. Both of these are important biographical experiences that influence the directors and the context of their work.

Another point in common between the two filmmakers is the fact that both Cardoso's and Sousa Dias's early projects focused on women. Sousa Dias's first project, *Processo-crime 141/53—enfermeiras no Estado Novo* (Case-Crime 141/53—Nurses during the New State, 2000), was about how the repressive dictatorship restricted the lives of women. Unlike this early work, her subsequent documentary films deviate radically from convention in formal terms. Susana de Sousa Dias's first full-length documentary, *Natureza Morta* (*Still Life*, 2005), paints a panorama of the Salazar dictatorship using only images and sound. She takes clips from propaganda films and photographs produced and taken by the regime, making a compilation she then plays with no spoken discourse. Both her masters thesis and doctoral dissertation, completed while working on her documentaries, focused on the relation between cinema, archive, and memory. In *48* the director chooses to use only mugshots of political prisoners from the same PIDE archives turning them into portraits with movement. The camera films over the still photographs in slow motion. Where Cardoso used footage or images to challenge particular constructions of nation, Sousa Dias also aims to raise consciousness by using imagery created by the Salazar regime to deconstruct the dictatorship's hegemonic narrative.

The audience hears the voices of the people represented in the pictures as they narrate their horrific and humiliating experience in jail. They also share their understanding of what the dictatorship signified for them, and give impressions of their sense of identity, loss, the meaning of life, and the passage of time. The individuals are interviewed by the director, whose voice we never hear but whose questions can be inferred in the prisoners' answers. Even though the filmmaker is absent, her existence is manifested. This strategy of partly hiding the presence of the filmmaker is also evident as we saw in *Kuxa Kanema*. There is one interview in Cardoso's documentary where we see a black shadow; part of the back of her head and hair (see Figure 6.6). In this scene, Cardoso is not behind the camera but at the table with her interviewee. Likewise, we infer that Sousa Dias is sitting with the prisoners at a table on the other side of the portrait, or on the other side of the black screen, since the camera interpolates a black screen with the filming in and out of each of the photographs. Thus, both directors hide themselves, but make that hiding visible albeit in darkness. This technique is a way of representing (or visualizing) invisibility and resonates with my earlier discussion of how historically the role, presence, and contributions of women filmmakers have been largely overlooked. In their films the directors cast themselves as dark shadows or as unseen yet marked appearances that act invisibly as interlocutors and listeners, observing, seeing, and listening to others.

While the directors I study are far from embracing themselves as subjects of their work, they do shrewdly include their figural presence, placing their roles (and biographies) into the framework of the film. This forces viewers to reflect on the filmmaker's function as a mediating and creative actor, one often taken for granted and usually assumed to be male. The films are clearly concerned with how subjective and political experiences intersect, asking us to contemplate how images of selfhood and nationhood, often linked, are aesthetically constructed. Instead of making a film about themselves, or claiming their subjectivity has no influence over their filmmaking, they manifest themselves indirectly. This subtle presence forces spectators to ponder the relevance of the filmmaker, and to question the role such an interceding figure plays in conveying and addressing polemical topics that they have a stake in. It also reminds us that a woman is

Figure 6.6 Camilo de Sousa (First Run/Icarus Films, 2003).

doing the seeing, the listening, and the directing and is careful and conscious of her role.

In *48* the viewer is especially cognizant of the visual process – that is, the film – in its attempt to remember or represent these stories of violence. As we look at the pictures, we hear the prisoners in the private physical environments where Sousa Dias recorded and interviewed them. Scott MacDonald writes, 'Their environment becomes ours, and it is as if we and the ex-prisoners are sharing a space from which together we can contemplate their past.'[17] The sound in the background is thus an integral part of the project, as we hear their voices, but also other noises, random sounds, a plane flying overhead, traffic. The prisoner's physical presence is marked bodily by the sounds they make, their heavy breathing, the sound of their tears and the tapping of their fingers on a table as they point, most probably, to their photograph. We hear the anguish and pain in their voices, whispers, grunts, moans, and objects being moved around. We hear their silences. As we contemplate the photographs or the dark screen, it is as if their thinking made a noise as well, or as if their remembering could be heard or seen in the darkness. Besides the sense of shared space that MacDonald notes, and becoming involved ethically in the personal narratives told by the former dissidents, the film creates an important analogy that connects us to the film's process. The prisoners are asked in their interview to contemplate their own images and take their time before speaking. As viewers we are also asked to reflect on the black screen and the slowly appearing photographs. We undergo the same difficult process following the slow course the camera and filmmaker take, thus ultimately being involved in what becomes a collective creative endeavour of remembering and redefining historical memory. The film sets in motion, both thematically and formally, a consideration of how memory, history, and politics shape individual and collective identity and resilience.

Like the forgotten filmstrips in *Kuxa Kanema*, which are given intensity and movement in the sequence organized by Cardoso, Sousa Dias's framing and filming of the mugshots turns the still into a literally and affectively moving picture. *48* exposes the falsehood of the regime, and viewers are invited to think about the historical context and the political implications. Yet viewers have nothing but slowly moving images before them, and are thus, like the filmmaker and the dissidents, similarly compelled to reflect on the significance of the image, to ask what makes a moving image, or a film, and to meditate on the relationship between these concepts and political and historical narratives. The documentary seems to use conventions of the genre – it includes what seem to be interviews, there is technically a voiceover – the prisoners speaking – we see 'real' images – the archival photographs – and yet *48* is anything but a conventional documentary. In fact, the allusions to the formal conventions of documentary filmmaking are there perhaps to make us aware of these strategies' limitations and for us to conceive of a different creative mode of filmmaking. Instead, what is at stake is the film as a reflection, an exercise, an essay; or a woman's idea of how to create new ways of narrating traumatic stories, and of contemplating both the creative potential and the indefinite nature of visual imagery.

One important way Sousa Dias reflects on the making of image and the materiality of the visual is to use the slowness of the camera. On the one hand, the fading in and out of the close-ups, or the literal visualizing of the images, seeing them from different perspectives, thematizes not only the workings of memory but also the process of cinematographic reflection (see Ribeiro de Menezes in this volume). The different nuances characterize the visual and point to their varied experiences and the diverse ways in which these different individuals faced the past and the atrocities they endured. Despite the emblematic sense of collectiveness conveyed by the series of repeated mugshots and the border shown on the photographs, the portrait-like quality gives each prisoner a powerful individual identity, and as the prisoners' testimonies make clear, not all prisoners were treated equally by the state police. The character's personal memory, although anything but discernible or complete, is immediately made part of our social memory conflating autobiographical and historical memory.

On the other hand, the slowness of the camera and the long interpolations of the black screen also theorize the actual production of images. The first prisoner surrenders her identity and says, 'I began to live for others,' and her picture disappears replaced by a black screen. From the outset of the film there is a sense in which this transitional plane, marked by the darkness, is actually a meeting place; something like the visual representation of a collective consciousness. But because the subsequent images always emerge from this darkness, coming evermore into focus, the blackness is also like a darkroom where photographs are developed. As if the camera were developing the photographs anew, creating a moving image, the film materializes and resituates the photograph giving it cinematic import. This rebirth of the image, or conversion from darkness to light, is possible, it is suggested, with filmmaking. As viewers and filmmakers, we have to imagine and reimagine light from darkness. One male prisoner on the verge of tears says at the end of his monologue describing the atrocities, 'it was something unimaginable, truly unimaginable', calling upon us to do just that, to contemplate and reflect upon the unspeakable, its consequences, and meanings. The blank aspect of the black screen encourages viewers to access their own imaginaries. These dark empty screens or this other side of the screen (behind the portrait) compel us to ask what might be hiding in that darkness, what can become light, what might be possible with film. How many people fought clandestinely against the regime, how many were hiding, tortured or killed? The darkness can likewise be conceptualized allegorically, as signifying the historical period or political context as a time of desolation, a dark hole emblematic of what happened during the regime: stories were hidden, silenced, lost, removed from sight or covered over. Viewers faced with this darkness imagine and fill the emptiness with a collective historical consciousness and awareness. Still, the repeated analogies the film creates between reviving that historical memory and conceptualizing the potential of the visual or the power and movement of the image make us think beyond the content, as we become increasingly attentive to the director's aesthetic intentions and prospects of telling stories with moving images.

The close-up shots reveal deformations, stains, smudges, and discolourations highlighting the importance of the materiality of the photograph. This focus on the materiality of the images is reflected in the prisoners' attention to their physical appearance. They discuss their hair colour, hairdo or loss of hair, and describe the clothing they are wearing. One man remembers how he put on several coats and sweaters as protection against the beatings he predicted he would suffer. They talk about the tone of their skin, their glasses, the wrinkles on their face and whether they had gained or lost weight. Their facial expressions, as two political prisoners emphasize, are one of the few things under their control, and thus they would often smirk or sneer into the camera (see Figure 6.7). This focus on their bodies and appearances as they in turn share experiences of being beaten, tortured and undressed reinforces the way in which the materiality of the torn, stained, discoloured photos echoes the individuals' physical and mental torture.

At times the prisoners talk about not being able to recognize themselves in the photo or in mirrors. Often arrested together, families and couples would not recognize one another when reunited. A young girl was convinced her father did not have legs because she had always visited him in jail and only seen his upper body. Recognition of the self and of the body is likened to identifying an image, a reflection, an impression. The film connects the photograph's materiality to bodily and subjective experiences. The historical violence registered first by the

Figure 6.7 Prisoners controlling their facial expressions (Alambique, 2011).

photograph and again by the director's composition outlives time and pain. The archival material, like the tortured bodies, survives the repression. Giving the photographs a moving or cinematographic existence is a way of caring for these bruised, crying, bleeding bodies. This makes the fact that half of the prisoners whose stories we hear in the film are women especially important. Issues of gender and sexuality come up repeatedly in the female prisoners' personal testimonies as they discuss their restricted lives under the regime and the specific trials they faced in jail. Some of the women share the difficult experiences they had being interrogated while menstruating and the pitiful conditions they endured. Like the many tears that are shed throughout the film which we hear in the background in the prisoners' testimonies, this female loss of blood is also cathartic. It reinforces the way in which the materiality of the photograph is embodied with traumatic personal, historic, and gendered experience. Like Cardoso, Sousa Dias's visual composition is a formal reflection that acts as a form of memory and gender politics but that primarily reflects upon a woman filmmaker's task as a maker and caretaker of images in portraying political history.

Despite the brevity of its laconic and minimalist title, *48* ironically refers to the extremely long period, forty-eight years, of authoritarian rule in Portugal – the longest in twentieth-century Europe. Like the oppressive political regime some of the prisoners' sentences were also anything but brief. One female prisoner, when referring to a comrade who was in jail for twenty-four years, says, 'Twenty-four years are not twenty-four days.' What a poignant coincidence that these two numbers should add up to forty-eight. The prisoners are insistently preoccupied with numbers and references to time; they mention dates, years, months, days, weeks, and seasons when talking about the length of time they were imprisoned, or subjected to sleep deprivation, or spent without seeing a family member. Arrested multiple times some of the prisoners rely on these numbers to give sense to their experiences. On the other hand, the paradox inherent in the title is echoed in the ironic fact that the linear and chronological preoccupation of the prisoners is also meaningless. Many protest the lost time admitting time stood still for them while in prison, while others see no difference between an earlier and a later photograph (see Figure 6.8). While we collectively mourn the half-century squandered and the prisoners' lost time, we also visualize these moving portraits of real life. By making the film, adding the numbers, assembling the images, listening to the stories and seeing the photographs, Sousa Dias and her viewers have a lot to gain from that collective sense of loss.

Kuxa Kanema and *48* follow Paula Amad's advice in her insightful work, in which she states that when studying archives 'one should not have to make a choice between an analytic framework devoted to original context and documentary evidence versus one attracted to aesthetic formalism and theoretical abstraction'.[18] In many ways the visual testimony both filmmakers use to compose their evaluation of political history acts as a counter-archive, to use Amad's terms, in the sense that the directors' mediating process, or their gendered filmmaking politics and practices both question dominant narratives

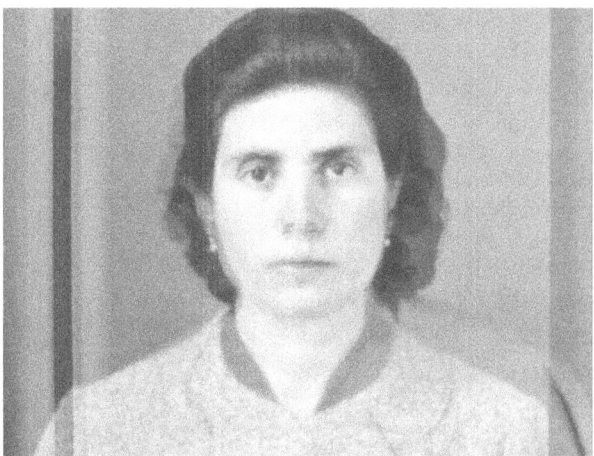

Figure 6.8 A dissolve between an earlier and a later photograph in (Alambique, 2011).

and critique the positivist conception of the archival image as the source of a complete or absolute historical knowledge. *Kuxa Kanema* and *48* broaden our notions of archive and documentary in relation to complex, traumatic, and violent political contexts; they are essays attempting to rethink the implications of film and archival imagery in narrating political stories. While *Kuxa Kanema* follows more of documentary's conventions and *48* is more explicitly experimental, they are both composition works, which bring together old footage to question or reflect upon the capacity of film, the ambiguity of the visual and the possibilities created when we relate the moving image to memory, politics, and history. While viewers and filmmakers are ethically and politically implicated here, they are first and foremost, along with the two women filmmakers who are very aware of their creative power and role, reassessing the image and the art of filming as a deceptive aesthetic medium that can integrate voice, body, hope, and suffering in remembering and rethinking historical memory.

Notes

1 Jaimie Baron, *The Archival Effect: Found Footage and the Audiovisual Experience of History* (London: Routledge, 2014), 7–9.
2 Bill Nichols, *Introduction to Documentary*, Third Edition (Bloomington: Indiana University Press, 2017), xi.
3 Patricia Aufderheide, *Documentary Film: A Very Short Introduction* (Oxford: Oxford University Press, 2007), 2; emphasis in original.
4 Paula Rabinowitz, *They Must Be Represented: The Politics of Documentary* (New York: Verso, 1994).
5 Diane Waldman and Janet Walker, *Feminism and Documentary* (Minneapolis: University of Minnesota Press, 1999), 6.
6 Manuela Penafria, *O paradigma do documentário: António Campos, cineasta* (Livros LabCom, 2009), 5.
7 Ibid., 15.
8 See for instance, Paulo Cunha, *Uma nova história do novo cinema português* (Lisboa: Outro Modo Cooperativa Cultural, 2018).
9 Ana Catarina Pereira, *A Mulher-Cineasta: da arte pela arte a uma estética da diferenciação* (Covilhã: LabCom, 2016), 96.
10 Jorge Leitão Ramos, 'Margarida Cardoso', *Dicionário do cinema português 1989–2003* (Lisbon: Caminho, 2005), 118.

11 Victoria Pasley, '*Kuxa Kanema*: Third Cinema and Its Transatlantic Crossings', in *Rethinking Third Cinema: The Role of Anti-colonial Media and Aesthetics in Postmodernity*, eds Frieda Ekotto and Adeline Koh (Berlin: Lit, 2009), 121.
12 Ibid., 113.
13 http://filmthreat.com/uncategorized/the-ten-best-and-worst-unseen-films-of-2004-2/ and http://filmthreat.com/uncategorized/kuxa-kanema-the-birth-of-cinema/ (accessed 22 October 2019).
14 Robert Stock, 'Archival Images and Audiovisual Testimony – Negotiating the End of Empire in the Documentary Films *Guerra colonial. histórias de campanha em Moçambique* (1998) and *Natal 71* (1999)', *International Journal of Iberian Studies* 27, nos 2–3 (2014), 186.
15 Eric Allina-Pisano, 'Kuxa-Kanema–The Birth of Cinema', *The International Journal of African Historical Studies* 38, no. 2 (2005), 395.
16 Robert Stock, 'Cinema and Conflict in Postcolonial Mozambique: Archival Images as Illustration and Evidence in *Estas são as armas* (1978)', *Mediations of Disruption in Post-conflict Cinema*, eds Adriana Martins, Alexandra Lopes and Mónica Dias (London: Palgrave Macmillan, 2016), 86.
17 Scott MacDonald, 'Susana de Sousa Dias', *Avant-Doc: Intersections of Documentary and Avant Garde Cinema* (New York: Oxford University Press, 2014), 26.
18 Paula Amad, *Counter-Archive: Film, the Everyday, and Albert Kahn's Archives de la Planète* (New York: Columbia University Press, 2010), 20.

7

Affect and the archival turn: Documentaries by Inês de Medeiros and Susana de Sousa Dias

Alison Ribeiro de Menezes

Memory studies have engaged for some time now with the broader 'archival turn' in the humanities, in which, to quote Ann Laura Stoler, the archive has moved from functioning as a source to becoming a subject in itself.[1] Of course, such a focus on the archive is not unexpected, given memory's concern for individual narratives, as well as their intersections with, and challenges to, collective fictions of identity, belonging and shared histories. Natalie Zemon Davis's *Fiction in the Archives* in the late 1980s made us aware of the inherent narratability of archived materials, as well as of the concealed narratives that archives may unwittingly conserve.[2] And the archive, as Carolyn Steedman reminds us in *Dust*, contains 'half-told stories' and 'discontinuities' that, through varying contextualizations, can be used to unexpected ends.[3] In this sense, argues Steedman, any user of an archive effectively 'steals' its contents and misuses them.[4]

Historians have, of course, always been conscious of the incomplete, limited and limiting nature of archives, viewing them as one of many sources to be marshalled – manipulated even, depending on adherence to the historian's craft – in service of a particular argument. Nevertheless, recent scholarly focus on the constructed and generative nature of the archive largely takes its cue from the work of Michel Foucault and Jacques Derrida, and their use of the archive, in the words of Ernst van Alpen, as a 'metaphorical construct' to articulate ideas about 'knowledge, thinking, memory and power'.[5] For Foucault, the archive shapes what can and cannot be said; for Derrida, the archive is a feature of mental life, a 'fever' or compulsion to archive.[6] And the result, according to van Alpen, has been a very real 'postmodern turn' in archival science, away from a positivistic approach towards an understanding of archives and archivists as agents who shape cultural and social memory.[7]

It is partly this that Stoler studies with regard to archives of Dutch colonial rule in Indonesia, locating not 'the finite boundaries of the official state archives' but feeling along their grain to tease out 'their surplus production, what defines their interior ridges and porous seams'.[8] Stoler's conceptualization of her task relies on visual imagery of light and shade, shadow and illumination, as much as on a tactile view of archival documents as granular objects of study: her aim is to 'linger' in the archive's 'opacities, to muddy its reflection, to refract away from its shadow'.[9] The archive, for Stoler, has a pulse through which one can feel displaced histories, 'contrary and subjacent' but – and this is the crucial point – not necessarily subaltern. Archives are thus not to be read as 'skewed and biased sources' but as 'condensed sites of epistemological and political anxiety … transparencies on which power relations were inscribed and [which were] intricate technologies of rule in themselves'.[10] Despite her emphasis on tactility, it is striking that Stoler turns to visual metaphors to explain her engagement with the archive, using, in the latter quote, the photographic transparency – a positive photograph printed on plastic or glass and viewable using a projector – as an image of the operations of power within and through the materials she examines. She works ethnographically to uncover 'unevenly sedimented deceptions and dispositions that accumulated as acceptable or discarded knowledge', pointing to layered stories with 'crosscurrent frictions, attractions, and aversions that worked within and against those assertions of imperial rights'.[11]

Here documents may be secret, but they also secrete.[12] Stoler's work is almost haptic, in Laura Marks's sense of the term, aligning visual-tactile-affective readings with issues of memory and concerns for the future. The visions she uncovers by reading along the grain of the archive highlight her topic of study, the intimate workings of colonial rule and the politics of race, 'through tone and hue, through frames of different scope, and contrasts of different intensity'.[13] Her objective is thus to shift from

> the high-gloss print of history writ-large to the space of its production, the dark-room negative: from direct to refracted light, from 'figure' and 'field' – that which is more often in historic relief – to the inverse, grainy texture of 'surfaces' and their shifting 'grounds'.[14]

Stoler engages the archive rather as Marks develops the haptic in cinema, where she emphasizes 'the tactile and contiguous quality of cinema as something we viewers brush up against like another body'.[15] For Marks, intercultural contact and exchange is an inherent part of the haptic, in which 'the body is a source not just of individual but of cultural memory'.[16]

Drawing upon Stoler's nuanced exploration of the archive's store of histories in a minor key, in this essay I examine two recent documentaries by women filmmakers who have taken the rediscovery of what might be termed 'archival materials' in the broadest sense as the starting point for an exploration of memories of the Salazar dictatorship. These films are Inês de Medeiros's *Cartas a Uma Ditadura* (*Letters to a Dictator*, 2006) and Susana de Sousa Dias's *48* (2010). Born in Austria and moving to Portugal after the Revolution, Inês de Medeiros is perhaps best known as an actress, occasional director and more recently left-wing politician. In 2017 she won a surprise victory for the Socialist Party, becoming president of the *Câmara Municipal* (City Government) of Almada. She has remarked that documentary is the genre that she most identifies with, perhaps because of her strong political interests, and this is evident in *Letters to a Dictator*.[17] The film draws not on an established archive, but on a chance archival find in a second-hand bookshop: a box of letters motivated by the efforts of what would seem to be an elite group of women to provide rearguard support to Salazar following the 1958 challenge of General Humberto Delgado for the presidency of the republic.[18] This challenge shook the foundations of Salazar's New State and, in the words of Filipe Ribeiro de Meneses, 'The government was forced to act, under the pretense of ensuring public order, to curb the Delgado campaign, and then to resort to election-day chicanery in order to secure a positive result for its candidate, Admiral Américo Tomás'.[19]

Susana de Sousa Dias is an independent filmmaker and co-founder of the production company Kintop. In addition to *48* she has completed two companion documentaries, *Natureza Morta* (*Still Life*, 2005) and *Luz Obscura* (*Obscure Light*, 2017). Like *48*, they draw on PIDE archive images to confront the legacies of Salazar's dictatorship. These works constitute, in the words of Mariana Souto, 'a mourning reflection', using material produced by the New State but subverting its original intent.[20] *Still Life* is structured around the figure of Salazar,[21] with original footage, slowed considerably and interspersed with PIDE photographs. The spoken word is absent, with a grating soundtrack that includes the noise of heavy doors banging, evocative of the imprisonment experienced by the political prisoners depicted in the photographs. In contrast, *48*, which is titled for the length of the dictatorship in years, privileges spoken testimony but without contemporary footage of the former prisoners bearing witness. *Obscure Light* continues the approach of *48*, focusing on the story of one political prisoner, Octávio Pato. The voiceover in this instance comes from the memories of his children, and silences and pauses in the witnessing indicate an open space for remembering. This latest film thus examines the intersections of PIDE and family memory, revealing the hidden connections that lie behind the public persona of a political prisoner.

In *Letters to a Dictator* and *48* we see contrasting deployments of the archive. Medeiros sets the newly discovered letters to Salazar in their historical context, notably through the use of original footage with voiceover commentary, and offers the reflections and memories of some of the women who wrote them five decades earlier. There are respects in which, through analysis, the film permits a reading along the archival grain, notably with regard to gender issues. However, it does not actively direct the viewer towards this. Sousa Dias, in contrast, reads within and through the PIDE photographs to give expression to silenced and forgotten experiences of torture. The absence of evidence of torture leads her to read the photos not only *along the grain* but through studied close-ups, finding hidden elements within their texture.[22]

Both films give voice to memories, expanding the archive beyond the evidential to include individual experience and personalized testimony set within the frame of shared or collective remembrance. In Medeiros's documentary, original images and film footage act as a historical grounding, and her use of interviews offers embodied testimonies. Medeiros thus creates the sense of a direct encounter for the viewer, though there remains a narrative voice that functions as a guide or interpretative frame. This is, as Bill Nichols notes in *Speaking Truths*, an oratorical but not a dogmatic narrative voice, one that 'externalizes evidence'.[23] In Sousa Dias's works, in contrast, the recovered image is opened up through a technical expansion of film time and the animation of the flat surface of a still, two-dimensional photograph. Her film, of course, is itself a two-dimensional construction of light and shade, but the changing tones and qualities of light, allied to the verbal testimony of former political prisoners who are effectively disembodied voices (they do not appear in the present but only via their PIDE photo), add the illusion of depth and create the paradoxical sense of viewing an 'animated still'.

Sousa Dias thus leads the viewer to internalize the evidence through her highly manipulated footage, and she innovates aesthetically much more than Medeiros, engaging the spectator in what Jill Bennett calls 'transactive art'. In contrast to a more straightforwardly communicative art – exemplified here by

Medeiros' work, which nevertheless has considerable value in the memory sphere – transactive art sets out to examine 'how affect is produced within and through a work, and how it might be experienced by an audience coming to the work'.[24] This is something that we see in particular in Sousa Dias's handling of light and sound and their relation to voice, testimony and embodied witnessing. In what follows, I discuss the deployment of affective strategies in each documentary, focusing first on the sentimental resonances of particular words within Salazarist society in Medeiros's work, and then on the disruptive disjunctures that emerge between sounds and images in Sousa Dias's film.

Affective words

Over two and a half decades ago, Janis Hunter Jenkins explored the workings of what she termed the 'state construction of affect' in a study of mental health issues confronting Salvadorian refugees in the United States who had fled political violence and persecution. Her central proposition derives from 'the essential role of culture in constructing emotional experience and expression', and thus from the related point that in a dictatorial or politically controlled context, we find an ideologically driven 'culturally standardized organization of feeling and sentiment'.[25] Focusing on the words used by the refugees to describe violence and its effects, as well as the emotional terms they choose to refer to their lost homeland and condition of exile, Jenkins opens up not only the 'repertoire of affective themes and strategies' which the repressive Salvadorian state deployed[26] but also the refugees' engagement with them. Stoler develops this approach in *Along the Archival Grain*, focusing in her study on how the Dutch colonial state deployed a vocabulary of emotion and sentiment to create structures of feeling capable of orienting responses, engendering loyalties and channelling soft power. The state thus generated consent 'by shaping appropriate and reasoned affect, by directing affective judgements, by adjudicating what constituted moral sentiments (that is, affectively informed good reason) – in short, by educating the proper *distribution* of sentiments and desires'.[27] She continues, '*Statecraft was not opposed to the affective, but about its mastery.* Like Foucault's notion of "governmentality", statecraft joined the care and governing of the polity to the care and governing of the affective self'.[28]

This emphasis on the state construction of affect and its measures to control emotion on a social level emerges from the interviews in *Letters to a Dictator*.

Medeiros's film illustrates the manner in which 'the inextricable interrelatedness of domestic and public concerns that characterizes the Lusophone imperial and postimperial archive', to quote Anna M. Klobucka and Hilary Owen, extends to metropolitan Portugal under Salazar.[29] The film opens with a quotation from Salazar, dated 1952, declaring that women have such a longing for freedom that they do not understand happiness in life comes from the renunciation of its pleasures and not from their enjoyment. It then cuts, with the slow motion inclusion of newsreel 'found footage',[30] to the adoring gazes of Portuguese women greeting Salazar at his official residence, São Bento, on his seventieth birthday. Slowing these archival images creates the paradoxical sense of a clamorous longing from which the viewer is distanced, since any sound of the crowd has been replaced by a violin accompaniment with a rather insistent melody. We cannot but reflect that the desiring gazes of these women articulate a tension between the emotional control the dictator points to as a supposedly feminine ideal and a euphoric celebration centred on his person. *Letters to a Dictator* could easily be read as a fascist expression of women's fortitude which ends up exposing contradictions, in Ana Paula Ferreira's words, in 'Salazar's measures to turn the home into the ideal birthing ground of nationalistic, authoritarian rule'.[31]

The film first presents the letters to Salazar, collected in a box, a classic memory metaphor (see Figure 7.1). The camera pans over them in close-up, revealing their unique character as historical documents written by different hands, though with not dissimilar handwriting styles. Extracts are read out in a cacophony of multiple voiceovers that recall Stoler's sense of the archive as containing narratives with 'storyed' levels.[32] What these opening frames set up is a contrast between the public nature of the newsreel images, which will soon appear in the film with the original soundtrack of the women chanting Salazar's name, and the intimate, dignified and respectful tone of the letters. Salazar then speaks, offering the women of Portugal metaphorical flowers in thanks for their devotion to the *cruzada nacional* (national quest). The dictator's priest-like paternalism, quietening the chants that interrupt his speech yet articulating a sort of chaste relation of desire and devotion, identifies Portuguese women as having one of four roles – mothers, wives, sisters and daughters. Collectively, he says, the 'warmth of their affection and the strength of their enthusiasm' undergird the New State and 'support us in our battles'.

Presented with letters they wrote to Salazar as much younger selves, at the request of a mysterious *Movimento Nacional das Mulheres Portuguesas*,[33] the

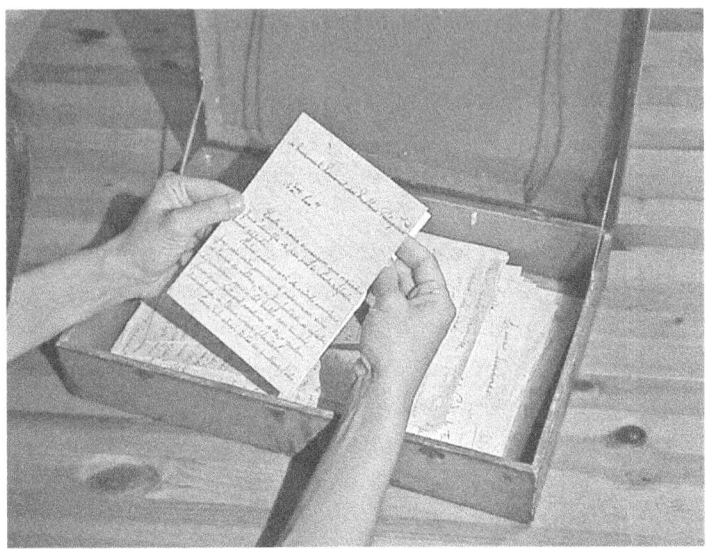

Figure 7.1 The letters written to Salazar (Alambique, 2014).

women interviewed in Medeiros's documentary articulate a gendered code of manners and values that superficially spans social classes. The film, however, stresses economic and social disadvantage visually, partly through the settings for the interviews and partly through the dress and postures of the women themselves. The better-off ones are filmed in formal, largely upper-middle-class living rooms with family photographs displayed on pianos and silverware and ornaments set out on tables. These ladies are clearly economically comfortable, well dressed and almost to a one wearing pearls. The less well-off sit at kitchen tables, wearing everyday clothes, and are more humble in their posture and speech. Some of the women are politically articulate (such as Madalena de Lencastre), others much less so.

The film's narrator identifies a series of shared themes in the letters, including the expression of gratitude to and admiration for Salazar. But there is, we are told, behind the set phrases a sense of the *medo* (fear), *tristeza* (sadness) and *isolamento* (isolation) that characterized life for women in 1950s Portugal. Each of these terms can act as an affective control of society through language, as can Madalena de Lencastre's suggestion, echoing Salazar's speech above, that this women's movement would be a domestic *tropa forte* (military force). Women's fortitude in the face of fear, sadness and isolation would thus protect and preserve the New State order, determining acceptable and unacceptable behaviour and imposing an affective socialization on both men and women. Danger, in one letter, is identified as one of the 'great calamities of the current world', and Portuguese womanhood is declared capable of protecting the nation from 'an ignominious and horrible future' so ensuring that 'the sun of happiness shines in the beautiful Portuguese sky'. The film presents the women's inner compass as in harmony with regime ideology.

One might easily interpret the film's closing reflections on words such as democracy, dictatorship, freedom and censorship as confirmation of this. For some of the women, the regime's key values of *Deus, Pátria e Família* (God, Fatherland and Family) are central, and they are evasive on the topic of democracy and dictatorship. However, Belmira, who is clearly less comfortably off, notes that it was not freedom but 'that people would live well' that she wished for. Nevertheless, two tensions emerge in the course of the film. The first is the ambiguity between a chaste sense of admiration for Salazar that actually tends towards desire, and the ghostly threat of uncontrolled emotion. The second is the role of charitable action, which opens a fracture line in the superficial expressions of gendered solidarity. With regard to the first, we hear that Salazar was 'someone very dear to women', receiving from one letter writer her 'most respectful affection' and from another her 'intense admiration'. A third bashfully notes that Salazar 'was a very handsome man'.[34] We hear, too, of the ambiguous role of Dona Maria, his housekeeper, and 'the pupils' Micas and Maria Antónia, the two young girls who lived with them as if forming a curiously orthodox yet chaste family. Salazar's celibacy, that of a man 'married' to his country, made him a flexible symbol of the ideal husband, father and son, able to appeal to several generations of women. The ambiguity in this relationship creates the sense of a suppressed threat of uncontrolled passion and disorder. There is, equally, no strong sense of virility, with the film conveying a rather untroubled surface that probes precisely because of the glaring absence of sexuality.

In these interviews, we see an echo of the manner in which, in New State films of the colonies studied by Patrícia Vieira, female desire is 'tamed and proven to stem from patriotism'.[35] While this ideology of *Deus, Pátria e Família* is well documented, it is important to note the affect implied by these terms, because it is precisely their emotive charge that explains their capacity to influence values and behaviour in daily life, beyond the strictures of fear and repression. Why might these women subscribe to a set of values that reinforce their inferior position within society? Because those same values give meaning to the women's lives and affirm a meaningful social role. In their final comments, all refer in some shape or form to a sacred higher principle, faith or implicit social structure. In other words, it is not enough to point to the regime's determination of ideology if we are to understand why it gained traction. What Medeiros's film does is attend to the affective links which, through the workings of emotive semantics, bridge the political and the private, collective ideology and its domestic acceptance. And this might then assist in understanding the vexed question of adherence to or complicity with a dictatorial regime that was impressive in its longevity.

This leads me to the second theme which gives rise to a conceptual tension in the film, namely the women's perceptions of lack, and their charitable contribution to society. The term that carries the strongest affective charge in this instance is *miséria*, meaning poverty or penury, something inspiring pity, and in certain usages a negative judgement. The film also makes frequent reference to *alegria* (joy), which becomes a pliable term ultimately denoting acceptance of one's situation. For Maria Hermínia Rodrigues, *alegria* is linked to respect for others and thus stability in a society in which everyone recognizes their place. *Miséria*, by implication, is a relative term, meaning physical need but not necessarily moral lack. From this, it is a short step to note that an austere lifestyle – such as that which Salazar himself cultivated – is morally good and noble. What matters for Maria José Fernandes Lopes is individual dignity, charity and serving others. A woman is above men if she is a 'good wife', a 'caring mother' and 'kind to poor people' – although Fernandes Lopes also states that she does not believe in the 25 April 1974 Revolution because she lost a lot of money as a result. Maria Manuela Oom naturally sees no contradiction between her weekly visits to help a poor family, which one could not miss all year, and her annual holiday to 'a nice house', when of course she did not keep up the visits.

Aside the inherent contradiction between the regime's view of women's proper place as at home or doing charity work, and the fact that many women needed to work to make ends meet, the film notes that charity work was a social outlet and thus a recognized role for better-off ladies. And only families who complied with the underlying values of the regime and its society received help. Charity, expressed through sentiments such as *miséria* and *alegria* thus established an affective economy of compassion and control. 'Sentiment', Stoler writes, 'is the negative print of the colonial archive's reasoned surface, the ground against which the figure of reason is measured and drawn.'[36] One might rewrite this comment to propose that sentiment in Salazar's Portugal was the domesticating force of the regime's contradictory ideology, ironing out its inconsistencies through an ambiguous appeal to a romance of happiness and security which found expression both through the alluring figure of an avuncular dictator who, as father, husband and son was all things to all women, and the social fulfilment that came from helping the deserving, accepting, submissive poor. As Maria Hermínia Rodrigues notes, she did nothing outside the house because her husband did not let her: '*não pode ser*' (it's not right), she remarks, using another highly emotive phrase of social censure and control.

Affective sounds

If my analysis of *Letters to a Dictator* focuses on words, unearthing their emotive and sentimental resonances within the space of the Portuguese dictatorship, that of *48* examines the intersections of image and sound. As Christoph Cox notes, cultural criticism and theory has generally been approached as an 'interpretative enterprise that consists in tracking signs or representations (images, texts, symptoms, etc.) through the associative networks that give them meaning'.[37] That is largely how I have viewed *Letters to a Dictator*, and it is an approach that I believe to be in keeping with the nature of the film itself. Susana de Sousa Dias, on the other hand, approaches sound as – in Cox's words – 'immersive and proximal, surrounding and passing through the body',[38] but also coming from it. She also explores disjunctures between images and words, drawing the viewer into an active engagement with her film in order to examine how, to quote Cox once again, 'while texts and images involve the spatial juxtaposition of elements, the sonic arts involve a temporal flux in which elements interpenetrate one another'.[39]

The development of a transactive aesthetic assists Sousa Dias's efforts in *48* in answering the question, 'How can one go beyond the semantic nature of the testimonial words and the visual representation of the actions or the consequences of the torturer?'[40] Sound possesses a materiality which – dissociated from its embodied production as voice in *48*, and allied to a technologically animated series of what were originally still photographs – moves beyond questions of the 'truthfulness' of the word and the 'authenticity' of the image. Sousa Dias's postulation is that, in the absence of any visual or documentary evidence of torture, and given the ethical impulse to honour and transmit the memory of torture experiences, the sound of testimony presented along with a paradoxical stretching of contemplative time, through what she calls 'montage within the shot',[41] reveals the 'lacunae and non-sayings' *secreted* (to borrow Stoler's word) by the archival sources used.

The PIDE photographs are not neutral indicators of identity, as Sousa Dias notes. All following a single format, they are 'strongly codified from the technical point of view but also from the ideological one': mugshots of political prisoners, they mark the individuals as 'miscreant'.[42] They also display a superficial aesthetic of transparency, seemingly eliminating any element of variability and hence doubt. Their relentless sameness erases individuality (a point that one might also make of the repetitive montages of *Letters to a Dictator*). These PIDE photos were produced precisely to be archived, but archived secretly and used as part of the repressive apparatus of the Salazar regime. They offer a contrasting vision of social control to the affective discourse of Medeiros's film, for the photos in *48* are visual objects denoting an archive of subversive reputations. Sousa Dias subjects them to a process that she describes as 'redemptive', exposing what the regime wished to hide.[43] Taken on arrest, the images mark the moment when the individuals became political prisoners. However, once allied to a testimonial reflection from each prisoner in the present, their original purpose is subverted, opening up cracks in time to present the past itself not as an act but a 'fact of memory'.[44] Sousa Dias thus concludes:

> By presenting historic situations beyond the historicity of the event, by seeking to integrate the set of movements and counter-movements which permeate the images (as well as the words), coalescing diverse temporalities into the same moment, we can subvert the principle of referentiality and the logic of the representation – in other words, we can go beyond the idea of cinema as an 'open window on the world'.[45]

Sousa Dias's manipulations of still images create, in her terms, a 'landscape which can be entered',[46] evoking Bennett's transactive art which makes demands on the viewer, turning still photos into objects impregnated with time and memory's secretions.[47]

Within *48*, we find series of photos of the same individual over time, stressing the length of the dictatorship and the constancy of prisoners' political resistance. We also encounter husbands, wives, sons and daughters, establishing a genealogy of opposition. Both these points could be taken as evidence of the ideological shaping of the narrative by the director. More interesting, however, is the creation of what Sousa Dias labels 'montage within the shot'. Seeking to animate still, two-dimensional photographs, Sousa Dias uses shifting tonalities of grey created via a lightening and shading of the images, to hold the viewer's contemplation. Her work in this regard recalls Stoler's metaphor of the archive as made up of areas of light and shade, shadow and illumination.

The PIDE images thus seem to acquire the qualities of an oil painting, whose surface changes as light reflects off it from different angles, adding the illusion of movement. Beyond the question of how one might make a still image engaging, however, is that of the director's addition of micro-movements and the slowing down of the original footage at the editing table. This technological manipulation literally stretches time, which seems to alternate between such micro-movements and larger temporal change, for we also see photos taken throughout the dictatorship, and in these not only do generations appear but so do changing fashions in clothes. This is particularly the case for the third witness, Sofia Ferreira, of whom there are three separate photographs, showing her ageing[48] (see also Estela Vieira's piece in this volume).

One of the themes that Sousa Dias herself extrapolates from the images is the question of masks and concealed or revealed identities. Linked inherently to the mugshot as a form of anatomical identification, the mask thus offers an opportunity to flout the photographic object's intended function. António Dias Lourenço and Domingo Abrantes both explain how prisoners could use facial expressions as a form of resistance, for the PIDE could not control these. Thus, as Dias Lourenço notes, a prisoner could deny the officers the *alegria* of seeing a tortured visage. For Abrantes, adopting 'caras medonhas' served a similar purpose. Prisoners could, then, exert a sense of agency though this gesture of resistance or non-compliance. Maria Galveias describes her countenance as 'that face there' distancing herself from her photograph. For Maria Antónia Fiadeiro, arrest was the completion of a generational circle, since her parents had been political prisoners. She is seen with a broad smile, which she felt ashamed of for a time, but now regards with enormous satisfaction (see Figure 7.2). Reviewing

Figure 7.2 Maria Antónia Fiadeiro's broad smile (Alambique, 2011).

these PIDE photos today permits one, she says, to discover the truth about historical Portugal through very small gestures: a Portugal of silence and secrecy in which private life was highly repressed, censored and self-censored. Fascism, she concludes, amounted to cynicism and hypocrisy, a mere masquerade.

While these images certainly show individuals who have suffered, 'proof' of their torture can, in fact, only be revealed by their spoken testimonies. Their stories are inaccessible to the viewer in the absence of their words and the sound of their embodied gestures. It is noticeable that the opening credits of *48* roll by in silence, offering historical context on the New State and creating a reflective mood that is then interrupted by the sound of an intake of breath as Georgette Ferreira's photo emerges from the blackness of that opening screen. We then hear her uttering the first words of the documentary – 'I remember' – which comes across as surprisingly affirmative, since her voice is somewhat hesitant. In many cases, the sound of the witness breathing or sighing punctuates their memories, and the documentary ends with a reflective sniffing from Álvaro Pato. These vocal gestures work against any sense that the testimonies in *48* are simply disembodied voices, for the viewer becomes acutely conscious of forms of communication beyond the visual and verbal. Nevertheless, of the sixteen testimonies in *48*, there are two for which no photos are provided. This is because, as Sousa Dias notes, there are no surviving judicial photographic records of the prisoners she interviewed.[49] These colonial prisoners thus have suffered a 'double erasure'.[50] A poorly illuminated, rather eerie bush landscape, with a barbed-wire fence and a barren tree, fades in and out as we listen to the testimonies of Amós Mahanjane and Matias Mboa, Africans whose racial identity can only be surmised from their accents. As the director explains, this nocturnal landscape, intermittently lit by a searchlight, was filmed by soldiers of the Portuguese army in Guinea-Bissau during the Colonial War. It functions as a contrast or foil to the granular readings of the PIDE photographs, in that it remains 'a landscape "of surface", not a landscape that can be "entered"'.[51] Original footage does not work to offer a historical grounding, as in Medeiros's documentary, but to block any engagement on the part of the viewer and so establish a sense of opacity. Following on from a long series of photographs and testimonies which have drawn us in, this exclusionary push is all the more effective for concluding with the exclusions of colonial history.

Archives are truly seen by Sousa Dias to be (citing Stoler's words again) 'condensed sites of epistemological and political anxiety … transparencies on which power relations were inscribed and intricate technologies of rule in themselves'.[52] And archives have a 'pulse', offering living breathing stories, with images that become almost a series of skin contacts (echoing Marks) affecting the viewer. The disruption of that final landscape footage, moody and lifeless, distancing us from the identification we feel with the individuals whose PIDE photos we have seen, exemplifies this clearly. But what does it mean to view these PIDE images (or the black void of their absence) and hear these testimonies? What does it mean to enter them and take their pulse? To feel them create skin contact? What precisely do I mean by transactive art in this context, and what sort of transaction might occur in these affective encounters?

What we experience with *48* is, in Bennett's terms, 'an embodiment of sensation that stimulates thought ... affect that leads us somewhere'.[53] If sound is, as Jeffrey Jerome Cohen suggests, 'a vibration that travels through the air and implants itself in the flesh',[54] then the sounds that we receive from *48*, allied to the subtly animated images which our eyes focus and transmit to the brain as these sound waves bounce off our ear drums, must have the capacity to move us, to affect us, to effect some transaction within us as viewers. This precedes a cerebral response, involving an embodied reaction as we receive the testimonies with their sonic gestures at the same time as we receive the movements of light and shade on screen. While the sounds and images of *48* might seem characterized by temporal and spatial disjunctures and dislocations, our impulse as viewers is to make them cohere. The sounds of *48* do not just pass through the bodies of those on screen, but also the bodies of we who witness their witnessing, establishing a creative exchange in which Sousa Dias's visual 'montage within the shot' contains a sonic dimension fundamental to our interpretative efforts.

Our response, then, moves between the embodied and the cognitive, establishing an oscillation that recalls Kaja Silverman's notion of 'heteropathic identification' as a form of openness to the other that enables encounter without appropriation.[55] I do not mean here a one-way movement of transference, but a restless oscillatory movement of identification and separation, the entangling of embodied and cerebral responses – and, hence, a recycling of affect in two senses. First, there is the obvious reuse of images by Sousa Dias, not only in taking them from archives and adapting them to new uses but also in recycling these images across her own films. Second, there is the recycling of affect between the speakers of *48* and its viewers, drawn in by an affective montage yet pushed out by that final landscape footage and our wider desire to make sense of what we see as we watch it, drawn to empathic engagement yet aware of the dangers of appropriating experiences that are not our own.⁵⁶ In these oscillations the archive becomes both absence and excess, a space to be animated by the filmmaker, her subjects and the viewer in an exchange which opens out towards an understanding of the other without assuming a fullness of knowledge or a plenitude of experience. The archive here is potential, but its pulses are felt through embodied exchanges that are provisional, shifting and dynamic.

Conclusion

Letters to a Dictator and *48* would seem to exemplify Jaimie Baron's suggestion that the archive now exerts an 'epistemological seduction' feeding a 'desire for revelatory truth about the past'.⁵⁷ They both also point to the expansiveness of the archive, which is no longer a limited and limitable source, but one that can be repurposed in myriad ways. With her focus on the visual archival source as an 'experience of reception,'⁵⁸ rather than an official record or a physical location, Baron points to a conception of the archive as a relationship produced between elements of a film and its viewer. Nevertheless, the films studied here exemplify this shift towards reception in different ways. *Letters to a Dictator* offers an archived past that can be opened up to analysis along the grain, posing questions about the state organization of affect but working with a communicative purpose that keeps the viewer at a distance. *48*, on the other hand, demands affective engagement, feeling into the grain. It pushes beyond questions of truth and authenticity towards formal questions about the possibilities of the archive as a source of affective transactions not only with the past but also in the present, and with a view to the future.

Sousa Dias's film certainly embraces the archive as subject in itself, but it also moves beyond this, animating archival materials in ways that recall Marks's notion of the haptic. Marks, as I noted earlier, proposes that intercultural contact and exchange is an inherent part of the haptic, in which 'the very circulation of a film among different viewers is like a series of skin contacts that leave mutual traces'.⁵⁹ Skin here might be envisaged as both an embodied organ that enables contact and a boundary that signals (permeable) limits. The skin may, at least in trauma theory, be regarded as a bodily surface that registers wounds and sores,⁶⁰ but it is also the bodily organ that transmits sensation and enables affective exchanges – border crossings, in effect. These border crossings are liminal contacts where we jump in our skins on hearing the hissing of an intake of breath recalling the grinding memory of torture in *48*, or hear the clanging doors that are characteristic of shifts between PIDE photos in *Still Life*. And we jump momentarily in our skins, even as we know we are watching these images in the comfort and safety of an upholstered cinema seat.

Notes

1. Ann Laura Stoler, *Along the Archival Grain: Epistemic Anxieties and Colonial Common Sense* (Princeton: Princeton University Press, 2009), 44.
2. Natalie Zemon Davis, *Fiction in the Archives: Pardon Tales and Their Tellers in Sixteenth-Century France* (Stanford: Stanford University Press, 1987).
3. Carolyn Steedman, *Dust: The Archive and Cultural History* (Manchester: Manchester University Press, 2001), 54.
4. Ibid., 75.
5. Ernst van Alpen, *Staging the Archive: Art and Photography in the Age of New Media* (London: Reaktion, 2014), 12. Stoler argues that the 'archival turn' had already begun before Derrida published *Archive Fever*, suggesting in addition that there might be a valuable disciplinary contrast to bear in mind (*Along the Archival Grain*, 45): 'One could argue that "the archive" for historians and "the Archive" for cultural theorists have been wholly different analytic objects: for the former, a body of documents and the institutions that house them, for the latter, a metaphoric invocation for any corpus of selective collections and the longings that the acquisitive quests for the primary, originary, and untouched entail.'
6. Ibid., 13.
7. Ibid., 14.
8. Stoler, *Along the Archival Grain*, 14.
9. Ibid, 15.
10. Ibid., 20. Stoler notes that she uses 'displaced histories' in line with Foucault rather than De Certeau (*Along the Archival Grain*, 20, n. 9).
11. Ibid., 22.
12. Ibid., 27.
13. Ibid., 107.
14. Ibid., 108.
15. Laura U. Marks, *The Skin of the Film: Intercultural Cinema, Embodiment and the Senses* (Durham and London: Duke University Press, 2000), xii.
16. Ibid., xiii.
17. Cátia Bruno, 'Inês de Medeiros: A vida e as polémicas da mulher que tirou Almada al PCP', *Observador*, 5 October 2017. https://observador.pt/especiais/ines-de-

medeiros-a-vida-e-as-polemicas-da-mulher-que-tirou-almada-ao-pcp/ (accessed 12 July 2019).

18 It should be borne in mind that Salazar was never president of the republic, holding the post of president of the Council of Ministers, or prime minister, from 1932 to 1968.

19 Filipe Ribeiro de Meneses, *Salazar: A Political Biography* (New York: Enigma, 2009), 420. Following Tomás's victory, the regime changed the voting rules for the election of the president of the republic, bringing the process under Salazar's direct control. In 1965, Delgado would be murdered in Spain, close to the Portuguese border, by the PIDE.

20 Mariana Souto, 'Susana de Sousa Dias and the Ghosts of the Portuguese Dictatorship', *Comparative Cinema* 6, http://www.ocec.eu/cinemacomparativecinema/index.php/en/27-n-1-portuguese-cinema/298-susana-de-sousa-dias-and-the-ghosts-of-the-portuguese-dictatorship (accessed 29 August 2018).

21 Susana de Sousa Dias, '(In)visible Evidence: The Representability of Torture', in *A Companion to Documentary Film*, eds Alexandra Juhasz and Alisa Lebow (Oxford: Wiley-Blackwell, 2015), 495. *Natureza Morta* mixes propaganda images produced by the New State with the director's own filming of still police photographs, slowing down the speed and seeking out hidden dimensions in a Benjaminian sense. On the film, see Susana de Sousa Dias, '*Natureza Morta*', *Lumière*, http://www.elumiere.net/exclusivo_web/reel12/sousa_01.php (accessed 5 July 2019). For a discussion of *Natureza Morta*, see Alison Ribeiro de Menezes, 'The Enchantment and Disenchantment of the Archival Image: Politics and Affect in Contemporary Portuguese Cultural Memories', in *Film, History and Memory*, eds Jennie M. Carlston and Fearghal McGarry (Basingstoke: Palgrave Macmillan, 2015), 66–82.

22 Sousa Dias's earlier work with *Natureza Morta* had included exploration of the Benjaminian notion of 'unconscious optics', using technology (in this case, slow motion footage) to expose previously unnoticed or hidden details; see Ribeiro de Menezes, 'The Enchantment and Disenchantment of the Archival Image', 73.

23 Bill Nichols, *Speaking Truths with Film: Evidence, Ethics, Politics in Documentary* (Oakland, CA: University of California Press, 2016), 107 and 99 respectively.

24 Jill Bennett, *Empathic Vision: Affect, Trauma and Contemporary Art* (Stanford, CA: Stanford University Press, 2005), 7.

25 Janis Hunter Jenkins, 'The State Construction of Affect: Political Ethos and Mental Health Among Salvadorean Refugees', *Culture, Medicine and Psychiatry* 15 (1991): 140.

26 Ibid., 143.

27 Stoler, *Along the Archival Grain*, 69; emphasis in original.

28 Ibid., 71; emphasis in original.

29 Anna M. Klobucka and Hilary Owen, 'Introduction', in *Gender, Empire, and Postcolony: Luso-Afro-Brazilian Intersections*, eds Hilary Owen and Anna M. Klobucka (New York: Palgrave Macmillan, 2014), 6.
30 The narrator of the newsreel mentions the event as a celebration of Salazar's seventieth birthday; the images must therefore be from 28 April 1959.
31 Ana Paula Ferreira, 'Home Bound: The Construction of Femininity in the *Estado Novo*', *Portuguese Studies* 12 (1996), 135. For a subtle discussion of the tensions inherent in 'the "secret" of sex inhabiting within the *luso* family-nation', see Ana Paula Ferreira, 'Loving in the Lands of Portugal: Sex in Women's Fictions and the National Order', in *Lusosex: Gender and Sexuality in the Portuguese-Speaking World*, eds Susan Canty Quinlan and Fernando Arenas (Minneapolis: University of Minnesota Press, 2002), 110.
32 Stoler, *Along the Archival Grain*, 183.
33 The film notes that it is not mentioned in historical studies of the period, and Anne Cova and António Costa Pinto do not reference it in their survey of twentieth-century Portuguese women's movements, 'Women Under Salazar's Dictatorship', *Portuguese Journal of Social Science* 2 (2002): 129–46. Nevertheless, Medeiros does include footage of newspaper reports of the time mentioning the movement and its objective of encouraging those few women who had a vote to participate in the 1958 election.
34 Ferreira notes ('Loving in the Lands of Portugal', 127, n. 27) that contrary to other fascist regimes, Salazar did not exploit the 'erotically charged figure of the dictator to mobilize the masses'. Nevertheless, there is more than a hint of a concealed appreciation in some of the interviews in *Cartas*.
35 Patrícia Vieira, 'Filming Women in the Colonies: Gender Roles in New State Cinema About the Empire' in Owen and Klobucka, *Gender, Empire and Postcolony*, 81.
36 Stoler, *Along the Archival Grain*, 101.
37 Christoph Cox, 'Beyond Representation and Signification: Toward a Sonic Materialism', *Journal of Visual Culture*, 10, no. 2 (2011), 146.
38 Ibid., 148.
39 Ibid.
40 Sousa Dias, '(In)visible Evidence', 483.
41 Ibid., 497. Space precludes a discussion here of Sousa Dias's exploration of shifting perceptions of perpetrator and victim in the 'era of the witness' (as Wieviorka puts it). She argues that both perpetrator and victim have come to be 'bathed in the same light' ('(In)visible Evidence', 489), and thus an objectionable moral levelling has occurred. See Annette Wieviorka, *The Era of the Witness*, trans. Jared Stark (Ithaca, N.Y.: Cornell University Press, 2006).
42 Ibid., 492.

43 Ibid., 493.
44 Ibid., 494; Sousa Dias here quotes Georges Didi-Huberman's *Devant le temps: histoire de l'art et anachronisme des images* (Paris: Minuit, 2000), 103.
45 Ibid., 494.
46 Ibid., 502.
47 It is interesting that Irish filmmaker and Turner Prize Winner Willie Doherty has entitled one of his memory films *Secretion* (2012), drawing upon vegetal and organic images to evoke the leakages of the past and its bleeding into the present.
48 Witnesses are listed by order of appearance at the end of the film, permitting the identification of individual testimonies while retaining within the documentary itself a sense of shared experience and collective testimony.
49 Sousa Dias, '(In)visible Evidence', 502.
50 Ibid.
51 Ibid.
52 Stoler, *Along the Archival Grain*, 20.
53 Bennett, *Empathic Vision*, 8.
54 Jeffrey Jerome Cohen, 'Posthuman Environs', *Environmental Humanities: Voices from the Anthropocene*, eds Serpil Oppermann and Serenella Iovinio (London and New York: Rowman and Littlefield, 2017), 38.
55 Kaja Silverman, *The Threshold of the Visible World* (New York and London: Routledge, 1996), 86. 'Heteropathic identification' implies an oscillation between proximity and distance, between identification and separation, that encourages the spectator to engage with an image without asserting ownership over the experience it expresses.
56 Bennett evokes Dominick LaCapra's notion of 'empathic unsettlement' as 'the aesthetic experience of simultaneously *feeling for* another and becoming aware of a distinction between one's own perceptions and the experience of the other' (Bennett, *Empathic Vision*, 8; emphasis in original).
57 Jaimie Baron, *The Archive Effect: Found Footage and the Audiovisual Experience of History* (London and New York: Routledge, 2014), 7.
58 Ibid.
59 Marks, *The Skin of the Film*, xii.
60 Claudia Benthien, *Skin: On the Cultural Border Between Self and World* (New York: Columbia University Press, 2002), 3.

8

The essay film and Rita Azevedo Gomes's *Correspondences*

Ana Cabral Martins

This chapter proposes an analysis of the concept of the 'essay film'. This is a term that has gained widespread appreciation in recent years as a particular type of cinematic practice, the bearer of its own history, tradition and canonical texts. The chapter examines this concept in tandem with Portuguese director Rita Azevedo Gomes's film *Correspondências* (*Correspondences*, 2016), questioning whether the film can be categorized as an essay film. The term 'essay film' often proves to be a somewhat cryptic, if deceptively straightforward, means of defining a particular mode of filmmaking. This is because the essay film has been both taxonomically valuable and very flexible in terms of defining inassimilable objects, allowing for inventiveness within its categorization.

Timothy Corrigan places the essay film somewhere 'straddling fiction and nonfiction, news reports and confessional autobiography, documentaries and experimental film'.[1] Azevedo Gomes's career has similarly straddled an *in-between* space, as the filmmaker has worked either in purely fictional territory or within a more or less essayistic space. As José Moure states, transferring the notion of the 'essay' from the literary to the cinematic lexicon is a gesture that demonstrates a determination to be affiliated with a specific literary experience and perspective on the world – which one could easily ascribe to Azevedo Gomes's intentions regarding *Correspondences*, as this film, even more so than her earlier work, aspires to affiliate itself with a very particular literary mood, experience and generation.[2] The essay film could not be a more appropriate lens for the analysis of *Correspondences*, a film that was inspired by the letters exchanged between the Portuguese poets Sophia de Mello Breyner Andresen and Jorge de Sena, during the latter's exile. Jorge de Sena left Portugal for political reasons in 1959 and never returned. He lived in exile in Brazil and, later, in the

United States. Through their letters, the film 'builds a dialogue between longing and belonging'[3] and establishes a fictionalized correspondence with our own lives. Throughout this chapter, the intention is to explore the malleability of the term 'essay film' and, then, to take *Correspondences* as a case study, questioning whether it can be categorized as an essay film and in what capacity, and thus establishing a direct line between the literary heritage of the concept and the literary origins of the film's subject.

The film critic Jorge Mourinha anticipates the presence of Azevedo Gomes's film at the 2016 Locarno Film Festival by describing *Correspondences* as an 'out of the box object, an audiovisual essay.'[4] The presence of *Correspondences* at the Swiss festival is an indication of an ongoing international responsiveness to Azevedo Gomes's cinema. *A Vingança de uma Mulher* (*A Woman's Revenge*, 2011), the filmmaker's previous film, travelled around the world for years after its premiere, leading to international retrospectives of her work, including at the Buenos Aires International Festival of Independent Cinema (BAFICI) in 2014. Similarly, *A Portuguesa* (*The Portuguese Woman*, 2018), Azevedo Gomes's latest film,[5] premiered at the Argentinian film festival, Mar del Plata, in November 2018, and began its European tour at the Berlin Film Festival, having subsequently been awarded the Golden Lady Harimaguada at the Nineteenth International Film Festival of Las Palmas de Gran Canária. Azevedo Gomes's cinema has almost always been undertaken in financially precarious conditions, and the filmmaker has never really settled within a particular genre or category. According to Jorge Leitão Ramos, Azevedo Gomes's oeuvre has been built 'under the sign of austerity and aestheticism, of literature and artistic refinement',[6] which often isolates her work from recent Portuguese cinema. This feeling may have emerged precisely because of her tendency to work in an 'in-between' space when it comes to her cinema.

Azevedo Gomes's first contact with the world of cinema was as an 'assistant and an actress in several shorts by the painter Noronha da Costa',[7] having also worked as a costume designer – in *Francisca* (Manoel de Oliveira, 1981) and *Notre Mariage* (Valeria Sarmiento, 1984) – and set decorator – in *Der Rosenkönig* (*The Rose King*; Werner Schroeter, 1986). She directed her first film in 1990, *O Som da Terra a Tremer*. Ramos describes this film as 'floating between fiction and reality, between the real and the imagined', though he also chides it for being too 'literary'.[8] In *Frágil como o Mundo* (2003) a strong literary quality becomes apparent in Azevedo Gomes's filmmaking. She is already bringing Sophia de Mello Breyner Andresen's texts to the screen here, since the title cites her poem *Terror de te Amar num Sítio tão Frágil como o Mundo*. This literary quality is present in both *Altar* (2002)[9] and *A Woman's Revenge*, which is based on the short story 'La Vengeance d'une femme' from *Les Diaboliques* by Jules Amédée Barbey d'Aurevilly.

Azevedo Gomes has, throughout her career, wandered from narrative fiction proper to forms that are 'more or less essayistic' in nature.[10] In conversation with Mourinha about the film, Azevedo Gomes explains her earlier plans regarding *Correspondences*, which she envisioned as a documentary film about the letters and the relationship between Sophia and Sena, although she was unable to 'make a formally correct, documental film' as she always knew she would transform it into something different. Azevedo Gomes talks of wanting to play with 'a diversity of materials, with technically pristine images, others less so, yearning for the lovely colours of Super 8, and the charcoal shades of the black and white. … I wanted to mix all that.'[11] Apart from trying to avoid a pure documentary approach, *Correspondences* also refuses to use visual elements as mere illustration: it 'shows actors, friends, artists and public figures (not all Portuguese) reading excerpts of letters or poems by Sophia and Jorge de Sena, interwoven with shots of places or evocations from their lives'.[12] Mourinha classifies it as 'closer to what one would call "essay film", on the threshold of *cinéma du réel* or "non-fiction"'. As such, he groups *Correspondences* alongside other Portuguese essay projects, such as Joaquim Pinto's *E agora? Lembra-me* (*What now? Remind me*, 2013) and Manuel Mozos's *João Bénard da Costa: Outros Amarão as Coisas que Eu Amei* (*Others Will Love the Things I Have Loved*, 2014).[13]

Towards a definition of the essay film

Suzanne Liandrat-Guigues and Murielle Gagnebin have presented the essay film as a genre that had, up until then, been marginal but enormously fruitful, though always treading a somewhat imprecise ground, defined by conflicting claims and marred by a certain incompleteness.[14] Citing Alain Ménil, they argue that not only does the essay film lack precise delineations but it also refuses to submit to any guidelines. The essay film is, therefore, characterized by the 'notable trait of non-consistency'[15] – or, even, as Denis Lévy writes, by encompassing 'all that is unclassifiable in cinema'.[16]

The debate concerning the unclassifiability of the essay film has continued over the years, with Nora M. Alter endeavouring to anchor its definition in a tradition relating to film and art installation, and attempting to establish it as a hybrid between fiction and documentary, going somewhat beyond traditional conventions and practices. Essentially, Alter's perspective sees the essay film as poaching from different disciplines and 'transgressing conceptual and formal norms'.[17] This characterization is, therefore, a decidedly in-between category, neither narrative fiction nor documentary and Alter deems it to have become, at the time, 'commonly acknowledged as a third cinematic genre'.[18] Yet, it is also perceived as a multifaceted and layered production, a composite of different 'tracks', from the image, to the sound, to any chapter headings or writing that may exist, all in order to achieve 'complex levels of meaning that the audience must co-produce'.[19] If Alter begins by defining the essay film as a hybrid, she goes on to contrast the essay film with the more conventional genre of documentary. Where the documentary presents (or tries to present) an 'unambiguous truth and a relationship to history that is not arbitrary', the essay film, by contrast, is the ideal playground for contradiction.[20] This is meant to highlight the essay's 'inherent flexibility and transgressiveness' and, even, its tendency to be fragmentary. Analogously, according to Christa Blümlinger and Harun Farocki, the essay film permits 'the relationship between word and image' to be 'reconfigured anew again and again'.[21] Blümlinger and Farocki wonder whether the essay can 'transcend the boundary between fiction and reality or rather contest such a boundary'.[22]

Laura Rascaroli also attempts to narrow down the definition of the essay film, while still focusing on its inherent problems. Rascaroli identifies certain recurrent markers: the in-'betweenness' that emerges from the hybrid form of the essay film, a form that is transgressive, as well as self-reflective and reflexive because it is both the cause and the result of a 'personal investigation'.[23] For her, reflexivity and subjectivity are the two most essential characteristics of the essay, both literary and filmic. This subjectivity is connected to the fact that 'most if not all accounts of the essayistic also place emphasis on its personal, almost autobiographical nature'.[24] Similarly significant is the importance of the word in essayistic cinema. Working from André Bazin's review of Chris Marker's *Lettre de Sibérie* (*Letter from Siberia*, 1957), first published in 1958, Rascaroli expands Bazin's comments (which make specific reference solely to that film) regarding the category of essay film as a whole. She focuses on what she calls Bazin's conception of a 'cinema of the word'[25] and the use of written text read by a voiceover. This will be an interesting point to explore in a more in-depth analysis of *Correspondences* given the film's reliance on the written letters of both

Sophia (as she is fondly called in Portugal) and Jorge de Sena, and the voiceover delivery of many of their poems, as well as of the letters themselves.

In respect of essay film definitions, Rascaroli goes on to observe an emphasis on 'a personal authorial vision' where the 'centrality of a text read by a voice-over' can be more (Phillip Lopate[26]) or less (Timothy Corrigan[27]) prescriptive depending on the sources.[28] Rascaroli then returns to the writings of Paul Arthur,[29] owing to the fact that he draws attention to the use of found footage and collage as being widely used in essay films. The result of this aesthetic choice is a 'juxtaposition between the past tense of archival images and the present tense of the commentary'. Furthermore, she adds that due to the essay's deployment of the first person, Arthur considers it a very apt format to 'express oppositional positions, … indeed often used by women directors and artists of color'.[30] Subsequently, Rascaroli distinguishes the authorial voice as another specific element of the essay film, an (authorial) presence also identified by Arthur.

Timothy Corrigan's perspective on the essay film is particularly pertinent here because of his emphasis on the temporalities of the essay film – a form that can enact diverse temporal experiences. According to Corrigan, an 'essayistic temporality' is, fundamentally, about 'the timing of thought'.[31] This is a productive viewpoint from which to explore *Correspondences* as the film continually plays with temporality, especially when considering that precisely because the essay film operates 'outside or on the margins of conventionally coherent temporal patterns', it can offer unique access to several, conflicting temporalities.[32] In a similar vein, David Montero notes that an essay film offers 'an access (however oblique) to the domain of the lived experience'.[33] This access is constructed through a dialogue of utterances and images. Montero considers this 'dialogic manner' a characteristic of the cinematic essay as it helps to conceptualize 'what we see and experience, using what we know or have heard', positioning the essay film as 'an attempt to situate ourselves in relation to the world around us'.[34] Ultimately, Montero's argument regarding a 'dialogic approach' to the essay film, on which his book is based, focuses mainly on 'cinematic essays [that] combine and put in relation different discourses',[35] an element that is often neglected.

The reasons that Alter and Corrigan provide for the swift propagation and popularity of the essay film in recent years include the ubiquity and ease provided by digital technologies and the emergence of new media platforms for the distribution and exhibition of filmed content.[36] I highlight these because they are echoed in Rascaroli's work. She stresses the importance of technology in respect of the essay film as it 'facilitates a cinewriting that is increasingly personal and idiosyncratic',[37] but, nevertheless, inevitably political. This is also the case of *Correspondences*, due to the film's underlying themes, as well as the history it portrays. Rascaroli develops her exploration of the essay film by concentrating on the 'dialectical tension between juxtaposed or interacting filmic elements and, more precisely, the gaps that its method of juxtaposition opens in the text'.[38] These are, as Rascaroli defines them, 'in-between spaces',[39] which are integrated in a form that is, itself, something in-between.

In the section that follows, I will draw on the above-mentioned debates to explore various specific features of essay film as well as considering its value as a mode of classification for Azevedo Gomes's *Correspondences*. I am particularly interested in Alter's views regarding the essay film's lack of precise delineation and the evident poaching from different perspectives, which renders the films that belong to this category, and indeed the category itself, somewhat unclassifiable. I am also interested in exploring Rascaroli's notions of dialectical tension, in between-ness and in-between spaces in the essay film, specifically as regards its flexibility, transgressiveness and fragmentariness. Similarly, given the nature of the film in question here – which features the correspondence between two Portuguese literary figureheads – I would like to highlight the importance of the use of voiceover and the authors' own words, which contribute to the autobiographical and idiosyncratic elements that permeate the film. Corrigan's analysis of diverse temporal experiences outside conventionally coherent patterns will also be relevant to my reading. Finally, I will explore Montero's dialogic approach concerning *Correspondences*, alongside Alter's and Arthur's concepts of collage and juxtaposition.

Correspondences as an essay film

Relating Azevedo Gomes's *Correspondences* to the notion of the essay film positions this Portuguese filmmaker in a tradition of women directors such as Agnès Varda, Yvonne Rainer, Jill Godmilow and Ngozi Onwurah; plenty of characteristics or features connect these five women's oeuvres. The late Agnès Varda's *cinécriture*[40] (a term she coined for her own type of filmmaking) may not be connected to the essay film's ontology, but it remains a term affiliated with a necessarily literary experience. In her work, she eschewed working within one genre or style, mixing fact and fiction, and her cinema was self-reflexive and personal. Yvonne Rainer – a legendary figure in American contemporary art, film and postmodern dance – exhibited, in her early films, an aversion to following narrative conventions, combining autobiography and fiction. Jill Godmilow's *Far From Poland* (1984) is a fragmentary cinematographic work, constructed through dreams, documentary footage and re-enacted interviews that lead to a deeply personal collage film. Similarly, Ngozi Onwurah embraces heterogeneity and subjectivity, and challenges conventional narrative limits. If these women have 'adopted the essay as an instrument of creative struggle',[41] so too has Azevedo Gomes, whose instinct told her early on that *Correspondences*, initially imagined or conceived as a documentary, would be transformed into something else along the way.

Speaking of her filmmaking process regarding *Correspondences*, Azevedo Gomes could be responding to Moure's depiction of the literary essay as something that is exercised as *expérimentation* – a result of her creative labour and effort. The filmmaker specifically highlights her need to experiment in her cinema: 'I love to experiment because I think I am not sure exactly what to do. And when I am not sure what to *do*, I have to experiment' (my emphasis).[42] Additionally, Azevedo Gomes defines her cinema 'as "open to circumstances" rather than to chance',[43] which also converges with Moure's depiction of the literary essay as born out of '*expérience du monde, de vie et de soi*' (experience of life, self and the world).[44] As Montero argues for the essay to be seen not as a genre but as a form, he returns to Michel de Montaigne's 1952 *Essays* to consider how, similarly to Azevedo Gomes and *Correspondences*, the 'essayist does not know beforehand where his quest would lead and can only find out by actually writing the essay'.[45]

Rascaroli is also keen to distinguish experimentation as a key feature in essay films. She writes that 'experimentation and idiosyncrasy are intrinsic to a form that is always and necessarily unique and original'.[46] Therefore, each director 'embraces the textual and rhetorical strategies of the essay, but articulates them in very different ways'.[47] 'Experimentation' becomes, then, a key descriptor regarding *Correspondences* given that the film had a prolonged shooting schedule, dictated by the small team, 'improvised according to the availability of the participants and the encounters staged throughout the process'.[48] This underlines, from the start, how well *Correspondences* fits the notion of the essay film as a hybrid (see Alter), as it is easily contrasted with the stricter genre of documentary. Unlike documentary, *Correspondences* never presents (or tries to present) an 'unambiguous truth and a relationship to history that is not arbitrary'.[49] On the contrary, it allows – just as the essay film does – 'for contradictions and play'.[50]

The film 'plays with fact and fiction, untruths as much as truths, poses problems without answers, and is deeply self-reflexive'.[51] Its evocations are not factual; its contemplation is not restrictive. Azevedo Gomes's *Correspondences* also resides, then, somewhere 'in-between', at the same time as it also fosters a sense of play.

Two and a half hours in total length, *Correspondences* visually articulates Sophia and Sena's epistolary back and forth (in an exchange that shows the depth of a friendship going beyond geography and literature) using a mixture of dramatization, confession and impressionistic visuals. Azevedo Gomes opens *Correspondences* up and expands the film through multiple 'tracks': not only does it recover and present the letters but it also allows for and creates subtle and infinite correspondences and connections between images, words, songs, photographs, family films, memories and remarks on the life of the writers themselves, the life of the Portuguese director herself and even our own recollections and experiences as spectators. In this essay film, history, politics, past and future – and even the process of shooting the actual film – are continually juxtaposed and constructed/built upon.

In a key sequence exemplifying this journey through time, the camera looks up, slanted, to an office that's clearly contemporary, given the presence of a very recent model of Apple's iMac (see Figure 8.1). A woman is seen holding up a photo and otherwise apparently working in this office. As it is shot in similar fashion to many of the moments in the film that display the process of shooting

Figure 8.1 The filmmaker at work (C.R.I.M., 2016).

Correspondences, it seems likely that we are watching Azevedo Gomes herself, working on the film we are viewing. Then, swiftly, we jump to another scene – a POV shot, as the camera is moving, placidly, along a path in an orchard. The image is tinted magenta, aesthetically denoting the notion of a time past. Scoring these two scenes is the seventh song in Pergolosi's *Stabat Mater*, 'Eja mater fons amoris'. Its operatic musical style is meshed with quotidian sounds (cupboards opening, things or people moving around) from the office we just left, even as we (and the camera) wander through the orchard. As the camera continues to roam, now showing a waterfall, a voice reads a new letter from Sena to Sophia (and her husband Francisco) that wishes her a happy birthday and continued friendship, as he has recently moved to Brazil. The magenta tint disappears. A crisp, clear image shows a window frame next to some greenery and flowers, while a female voice reads Sophia's answer. The text recited, the words written by Sophia, denote a void created by Sena's absence: she speaks of missing her friend's support in a country and in a reality she doesn't recognize, while also talking about how her writing process has recently changed.

The sequence evokes much of what I described above regarding the film's multiple 'tracks' as it incorporates history and politics through the words both spoken and read. Time is indicated by the date read out loud ('Assis, 30 October 1959') and by the magenta tint upon the image, as well as the process of constructing the film, denoted by the office and its very contemporary technology, and also the more obvious shot of the film crew setting up to start, we imagine, the filming process. These images flow into one another, a constantly contrasting, but not conflicting, construction. This flow creates – and is exemplary of – a kind of correspondence between the film's diverse temporal experiences, eschewing, as Corrigan discussed, conventional patterns of coherence. As in other moments in *Correspondences*, this contrasting construction creates a connection and a harmony between what is spoken and what is shown, through a constant, and connecting, juxtaposition.

Time is relevant to reading *Correspondences* as essay film in respect of the letters between Sophia and Jorge de Sena, because these letters also function as a map of their self-expression as individuals, all the more so since the letters convey details of 'daily life and experience', which Corrigan has identified as a practice characteristic of essay film.[52] For Mourinha, *Correspondences* is 'a leisurely essay film about the ability of poetry and writing to capture moments in time and preserve them in amber for the future'.[53] Importantly, the film functions as both a 'capsule of a historical moment in Portugal where poetry and exile seemed to be the only windows out to the world' and, at the same time, a 'scrapbook of the director's own life and experiences'.[54] This last element embodies something that is repeatedly noted as emblematic of the essay film, the 'personal investigation'.[55]

The film is focused on the two writers and centred on their interiority, which is underlined in particular ways. One of the many 'correspondences' the film makes is between the environments related to Sophia and to Sena. They each inhabit a different universe – even though they are connected through friendship and admiration – but Azevedo Gomes displays her understanding of each writer's individuality. The aesthetic that denotes Sophia's universe is cleaner, with a starker image. It's also, as Bernardo Vaz de Castro points out, in his review of the film, 'punctuated by white statues, footage from Greece, by the long awaited "new day clean and whole" in Portugal'.[56] Jorge de Sena's corresponding aesthetic is often marked by 'movement, where images result from the ephemeral quality of places, from his inability to put down roots wherever he went'.[57] The sequence described here denotes this in a very understated manner. Jorge de Sena's reading aloud of a letter is accompanied by magenta-tinted moving images that are unmoored from any home life. As soon as Sophia's letter is read, the image from the Super 8 aesthetics shifts to a much crisper digital look, displaying a tableau of quiet domesticity.

Correspondences conforms to a particular type of essayistic subjectivity as a 'form of cinema [that] is able to express authorial subjectivity at different levels'.[58] In the case of this film, authorial subjectivity is expressed by the authors of the letters and poems, as well as by the director. Rascaroli argues that while the 'inscription of the authorial figure can be very direct, for instance by making the filmmaker's body visible and his/her voice audible' it can, in other examples of cinematic essay films, 'be more indirect, for example through the use of a narrator / spokesperson, or of intertitles, or of musical commentary, camera movements, etc.'[59].

It's also relevant to consider another important juxtaposition in *Correspondences*. In a more conventional film – especially a film with more 'conventionally coherent temporal patterns', to use Corrigan's words, – certain aspects of the writers' biographies or lives, whether intimate or public, would surely be on display. In this instance, however, just as she eschews convention, Azevedo Gomes also chooses to focus and home in on the writers' interiority (their poetry and their letters) as it relates to topics that range from physical absence to political dictatorships. At the same time, the director continuously presents contrasting images that address the intimacy of domesticity, distance and isolation. If images of a home life are symbols of friendship and closeness, distance and isolation are suggested through footage that exhibits bare beaches and bodies of water, which Vaz de Castro sees as actual 'physical limits caused by separation'.[60]

Azevedo Gomes is able to echo and reflect Blümlinger and Farocki's notion of the essay film as a facilitator of cinematic flexibility through her work in *Correspondences*. Again and again, with each juxtaposed image and text, she is able to construct a tapestry that relentlessly reconfigures what is heard and what is seen, contesting the boundaries between what is fictionalized and what is real, creating a permanent, if not limbo, at least a place outside of such boundaries. Throughout her filmography, Azevedo Gomes has included elements of fantasy while still allowing what is real to shine through her cinema. An example of this would be the very real moment when the actress Rita Durão is shown fluffing a line from a poem and then going on to perform it with great expression. Often, the balance that Azevedo Gomes strikes between lyrical and real highlights their respective weight and beauty. By showing Durão's mistake, Azevedo Gomes shines a light on the messy, often unseen process of filming Durão's recitation, cutting through the illusion to provide a humorous moment. By subsequently showing Durão's pristine recitation, and highlighting the contrast, the director calls even greater attention to the words that have been spoken by Durão and selected and written by Sophia.

The fact that Azevedo Gomes uses collage to structure her film is a further strong indication of the applicability of the term 'essay film' to *Correspondences*. Going back to the writings of Rascaroli and Arthur, collage is 'widely used in essay films', as is the 'juxtaposition' of images and words, past and present tense. Just as the 'sense-deranging surrealists ... famously found accidental poetry in the juxtapositions' (juxtapositions they themselves created by 'randomly walking into and out of films')[61] so too does Azevedo Gomes in *Correspondences*. This film is a collage of shots. They follow one another without any particularly evident rhyme or reason. The thread is their epistolary communication read out loud. It would be easy to label the film as unfocused, but there is a strategy behind the mixture. Its lack of palpable structure creates a sense of displacement and disorientation, causing the spectator to drift in and out of the film. Absence is always felt when the performers read the words of these now departed poets, whose words are transmitted and translated as each actor recites them in their own language and tone. Montero's argument, explained above, regarding a 'dialogic approach' that combines and puts in 'relation different discourses' is relevant to *Correspondences* as the film does effectively place Sophia's and Jorge de Sena's letters in relation to each other, to their poetry, to the images and to the words being spoken or their lives being evoked. This is exemplified by the existence of shots with different aesthetics that, in turn, create a 'correspondence not only between the spoken/listened to words and the images, but also between periods in Portugal's history and people of very disparate origins'.[62] The kind of dialogic approach that Montero considers and remarks upon is present in *Correspondences*, and it is this that allows the director to portray (and eventually, the audience to access) the subjects' lived experiences, which are achieved, or constructed, through a dialogue (or a correspondence) of utterances and images.

Within the film, there are examples of how Azevedo Gomes uses a visual juxtaposition that positions the image as a site for constructing revolving collages. This is evident, for example, in shots where she places, side by side and on top of each other, images that denote a kind of before and after, or an on-screen and an off-screen. Durão is made the object of the camera's gaze, but the crew that constructs this gaze is placed alongside her, separate but within the same frame (see Figure 8.2). The second of the two images is, again, a mirroring image, this time of a previous shot. Having been shown previously, in full colour and crisp digital image, an actor is then shown going through the papers strewn across the floor and reciting the corresponding letter from Jorge de Sena (see Figure 8.3). The film, then, jumps to a composition where two

Figure 8.2 Rita Durão (C.R.I.M., 2016).

Figure 8.3 An actor on the floor (C.R.I.M., 2016).

images, linked within the same frame, show different perspectives on the same moment when we, as spectators, see the apparatus of the film crew shooting the actor reciting. These two instances illustrate junctures at which Azevedo Gomes is showing the filming process of a recitation that has itself been shown previously. These collages are especially interesting juxtapositions given that they are also showing different moments in time, from the same shooting session, juxtaposing past and present tense.

As noted earlier, Alter, citing Theodor Adorno, also indicated 'fragmentariness' as a 'distinguishing feature of the most contemporary essay films'.[63] Furthermore, *Correspondences* makes present the past, not only through the recitation of the poets' letters and writings but also through evocations of their lives.[64] At the same time, the director stresses the temporal separation (while remaining communicative with the present) first by emphasizing the film's own production, then by offering tableaux, the contemporaneity of which is highlighted by technology (several instances of computers used as screens) and by the staging of the readings. Around the end of the first half-hour in the film's long running time, the film shows us a seated male figure, and beside and behind him, there is a computer showing previously seen footage, unfolding while he recites a text in French (see Figure 8.4). To the left of the frame, the glass pane from a window seems to provide access to another screen (perhaps that of a television) that shows the same footage running. This particular moment exemplifies the presence of two elements that seem to weave in and out of *Correspondences*: the presence

Figure 8.4 Dialogic framing (C.R.I.M., 2016).

of computer screens, upon which an actor is confronted with images that have already played before the eyes of the spectator, and the presence of windows, denoting a capacity for reflection that creates dialectical tension, through the juxtaposition or interaction of filmic elements. This 'dialogic' essence of the essay film is also present in *Correspondences* as Azevedo Gomes uses the letters exchanged and the poetry, written by the authors she films in dialogue with each other, to create dreamed or invented accounts of experiences in which she, the director did not participate but which, nonetheless, offer clues towards a specific, and a specifically Portuguese, historical moment. At the same time, just as it places Sophia and Jorge de Sena in dialogue with each other, it places Azevedo Gomes in dialogue with them, in dialogue with the team helping her make the film and in dialogue with a literary tradition that has haunted the director from her very first film.

The first-person voice – sometimes Sophia's, sometimes Sena's – is maintained through the people reciting their words, a kind of meta-textual first person that overlaps past and present, writer and reciter. Their correspondence – from 1959 to 1978 – is removed from its time, although it retains its historical resonance, and is transported to our contemporaneity, here marked by both the technology (from the screens I mentioned earlier to the filmmaking paraphernalia that is on display throughout the film) and the actors reciting their words. The constructed present tense of the recitation is both the *here and now* of real time and the *here and now* of the cinematic temporality that is preserved. The temporalities of this essay film constantly evoke different temporal experiences and, despite or rather because of their contemplative pace, exercise an unbroken dialectical tension.

Related to the question of the authorial voice, it would be remiss of me not to address the construction of the use of the first-person voice. Although Azevedo Gomes is focused on Sophia's and Sena's interiority – her focus relies definitively on the writers' poetry, creativity and intellectual ideas, and on their thoughts about distance, longing, their country and the stifling dictatorship – she does not seem to be concerned with considerations of gender representation and discourse regarding either Sophia or Jorge de Sena.[65] Yet, her own directorial authorship makes itself felt, and it impacts Azevedo Gomes's treatment not only of the correspondence but also of these two canonical literary figures. In this essay film, Azevedo Gomes presents contrasting images of intimacy and domesticity and of distance and isolation. The Portuguese director, however, does not equate domesticity with Sophia's voice, and her written words become the spoken words of others, both women and men. In fact, unless one knows their work well, it is often difficult to discern whose voice or whose words are being recited. Contextual clues do provide some clarity, as Sophia's poetry is distinct and Sena's letters are filled with nostalgia and, sometimes, frustration, but it is never obvious, as if the director were intentionally interweaving their voices as tightly as possible.

The actual voices of Sena and Sophia do make themselves known in interview excerpts. In one of Sophia's appearances, she recites one of her poems, *Musa ensina-me o canto* ('Muse, Teach Me the Song'), although it ends with her saying that she is losing her voice and must read it again. Instead of repeating her words, we are taken from the confines of her home life and transported through Sophia's words and Azevedo Gomes's imagery to Delos, in Greece, revisiting the eight days she once spent there. She later returns, in *Correspondences*, alongside her husband Francisco Sousa Tavares, speaking more forcefully than she does in her letters, against the PIDE, Portugal's political police force during the dictatorship. Later in the film, Jorge de Sena emerges reading his poem *Em Creta, Com o Minotauro* ('In Crete, With the Minotaur'), where he speaks of his life being 'broken into pieces by the world'.

Conclusion

The essay film, as we have already noted, does not conform to any specific guidelines. Azevedo Gomes has also carved a very particular, and particularly literary, niche in Portuguese cinema. She is a woman working in a cinematic in-between space, resisting clear genre distinctions and carving out an oeuvre that is highly idiosyncratic, while still inhabiting a tradition of women working in similarly disruptive and unconventional spaces. As Azevedo Gomes has embraced the essay film as an instrument of creative labour, so has her cinema involved approaches that warrant comparison with the works of women directors, such as Agnès Varda, Yvonne Rainer, Jill Godmilow and Ngozi Onwurah, by avoiding conventional forms and structures, mixing fact and fiction and embracing subjectivity, to create a fragmentary form of cinema that is the result of experimentation and juxtaposition, allowing for contractions and play (with time, words and multiple tracks and elements). *Correspondences* offers the perfect jumping-off point for considering her cinema in terms of its 'in-betweenness', as well as embodying multiple characteristics which inform the definition of essay film per se. As such, the film demonstrates how Azevedo Gomes eschews conventional tools and perspectives, in defiant opposition to the (cinematic) status quo.

Notes

1 Timothy Corrigan, *The Essay Film: from Montaigne, After Marker* (New York: Oxford University Press, 2011), 4.
2 José Moure, 'Essai de Définition de l'essai Au Cinéma', in *L' Essai et Le Cinéma*, eds Suzanne Liandrat-Guigues and Murielle Gagnebin (Seyssel: Éditions Champ Vallon, 2004), 252.
3 As described in various synopses of the film, namely through the production company's materials, such as a Vimeo excerpt available at: https://vimeo.com/182368833 (accessed 3 July 2019).
4 Jorge Mourinha, 'Cinema. Sophia e Jorge de Sena Vão a Locarno Com Rita Azevedo Gomes', *Público*, 3 August 2016, https://www.publico.pt/2016/08/03/culturaipsilon/noticia/-rita-azevedo-gomes-leva-sophia-e-jorge-de-sena-a-locarno-1740074 (accessed 3 July 2019).
5 Jorge Mourinha characterizes this as 'a film that owes everything to Oliveira, but could only have been done by a woman, and by a disciple. And as a homage, it must be said, it is not bad at all'. Jorge Mourinha, 'Um retrato de mulher à sombra de Oliveira iluminou a Berlinale', *Público*, 7 February 2019, https://www.publico.pt/2019/02/07/culturaipsilon/noticia/retrato-mulher-sombra-oliveira-1861100 (accessed 3 July 2019).
6 Jorge Leitão Ramos, *Dicionário do Cinema Português 1989–2003* (Lisbon: Caminho, 2005), 276.

7   Ibid., 275.
8   Ibid., 580.
9   Ramos cites a review from the Portuguese newspaper *Expresso* that states: '*Altar* is not a narrative film, nor a film of sudden emotional outbursts. It is made up of painting, texts (in three languages), fragments of music, stones and water.' Ibid., 36.
10 Mourinha, 'Cinema'.
11 Ibid.
12 Ibid.
13 Ibid.
14 Liandrat-Guigues and Gagnebin, *L'essai et le cinema*.
15 Ibid., 93.
16 Cited in Ibid., 137.
17 Nora M. Alter, 'Translating the Essay into Film and Installation', *Journal of Visual Culture* 6, no. 1 (2007), 44.
18 Ibid., 45.
19 Ibid., 48.
20 Ibid., 52.
21 Christa Blümlinger and Harun Farocki, *Christa Blümlinger/Harun Farocki: the ABCs of the Essay Film* (Berlin: Harun Farocki Institut & Motto Books, 2017), 6.
22 Ibid., 7.
23 Laura Rascaroli, 'The Essay Film: Problems, Definitions, Textual Commitments', *Framework* 49, no. 2 (2008), 24.
24 Ibid., 26.
25 Ibid., 29.
26 Phillip Lopate, *Totally, Tenderly, Tragically: Essays and Criticism from a Lifelong Love Affair with the Movies* (New York: Anchor, 1998).
27 Timothy Corrigan (ed.), *Film and Literature: An Introduction and Reader* (Milton Park, Abingdon, Oxon and New York: Routledge, 2011).
28 Rascaroli, 'The Essay Film', 32.
29 Paul Arthur, 'Essay Questions: From Alain Resnais to Michael Moore', *Film Comment* 39, no. 1 (2003): 58–62.
30 Rascaroli, 'The Essay Film', 26.
31 Corrigan, *The Essay Film*, 132.
32 Ibid., 139.
33 David Montero, *Thinking Images: The Essay Film as a Dialogic Form in European Cinema* (Bern, Switzerland: Peter Lang, 2012), 3.
34 Ibid., 4.
35 Ibid., 10.
36 Nora M. Alter and Timothy Corrigan (eds), 'Introduction', in *Essays on the Essay Film* (New York: Columbia University Press, 2017), 6.

37 Laura Rascaroli, *How the Essay Film Thinks* (New York: Oxford University Press, 2017), 5.
38 Ibid., 8.
39 Ibid.
40 Emma Jackson, 'The Eyes of Agnès Varda: Portraiture, Cinécriture and the Filmic Ethnographic Eye', *Feminist Review* 96, no. 1 (2010): 122–6.
41 Paul Arthur, 'Essay Questions', 59–60.
42 Mourinha, 'Cinema'.
43 Ibid.
44 José Moure, 'Essai de Définition de l'essai Au Cinéma', 25.
45 Montero, *Thinking Images*, 6.
46 Rascaroli, 'The Essay Film', 39.
47 Ibid., 40.
48 Mourinha, 'Cinema'.
49 Alter, 'Translating the Essay into Film and Installation', 52.
50 Ibid.
51 Ibid.
52 Corrigan, *The Essay Film*, 131
53 Jorge Mourinha, 'Connections in Invisible Ink: A Look Back at Locarno 69 on Notebook', *MUBI* (blog), 25 August 2016, https://mubi.com/notebook/posts/connections-in-invisible-ink-a-look-back-at-locarno-69 (accessed 3 July 2019).
54 Ibid.
55 Rascaroli, 'The Essay Film', 24.
56 It is a reference to a poem by Sophia about the day when the 25 April 1974 Revolution erupted. In it, she expresses her joy at a long-awaited day finally arriving. The poem is entitled '25 de Abril'.
57 Bernardo Vaz de Castro, 'Correspondências (2016) de Rita Azevedo Gomes', *À pala de Walsh*, 12 March 2018, http://www.apaladewalsh.com/2018/03/correspondencias-2016-de-rita-azevedo-gomes/ (accessed 3 July 2019).
58 Rascaroli, 'The Essay Film', 38.
59 Ibid.
60 Vaz de Castro, 'Correspondências (2016) de Rita Azevedo Gomes'.
61 Andrew Tracy, Ginette Vincendeau, Katy McGahan, Chris Darke, Geoff Andrew, Olaf Möller, Sergio Wolf, Nina Power, and Nick Bradshaw, 'The Essay Film', *Sight & Sound*, 5 August 2015, https://www.bfi.org.uk/news-opinion/sight-sound-magazine/features/deep-focus/essay-film (accessed 7 November 2019).
62 Mourinha, 'Cinema'.
63 Alter, 'Translating the Essay into Film and Installation', 54.

64 Azevedo Gomes is interested in interweaving the letters and poems with these evocations. I believe that, owing to the film's inclusion of evocations of the authors' lives (music they may have shared with loved ones, scenes described and how they may have happened), it deploys a practice that is closer to a documentary style such as 're-enactment' – which is also at the core of a kind of essay film deemed 'refractive cinema' (Corrigan, *The Essay Film*, 181–96). While re-enactment is not necessarily equivalent to evocation, it is quite similar. This similarity is centred on intention. Internally, both concepts, re-enacting and evoking, share the same aim of recalling something, which might be an event or a memory.

65 In *The Portuguese Woman*, however, Azevedo Gomes deals with concerns about the female condition, something that is very present in Robert Musil's text (which inspired the film) as the director acknowledges. She nevertheless eschews the 'feminist film' label. See for instance Paulo Portugal, 'Rita Azevedo Gomes. "Sinceramente, Nunca Pensei Que Estava a Fazer Um Filme Feminista"', *Jornal i*, 2 February 2019, https://ionline.sapo.pt/646146 (accessed 3 July 2019).

Section Four

Transnationalisms

9

Women's cinema, world cinema: Margarida Cardoso's *Yvone Kane*

Sally Faulkner

Drowsiness, the interstitial moment between sleeping and wakefulness, is the in-between state in which we encounter the protagonist some seven times over the course of Margarida Cardoso's second fiction film, *Yvone Kane* (2014) (see Figure 9.1). We meet Rita (Beatriz Batarda) as she apparently awakens into the trauma of a world in which she has lost her child (Clara, uncredited) to a drowning accident. However, the repetition of her awakening over the course of the film suggests that it is a process that is never complete. Matching the protagonist's suspension between dreaming and wakefulness, in the wider narrative of Cardoso's film we witness a number of further, and highly suggestive, incomplete processes. *Yvone Kane* takes us on multiple journeys, but these journeys are never complete: they hover instead in the in-between. There is an incomplete search into the biographical facts of the life of fictional revolutionary leader Yvone Kane (Mina Andala); into Rita's grief and incomplete recovery following the loss of her child; the study of Rita's mother Sara (Irene Ravache) and her sense of belonging as she hovers between life and death are never resolved; and the raped Niazoia girls' recovery from their attack stalls, as does the judicial investigation of the crime. Ultimately, the unnamed African country[1] of the film's shift from colonial past, through violent independence, to haunted post-colonial present remains caught in-between traumatic, censored pasts, silenced, resentful presents, and haunted, uncertain futures.

This chapter will explore *Yvone Kane*'s interstitial states and incomplete journeys by considering narrative events, and non-events, as well as what we might term Cardoso's aesthetics of the interstices: wide-angle and often split-screen framing; layering of reflections; ellipses and deferred explanations. Such an off-centre mode of film practice reveals an affinity between Cardoso and one

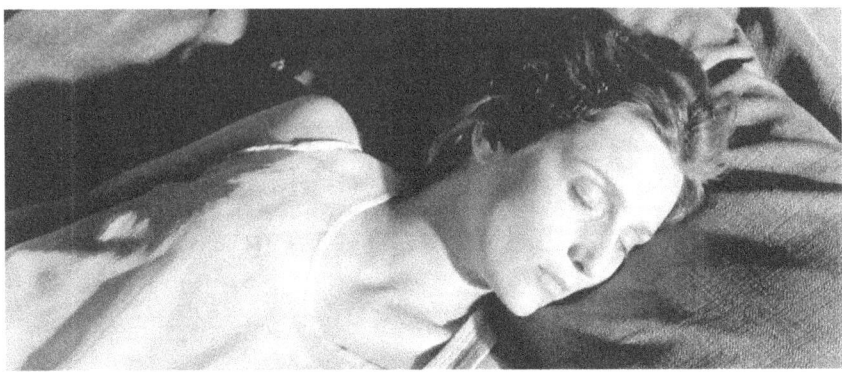

Figure 9.1 Drowsiness: Rita between nightmarish sleep and traumatic wakefulness (Midas Filmes, 2014).

of the most successful women directors of non-English language international film, Argentine Lucrecia Martel. Indeed, Cardoso has spoken of the influence of Martel on her work in interview.[2] This chapter will suggest, furthermore, that both directors occupy a precarious in-between space in contemporary world filmmaking, especially one that hovers between the 'women's cinema' and 'world cinema' of Patricia White's eponymous study of contemporary feminist film.[3] Considering questions of the local and of deterritorialization in the work of the two directors, the chapter will attempt to explain how Martel and Cardoso occupy this in-between space following distinct, if complementary, directorial trajectories. Until her latest film, Martel has fused a commitment to the local of her native Argentina with transnational, feminist art-house aesthetics, a combination that has appealed to international cinephile audiences. Working in a similar aesthetic mode, Cardoso, meanwhile, is committed to exploring wider African histories of the colonial and post-colonial periods. In the context of this highly sensitive terrain, in Portugal and beyond, a terrain that is also dominated by male authorship, Cardoso bids for, and achieves some success in attaining, a widely meaningful address by deterritorializing settings to an unnamed Africa.

The female auteur: Lucrecia Martel, Margarida Cardoso

Problematic for its erasure of the collective nature of cinematic creativity, the idea of the 'auteur', as feminist film critics have argued,[4] is nonetheless key. For any audience interested in diversity, female auteur studies provide a vocabulary to describe and defend the often select and fragile, but nonetheless critically important, space often occupied by women directors. The concept of the director as auteur has recently been helpfully framed in studies of cinephilia. Cinephilia, in Antoine de Baecque's widely used 2003 definition, is 'a way of watching films, speaking about them and diffusing this discourse'.[5] Post-war, classic cinephilia (or, in Thomas Elsaesser's filmic pun, 'Take One' cinephilia[6]) was born with the concept of the director as auteur, who controlled meaning in his or her work, as a literary author did, and about whom cinephile writers, who were often also directors themselves, wrote in journals like *Cahiers du Cinéma* (1951–).

On first examination we might assume that cinephilia is entirely international – a love of film that respects no boundaries of nation, as demonstrated by those pioneering French directors and writers' admiration for Hollywood B Films. Writing on auteurism in neighbouring Spain, a similar case to Portugal given its contemporaneous contexts of authoritarian dictatorship and censorship, Marvin D'Lugo makes the point that early, cinephilic accounts of auteurism written in *Cahiers* in the 1950 and 1960s tended to valorize a canon of auteur directors from France, the United States and Italy and ignored the question of the 'National' as any kind of organizing structure for criticism. They 'affirm[ed]', rather, 'a borderless community of spectators taking shape around the universality of the medium'.[7] In the Portuguese case, Paulo Cunha offers an account of the inspiration of *Cahiers* for cinephile directors in Portugal in the 1960s, noting that a division between an artistically and socially ambitious *cinema de autor*, as opposed to a *cinema comercial*, settled in the 1970s.[8] In the context of authoritarian dictatorship, in Portugal as in Spain, the concept of the ambitious individual voice of the auteur became meaningful in a context in which certain directors dared voice their dissent against the regime. Portugal's 1960s *Cinema Novo*, led by producer António da Cunha Telles and featuring directors such as Fernando Lopes, António de Macedo and Paulo Rocha – like its neighbour's *Nuevo Cine Español*, where producer Elías Querejeta played a leading role, alongside directors such as Basilio Martín Patino, Miguel Picazo and Carlos Saura – was therefore based on a specific act of cultural translation. The nation-less auteur of classic cinephilia became, from the perspective of making art under dictatorship, the valorization of the individual voice of anti-authoritarian protest in the particular national contexts of Portugal and Spain.[9]

Given that the cinephiles of the 1950s and 1960s were overwhelming male, the cinephile veneration of the auteur is problematic for feminist film studies. Geneviève Sellier put this most succinctly in the title of her 2005 critique of gender in auteur cinema.[10] Given that the 'auteur' was dependent on a single male voice, this was a cinema, Sellier argued, that wrote in the tense of the 'masculine singular'. I would suggest that this erasure of the feminine and the collective was actually deepened when the term 'auteur' was translated to authoritarian Portugal of the 1950s and 1960s, where its translation as '*autor*' meant it met with and reinforced the deeply patriarchal connotations of *autoridade* (authority) in the Portuguese context of the Salazar dictatorship.

However, the continued usefulness of the term 'auteur', including for feminist studies, lies in its adaptability to different strategies. As we have seen, auteurism in mid-century Portuguese and Spanish film was 'strategic'[11] in its employment of an anti-authoritarian, anti-establishment voice for political dissent, even as the singularity of that voice, and its consequent erasure of the collective, ironically replicated authoritarianism. Shifting again to a new context of the competitive market in world cinema in the 1990s, Catherine Grant has argued for an auteurism that is once again strategic as it deploys an authorial name as 'a commercial strategy for organising audience reception [and] a critical concept bound to distribution and marketing'.[12] In the new millennium, Miguel Gomes, for example, offers a particularly effective example of a 'media-savvy' auteur, using the festival appearances and online interviews that fuel contemporary (or 'Take Two')[13] cinephilia to underscore what we might term the Gomes 'brand'.[14]

It may be argued that a feminist cinema should be one of the 'Feminine, Plural', to invert Sellier's terms, in order fully to break with patriarchy, and offer a genuine 'Counter Cinema', to reprise the title of Claire Johnston's now classic manifesto piece (1973).[15] However, the examples of strategic auteurism discussed here, where the auteur can become a voice of political dissent in a national context, or a particularly effective marketing tool in a transnational one, explain its usefulness in the present discussion of the female auteur. It should also be stressed at this point that, given the immense difficulties in independent filmmaking, especially independent filmmaking beyond the English language, the deployment of an auteurist 'brand' by directors is a savvy strategy. Indeed, it may be even more savvy for independent, non-Anglophone and female directors, whose work might be perceived by world audiences as not only a niche (independent), or even a niche within a niche (independent and non-Anglophone) but, if you will, also a niche within a niche within a niche (independent, non-Anglophone and female-authored). As we will see, this is a fragile position for Argentine Martel to occupy, even with the weight of the rise of Latin American cinema since 2000 as her powerful context. For

Cardoso, though, who has only made two fiction films, and these ten years apart, it is especially fragile. Nonetheless, critics like Mariana Liz[16] and Horacio Muñoz Fernández and Iván Villarmea Álvarez[17] have suggested that we may be witnessing a rise in Portuguese film in the new millennium through increasing visibility at film festivals. 'Filmmakers including Pedro Costa, Miguel Gomes and João Pedro Rodrigues', writes Liz, 'have become household names for film festival, art-house theatres and cinephile audiences.'[18] With female examples less visible thus far,[19] the 2020s may be a particularly exciting moment for Portuguese female directors like Cardoso.

Returning to Martel, we may explain her success – and inspiration to Cardoso – as a skilful deployment of both types of strategic auteurism: political and marketing-led. Albeit reluctantly, she appears on the festival circuit, gives multilingual promotional interviews and has created a distinctive look wearing heavy-rimmed glasses or sunglasses. This look, for White, is brilliantly strategic: the glasses succeed in 'combining a stereotypically male-centred virtuosity and a female-coded mystery and accessibility in a queer kind of reticence'.[20] In parallel to this media-savvy strategic auteurism, Martel's work offers one of the foremost examples in contemporary world cinema of the development of an authorial signature, or distinctive filmmaking style. Off-centre framing, long takes, dissonant sound, a lack of establishing shots and narrative gaps may appear typical of the festival film or art film generally,[21] but Martel achieves auteurist distinction by deploying these aesthetics politically to create what Katy Stewart names 'the female gaze'.[22] For Stewart, Martel harnesses sonic and haptic – as well as visual – resources and as such 're-forms and remodels cinematic convention to create distinctly female expression in film'.[23]

Although lacking the powerful backing by the Almodóvar brothers and the Cannes Film Festival that Martel enjoys, Margarida Cardoso's strategic auteurism nonetheless bears comparison with the Argentine director. Not only an independent filmmaker but a non-Anglophone and female one, Cardoso also emerges from the context of Portuguese film, a 'small nations' cinema[24] without a domestic audience able fully to support native production. Cardoso has also, thus, albeit in a more limited way, deployed a media-savvy strategic auteurism, giving multilingual interviews to accompany public and festival screenings of her films,[25] and her first fiction film *A Costa dos Murmúrios* (*The Murmuring Coast*, 2004), attracted indicators of cinephile prestige such as inclusion at the Giornate Degli Autori at the Venice Film Festival. While Cardoso may have a smaller domestic context and thus far garnered fewer prestige accolades, she has likewise remained faithful to her own distinctive voice as a female auteur, a voice that bears ready comparison to Martel's.

Like Martel, Cardoso eschews establishing shots, deploys narrative ellipses that forestall easy intelligibility, employs off-centre composition in widescreen shots and occasionally disassociates sound and image, as at the start of *Yvone Kane*, where the sound of the wind dial precedes its image. Just as Stewart has shown that Martel deploys these characteristics to fashion a female gaze – rather than simply adhere to the aesthetic conventions of festival art films – I suggest that these are also deployed by Cardoso to create alternative female expression. In her words, she seeks to expose audiences to the 'vulnerability of the certitude we have in the image',[26] a description that readily applies to Martel's work also, and which is especially suggestive for a feminist reading of resistance to patriarchy.

The similarities between the two directors' aesthetics are thus multiple, from their resistance to mainstream cinematic convention, so crucial to feminist film, to the fascination both directors show for the formal and narrative possibilities of spaces like the swimming pool (especially important in Martel's *La ciénaga* (*The Swamp*, 2001) and *La niña santa* (*The Holy Girl*, 2004) and Cardoso's *Yvone Kane*) and the hotel (Martel's *The Holy Girl* and Cardoso's *The Murmuring Coast* and *Yvone Kane*). Key for my argument here is that Cardoso, like Martel, deploys an aesthetics of the interstices to portray in formal and narrative ways multiple unfinished journeys and unresolved situations that are critical for both feminist and post-colonial interpretations. I will argue finally that one key distinction between the two lies in their approaches to the local and to deterritorialization, from Martel's specific locations in her Salta trilogy, to the resolutely unnamed Africa of *Yvone Kane*.

Women's cinema

In a self-reflective moment towards the start of Cardoso's film, and the start of Rita's search into the biography of Yvone, the protagonist visits a museum. Accompanied by a young boy who reads a set narrative, Rita, and the audience, explore the history of the unnamed African country's move from colonial oppression to independence through a series of photographs and military memorabilia. Cardoso deploys her wide-angle frame to brilliant effect here, allowing us simultaneously to see the 'official' version of independence, yet also see in the same frame the parts of the museum that have been abandoned, or relegated as 'unofficial'. Further wide angles reveal the adult museum guide having a snooze, leaving the business of voicing the national narrative to the hesitant young boy reading a set script. Rather than rely on the wide angle only, Cardoso brings the question of the Women's Detachment into the dialogue and into the narrative when Rita enquires into its whereabouts. The boy takes her, then, into a neglected backroom: the light bulb only switches on only after a period of flickering, and the light it casts reveals a room of photographs and banners that are pealing and hanging off the wall (see Figure 9.2). Not only has the role of women been censored from the national museum, but, we later discover, the roles of white women and gay women in the struggle have also been further silenced by the removal of their photographs altogether, even from the backroom.

A neglected backroom of a museum containing an alternative version of national history is richly suggestive for a feminist reading. Recalling British pioneer Virginia Woolf's *A Room of One's Own* of 1929 and Spanish counterpart Carmen Martín Gaite's *El cuarto de atrás* (*The Back Room*, 1978), it suggests that a female history is a space that is recoverable through investigation. It might be difficult to cast the light of historical investigation on this space at first – the light bulb flickers before it works – but, once illuminated, that history might appear fully visible and complete. However, our discovery later in the film that this space is still censored, on both racial and heteronormative grounds, problematizes the simplicity of this thesis. *Yvone Kane* is in fact interested in the in-between and the interstices – the cinematic flickering on and off of that light bulb – rather than the steady illumination. Cardoso troubles the easily intelligible, focusing instead on the flickering, the in-between and the interstitial. Like Martel, in Stewart's

Figure 9.2 The neglected back room of the museum (Midas Filmes, 2014).

suggestive reading, Cardoso disrupts the securities of the cinematic conventions that created the conditions for the 'male gaze', as it was famously named in Laura Mulvey's 1975 essay. Cardoso does not create an alternative, yet equivalent and similar, 'female gaze', which would replicate the same power structures. In other words, she does not add and illuminate a Women's Detachment extra room in the museum that simply adds to, rather than challenges, its patriarchal emphasis. Instead, she focuses on the interstitial flickering – the process and its incompletion – to create in fact an alternative space for what we might call a distinctly female expression.

Let's examine the further incomplete processes and journeys of the film's narrative. *Yvone Kane* adopts some of the conventions of the detective thriller to describe Rita's investigation into the revolutionary leader's life. We identify with Rita *qua* detective as she pieces together the jigsaw: as well as accompanying her on her visit to the initial 'official' museum we are presented with the same evidence as her through her interviews. These include the mysterious Alex (Adriano Luz, a familiar face from his role as Forza Leal in *The Murmuring Coast*); the kindly university professor Elias (João Manja); helpful archive worker Andrea (Susan Danford); Natural History Museum guard Amélia (Rosa Vasco); cleaner Djalma (Alfredo Conja); Sérgio's brother Eduardo (Mário Mabjaia); and finally Yvone's former lover Sérgio (David Branco). We also share POV shots with Rita as she searches through archive material including photographs, newspaper reports and archived film footage in English as well as Portuguese. While all this seems almost too easy, what is key is the lack of resolution. At the start of her search the double reflection in the window captures both Rita and Alex in the same frame. While this might have conveyed their shared interest, the lack of resolution by the end of the film suggests we re-read this as a symbol of entrapment in the past. At the end of her search, a narrative ellipsis takes us from Rita's and Sérgio's search for the buried Yvone files on the unnamed border, to a close-up of the unearthed new material. However, we are only ever afforded this brief glimpse of the material and thus never know what it reveals, and the film's open ending means we never know if Rita continues or completes her search. We are left, instead, with Sérgio's unsettling description of his experience of the moment of Yvone's death – '*não senti nem um sinal*' (I did not sense anything) – a moment that we learn later coincides with that of Rita's own mother Sara's death, as confirmed by the cut to her funeral.

Likewise the mystery of Sara's sense of identity is never resolved. Unlikeable, irritable, Sara is searching for belonging. We meet her as she confronts the certainty of the diagnosis of her lung cancer as terminal, but her location is otherwise uncertain. Her request, in the next scene, regarding her burial place encapsulates this. She declares to the long-suffering servant and chauffeur Gabriel (Samuel Malumbe) that she wants to be buried in the community graveyard of the unnamed city, but only at its very periphery, which Gabriel rejects as not a graveyard at all. A few minutes into the film, then, we are encouraged to think of Sara in life as a future restless spirit or ghost, without a proper place, or conclusion. Her reunion with her daughter after what must be at least a decade – since she never met the young child Clara – is shrouded in mystery. Cardoso allows us to perceive mother and daughter in double reflections on the window pane as Rita collects her luggage at the airport, but for the actual moment of reunion she pointedly places the camera at the back of Sara's head, obscuring both Sara's and Rita's faces as they embrace, and leaving us only with the awkwardly grinning João (Gonçalo Waddington) in the shot instead. Similarly, when Sara is forced to reveal her illness to her daughter, Cardoso's camera remains outside with distant mother and daughter inside the house. In a parallel move to Martel's frequent obfuscation of her soundtrack, Cardoso only lets us hear the dog barking at this point, rather than the intimate mother–daughter confession.

Similarly, Sara's revelations about her political affiliations to Rita are obfuscated and inconclusive, as are her aggressive discussions about Catholicism with the maimed Mother Superior (Francilia Jonaze). Sara is the biological mother of a distant son who lives in London, and appears only in a blurry distant image on a TV set, in which he appears hidden visually by a moustache and acoustically by speaking his non-native language, English. Sara in fact has her most revealing conversation with her adoptive son Jaime (Herman Jeusse), who is implicated in the crime of rape and rejects her. He gives Sara an interestingly geographical explanation for his behaviour '*não sou bem daqui, nunca fui*' (I'm not quite from here, I never was') and then adds what I take to be the key to Sara's lack of sense of identity and place: '*sei que tu percebes*' (I know you understand).' This conversation takes place in the half-light of dusk and offers us this interpretation of a character who remains in a half-light. She is neither fully African (as the officer pointedly reminds her during the rape investigation) nor fully European (she does not even enquire after her lost granddaughter Clara). A brilliant portrait of the in-betweenness of the postcolonial subject, in temporal terms Sara is a future ghost or spirit (and even names herself thus in a conversation with Gabriel) and in spatial terms she is condemned to an eternal periphery at the edge of the community cemetery.

In-betweenness and incompletion characterize the film's opening narrative strand also. *Yvone Kane* begins with Rita and João's little girl Clara's accidental drowning in a treacherous river or sea current. The widescreen high-angle shot seems to be at first one of beauty, with the golden hues of the sandy shore contrasting with the flickering turquoise tones of the water, and future trauma only hinted at by the unsettling presence of the abandoned boat. The sequence also indicates inconclusiveness and uncontainability in a number of ways. First, as previously noted, the sound of the wind dial precedes, and thus cannot be contained by, the image. The repetitive clicking sound is exaggerated and becomes unsettling. When the sequence ends abruptly with Clara's failure to respond to her mother's cries, and her approaching the water as if hypnotized by the clicking, we realize that this is a nightmare sequence and that the horror of the drowning exceeds image and sound, and cannot be contained within the frame. Just as the pointlessness of the death exceeds explanation, so the sound exceeds the image, the horror exceeds the narrative and the extreme close-up of Rita's eye as she awakens means that her face exceeds the frame (see Figure 9.3). All of these filmic resources form part of an aesthetics of the interstices, which convey Rita's failure to understand, mourn or recover from the loss – displacing her attention instead on the compensatory Yvone Kane search. The Yvone search as a compensatory act is confirmed by Cardoso's description of the creative process in interview, in which she describes switching from an initial focus on Yvone's biography to one on Rita's trauma, memory and incomplete recovery.[27]

We only witness Rita's nightmare memory of the drowning twice. The fact that these instances occur at the start of the film might indicate recovery, with the final moments of extreme close-up of her sleeping face not preceded by the

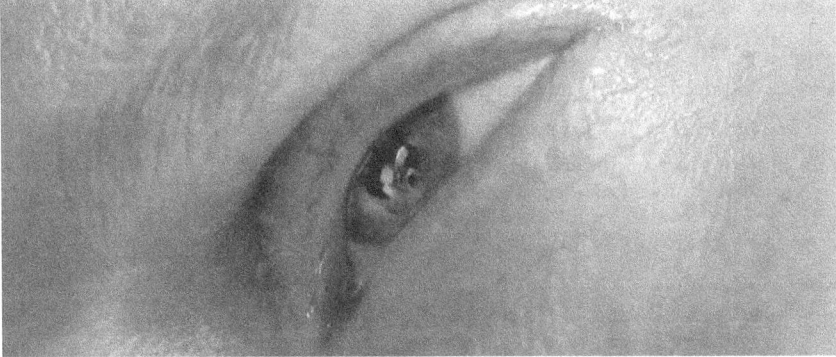

Figure 9.3 The extreme close-up of Rita's eye as she awakens (Midas Filmes, 2014).

nightmare. However, we understand that Rita's mourning and recovery are not complete owing to the evocative close of the film. Having travelled to a hotel under construction in the north of the country near the border, she finds, but does not use, the buried papers, and misses her mother's death and funeral. The film closes with her occupying the interstitial space of the window, looking out at a border hotel on the coast that it is undergoing repair (see Figure 9.4). She too is undergoing repair and the process is never complete. The spaces she occupies remain interstitial (the window, the hotel, the border, the coast), and a conversation with Gabriel reveals that time may be cyclical too rather than linear. While he informs her of her mother's death – the end point of a linear process – among Sara's final words are her reference to herself as a future ghost, echoed in Gabriel's self-description as a future spirit of the border hotel. When Rita makes a comment to him about visiting his house, which repeats her mother's earlier observation, it suggests that she too is trapped in troubling cyclical repetition. The film itself also draws full circle, for, just as the sound of the wind dial at the start precedes, and thus cannot be contained by, the image, the sound of the coastal waves at the end succeed the image, spilling out beyond it, and again, thus, cannot be contained.

It must be noted that all of the incomplete journeys and processes discussed thus far relate to the white European characters of the film – Rita's research, Sara's placelessness, Rita's grief. However grief-stricken, these characters are comparatively wealthy and educated. Rita does not appear to need to work and no one ever asks her for her report on Yvone; Sara works as a doctor and her salary pays for a large house and the services of three servants. Both Rita

Figure 9.4 Unfinished journeys and unresolved situations: Rita at the window of the coastal border hotel-under-repair (Midas Filmes, 2014).

and Sara are articulate and literate – they both converse effortlessly in both Portuguese and English, and are frequently seen reading (especially Sara) and writing (especially Rita). These characteristics might not be worthy of remark were they not to contrast so starkly with a further parallel investigation in the film's narrative, whose incompletion is especially troubling. As Rita begins her quest into the also highly educated and multilingual Yvone's biography, Sara is informed of the gang rape of two young girls from the province of Niazoai at the orphanage at which she works, an attack that Jaime witnesses and fails to prevent (see Figure 9.5). Never named, these girls' inability to speak Portuguese is twice stressed, and the only word we hear them utter is the chilling 'four' to number their attackers. While we learn they are disease-free following the attack, they remain mute throughout the film, and we learn of no progress in bringing the crime to justice, other than Rita's brief challenging of Jaime.

The multiple, incomplete journeys of *Yvone Kane* suggest, then, a cinema of the interstices that is especially propitious for articulating an alternative female voice which explores both feminist issues (the writing of women into history; the crime of rape) and post-colonial questions (Sara's placelessness, an experience that Rita looks set to repeat). I would suggest that white European Rita's loss of a child and her mother Sara's death from cancer, alongside the ups and downs of their mother–daughter relationship, are universal, family-related themes that are accessible to world cinema audiences.[28] The two narratives of investigation that pertain to the African female characters open up alternative, and highly contrasting, feminist questions that are also legible to world cinema

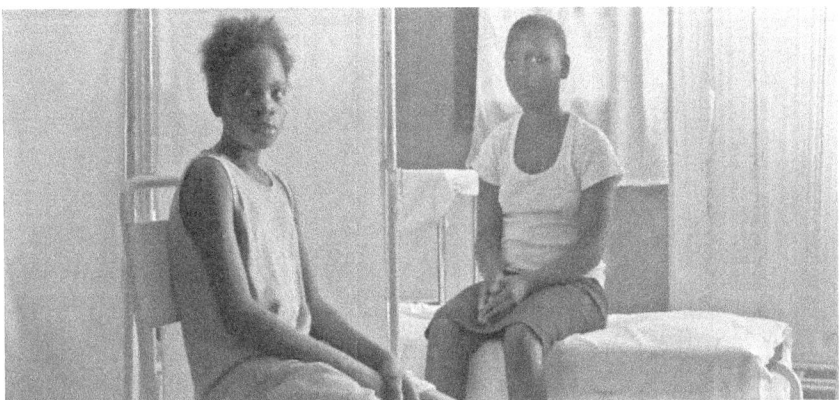

Figure 9.5 The Niazoia girls, whose rape remains an unresolved crime (Midas Filmes, 2014).

audiences. The incomplete investigation into the life of the powerful, articulate and educated Yvone Kane through Rita's detective work offers a reflection on the inclusion of women in the writing of history that is relatively familiar and thus comfortable for audiences. The stalled investigation into the anonymous and all but mute Niazoai girls' rape is, however, far more troubling. If Cardoso's cinema of the interstitial, the incomplete or the in-between is suggestive for feminist cinema, it is particularly impressive as it also creates space for us to contrast the powerful, articulate, educated women – journalists, doctors, politicians – with powerless, inarticulate and uneducated ones – the raped girls.

Women's cinema, world cinema

It is helpful, at this point, to return to Martel in order to assess Cardoso's success in occupying the fragile in-between space that is part of 'women's cinema' and 'world cinema', which White identifies in her book title. In what has now become known as her 'Salta trilogy' – her first three films set in her native north-west Argentina – Martel was insistent on this local space, even as the finance and distribution of the films were transnational. As Paul Julian Smith had it, writing in 2013,

> If Martel appeals, necessarily, to transnational systems of distribution, she clearly rejects the parallel trend of the deterritorialization of cultural production through her continued commitment to everyday life in the regional Salta, however filtered and defamiliarized that life may be through art-film aesthetics.[29]

Her latest feature, after a near ten-year pause due in part to illness, *Zama* (2017), saw a break with this local focus, as well as offering other Martel firsts: a literary adaptation, a period setting and a male protagonist. So successfully has Martel strategically built her female auteurism, *Zama*'s success demonstrated that she was able to shift time, space and gender while maintaining her recognizable off-centre directorial signature.

In *Yvone Kane*, her second fiction film, Cardoso ran a higher risk when deterritorializing her address in order to appeal to a world audience. Her filmography reveals that she has thus far followed a trajectory of increasing deterritorialization.[30] Her first documentaries, *Natal 71* (*Christmas 71*, 2000) and *Kuxa Kanema: O Nascimento do Cinema* (*Kuxa Kanema: The Birth of Cinema*, 2003), were specifically about post-independence Mozambique, a country in which the director lived from the ages of three to twelve (see also Estela Vieira in this volume). Her first feature film, meanwhile, *The Murmuring Coast*, was at once distanced in time, like Lídia Jorge's novel of 1988 on which it is based, unfolding in a colonial 1960s at once idyllic and inimical, but also specific to the place of a named country, Mozambique, and recognizable city, Beira. In *Yvone Kane*, however, Cardoso chooses a different tact. While the shoot also took place in Mozambique, the country remains unnamed, and the director avoids recognizable spaces, choosing instead generic ones, whose potential recognisability is frustrated by withholding establishing shots. We therefore see a graveyard, Sara's large house, an airport, an abandoned swamp-like swimming pool (another nod to Martel), an orphanage, a museum and archive, a school, the coast, but only glimpse the city that contains these spaces in brief travelling shots through the windows of the car as Gabriel drives. Its former leader Yvone Kane is fabricated (a mix of characters Cardoso had met and interviewed in the past) and even the flag is an invented patchwork of the flags of other nations.[31]

In its final section the location of the film is further deracinated to an unspecified 'north' and an abandoned hotel undergoing repair. Here, the deterritorialization is particularly effective. A transient space for travellers by its very design, the unspecified location of *Yvone Kane*'s hotel allows it furthermore to signify the modern and contemporary history of the continent. A leisure space under European colonialism (with Batarda's residency in the hotel as Rita recalling her earlier role as Evita, guest of the Stella Maris during the 1960s in *The Murmuring Coast*), we learn that the hotel became a detention centre during independence, with its swimming pool used for the torture and murder of dissidents. In her creation of this space Cardoso was inspired by a photograph of an abandoned swimming pool and hotel by French photographer Sophie Ristelhueber, specialist in the portrayal of the aftermath of war.[32] In the present, Cardoso's hotel and pool, like Ristelhueber's, are spaces abandoned as ruins. In the film, however, these spaces are undergoing repair by their new South African owners. While South African business investment in Mozambique characterizes the contemporary era, the new owners' entrapment in the hotel with the spirits of the past perhaps indicates a kind of punishment in the present for South Africa's radical destabilization of its African neighbours post-independence in the past.[33]

Further formal characteristics may have had mixed success, however, in underscoring this unspecified transnational address. Cardoso has revealed in interview that in order to secure co-production with Brazil, she appealed to the well-known Brazilian actress that plays Sara, Irene Ravache.[34] Natália Pinazza explains that 'Cardoso considered that Ravache's attempt to reproduce a European Portuguese accent made the character's accent unidentifiable, which contributed to the filmmaker's aim to deterritorialize the subject matter'.[35] While this 'unidentifiability' of accent effectively matches the character's in-betweenness, it may have contributed to a lack of connection between the character and Portuguese-speaking audiences.[36] Such are the risks to which directors who occupy the fragile in-between space of female-authored world cinema are exposed: what on the one hand may be appreciated as a suggestive in-betweenness may on the other be perceived as awkward deracination.

While matters of accent and language might have only concerned native Portuguese-speaking audiences, outside Lusophone territories viewing figures were also low. Portuguese and Luso-African audiences might have picked up on the links between the fictional figure Yvone Kane and Mozambique's Josina Machel and Angola's Sita Valles. International ones, however, seem to have failed to connect, with little context to guide them other than the transnationally legible iconography of that most famous of world revolutionaries, Che Guevara, which we see daubed on the wall of an abandoned outbuilding (see Figure 9.6).[37]

Cardoso's use of water imagery and the swimming pool suggests a further explanation for this disconnect. If we return to Martel, we see a director who, in the first two films of the Salta trilogy, made the narrative and aesthetic

Figure 9.6 The portrayal of Yvone Kane (Mina Andala) recalls the transnational iconography of Che Guevara (Midas Filmes, 2014).

uncontainability of the swimming pool – supposedly a container of water of course – an auteurist calling card.³⁸ If swimming pools are man's containing, or taming, of nature for swimming, in Martel's work, far from nature controlled, the images and sounds of constantly shifting liquid convey the uncertain and unruly questions of the film's narratives. In *The Swamp*, the rancid, swamp-like, abandoned swimming pool conveys family and societal breakdown, whereas the hotel pool of *The Holy Girl* underscores the uncontainability of the erotic awakening of adolescent girlhood. In the final scene of the 2004 film, holy girls Amalia and José swim in and out of sight in a shot of the pool that Sophie Mayer analyses thus:

> Framed eccentrically on a diagonal and from a canted angle [it] is not commensurate with the screen, nor is the camera ever submerged. Far from providing either surface gloss or visual depth, the pool remains opaque, impenetrable and polyvalent.³⁹

I would adjust this brilliant analysis slightly to suggest that, just as the shot fails to contain the pool, so the Salta society depicted fails to contain adolescent girlhood. Turning to Cardoso's *Yvone Kane*, given its deterritorialized address, narrative focus on incomplete journeys and aesthetic emphasis on the interstitial, we might expect a similar deployment of water imagery and the swimming pool as resistant to specificity. The argument might perhaps be made in connection with the opening image of the fast-flowing water of Rita's nightmare, which could convey the way her daughter Clara stands between life and death. Or perhaps it could be made in connection with the abandoned swimming pool of the hotel-under-repair as a symbol of this recently independent nation's in-between position, moving from a colonial past to a post-colonial future.

On closer examination, however, in *Yvone Kane* the use of water seems more specific, unlike Martel's use of the wide frame, which successfully holds in tension multiple interpretative possibilities as part of an aesthetics of the in-between. The fast-flowing water of the opening nightmare specifically signals the dangerous current that drowns Clara. The abandoned pool of Sara's house breeds mosquitoes carrying malaria. Thus, both contained water – the abandoned pool – and uncontained water – the current – convey death. For this reason the South African hoteliers' son will not swim: the water represents too much of a drowning risk.

Likewise the swimming pool of the abandoned hotel under renovation is not a fluid trope, but a specific one. A former leisure space, it became a site of torture and assassination, and is today, as the hotelier tells Rita in English, haunted by 'tormented spirits', who are 'looking for peace', a description that also applies to the living hotel guests: the mourning mother Rita, trapped by her loss, and the unnamed paraplegic man, trapped by his body. In a particularly effective sequence, Cardoso restages the torture and assassination of the past when Rita witnesses a group of drunken young male tourists smashing bottles in the empty swimming pool for laughs at dusk. Given the shadowy evening setting, Rita's lonely fearfulness and the men's unruly behaviour, we necessarily make the chilling association. The smashing and breaking of beer bottles in the present stand for the smashing and breaking of human bodies in the past. The banality of drunken male raucousness makes this acoustic association to the past all the more unsettling, recalling Hannah Arendt's 'banality of evil'.[40] When the young male tourists leave in the morning we see their boat is marked 'FAR-Q', bringing to mind a connection to further violent forces, the Colombian armed revolutionary group FARC. Thus, while Martel's images of water remain fluid, even when she locates them in the specific locale of Argentina's Salta, Cardoso's images set into specificity, even when she locates them in an insistently unspecific African location.

Falling in-between

As directors of 'women's cinema, world cinema', both Martel and Cardoso face multiple challenges to raise finance for their films, secure distribution and reach audiences. Born just three years apart in 1966 and 1963 respectively, these gifted filmmakers share similar interests in feminism and the post-colonial, and adopt comparable art-film aesthetics. Yet Martel has been highly successful, while Cardoso has struggled to raise finance and reach audiences.

We could of course attribute this to the prevalence of Spanish and Spanish-speaking markets over Portuguese ones, especially the North American Hispanic audience. We could attribute it to Martel's more secure beginning as part of the Argentine New Cinema of the 1990s, compared to Cardoso's hesitant context of 'small nations' cinema Portugal. We could also note Martel's powerful backing by the Cannes Film Festival, and the Spanish Almodóvar brothers' production company El Deseo from *The Holy Girl* onwards, a team of powerful producers without peer in the Portuguese industry to date.

As well as examining their similarities, this chapter has aimed to draw out differences in their modes of address, in connection with both the category women's cinema and the category world cinema. As women's cinema, Martel's feminism is I suggest lightened by an ambiguity or fluidity that critics like Catherine Grant have managed partially to pin down by analysing the decentring and undercutting that ripple under Martel's narratives as characteristics of queer cinema.[41] While Cardoso introduces a lesbian character in *Yvone Kane*, I suggest that this is part of her feminist process of giving a voice to those previously silenced, rather than her effecting a queering of her own narrative. Similarly, ambiguity and fluidity ripple under Martel's transnational film aesthetics as part of world cinema. If this aesthetic approach occasionally fails to connect with audiences (infamously, *La mujer sin cabeza* (*The Headless Woman*, 2008) was booed at Cannes), she has nonetheless remained steadfast in her approach, succeeding overall in using these ambiguous aesthetics strategically as her auteurist signature. A measure of the effectiveness of her strategy is the continued success of this aesthetic approach, even as she ventured for the first time beyond the local subjects and settings of the Salta trilogy to the colonial Paraguay of *Zama*.

Cardoso strikes a tricky balance in *Yvone Kane*. The film is named after a fictional revolutionary figure, it unfolds in an unnamed nation, and the attempt by Brazilian actress Ravanche to reproduce a European Portuguese accent for the key character Sara deterritorializes the narrative further. To explore the urgent feminist and post-colonial questions raised by the four stalled narrative journeys – into Yvone's past, into Rita's grieving, into Sara's identity and place, and into the orphan girls' rape – Cardoso for the most part deploys an effective aesthetics of the interstitial. The use of the widescreen is particularly successful in conveying this stalling and lack of resolution, as are the doubled window images (where we see the layered reflections of Rita by turns with João, Alex and Sara), the shots in the half-light of dusk, and the repeated images of the drowsy Rita suspended between sleep and wakefulness.

Occasionally, though, one senses that the urgency of the trauma and crimes addressed resists this fluid, interstitial address, which Martel proves can be so successful with transnational audiences. Unlike the Argentine director, Cardoso's water imagery specifies the unspecific, freezes the fluid. The flowing current of the opening nightmare is the killer of the little girl Clara. The swimming pool is not a fluid metaphor: it is a former site of torture, which must be buried by filling with sand. We do not see this, but bathing cannot wash away the trauma of rape for the orphan girls. Perhaps this mixed address – at times evocatively in-between, at times angrily specific – explains in part why *Yvone Kane* did not connect extensively with audiences. At times suggestively and successfully falling in-between women's cinema and world cinema, it also, at times, falls away from both.[42]

Notes

1. The film was shot in Mozambique.
2. Sally Faulkner and Mariana Liz, 'Portuguese Film: Colony, Postcolony, Memory – Q&A with Margarida Cardoso', 14 January 2016, available at https://www.youtube.com/watch?v=xO8pFfoDqwA (accessed 16 March 2019).
3. Patricia White, *Women's Cinema, World Cinema: Projecting Contemporary Feminisms* (Durham: Duke University Press, 2015).
4. Ibid., 2–3.
5. Translation in Thomas Elsaesser, 'Cinephilia or the Uses of Disenchantment', in *Cinephilia: Movies, Love and Memory*, eds Marijke de Valck and Malte Hagener (Amsterdam: Amsterdam University Press, 2005), 28.
6. Ibid., 30–1.
7. Marvin D'Lugo, 'Auteurism and Spain', in *A Companion to Spanish Cinema*, eds Jo Labanyi and Tatjana Pavlović (Malden, Oxford, Chichester: Wiley-Blackwell, 2013), 115.
8. Paulo Cunha, 'O novo cinema português. Políticas públicas y modos de produção (1949–80)', (PhD diss., University of Coimbra, 2014), 259–60.
9. On the Spanish case, see D'Lugo, 'Auteurism', 115.
10. Geneviève Sellier, *La nouvelle vague, un cinéma au masculin singulier* (Paris: CNRS, 2005).
11. Antonio Lázaro Reboll, Steven Marsh, Susan Martin-Márquez and Santos Zunzunegui, 'Strategic Auteurism', in Labanyi and Pavlović, *Companion to Spanish Cinema*, 152–90.
12. Catherine Grant, 'www.auteur.com?' *Screen* 41, no. 1 (2000), 102.
13. Elsaesser, 'Cinephilia', 36–8.
14. I take the term 'media-savvy', a translation of the Spanish 'mediático', from Núria Triana-Toribio, 'Auteurism and Commerce in Contemporary Spanish Cinema: *directores mediáticos*', *Screen*, 49, no. 3 (2008): 259–76. For a discussion of Gomes's self-presentation through interviews, see Sally Faulkner, 'Cinephilia and the Unrepresentable in Miguel Gomes's *Tabu* (2012)', *Bulletin of Spanish Studies* 92, no. 3 (2015), 352–3.
15. 'Feminine Plural' is part of the proposed title of a planned volume edited by Claire Williams and Maria-José Blanco: *Feminine Plural: Women in Transition in the Luso-Hispanic World*.
16. Mariana Liz, ed., *Portugal's Global Cinema: Industry, History and Culture* (London: I.B. Tauris, 2018).
17. Horacio Muñoz Fernández and Iván Villarmea Álvarez, 'Aesthetic Tendencies in Contemporary Portuguese Cinema', *Cinema Comparat/ive Cinema* 6 (2015): 39–45.

18 Mariana Liz, 'Introduction: Framing the Global Appeal of Contemporary Portuguese Cinema', in *Portugal's Global Cinema*, 2.
19 Ibid., 3.
20 White, *Women's Cinema, World Cinema*, 45.
21 Noting common formal traits in a cinema that supposedly stands apart from genre film is a move made by David Bordwell in his 1979 article 'Art Cinema as Mode of Practice', *Film Criticism*, 79, no. 4, 1 (1979): 56–64. Given that art film tends to circulate transnationally, work on the aesthetics of art cinema has now shifted to including those of world cinema, as Rosalind Galt and Karl Schoonover indicate in the title of their 2010 volume *Global Art Cinema: New Theories and Histories* (Oxford: Oxford University Press, 2010). Critics have stressed the tendency of these films to adopt a particular heightened realism (thus breaking Hollywood's Institutional Mode of Representation) that derives from post-war Italian neorealism, hence the description 'neo-neorealism' which Rosalind Galt, for example, uses in *Pretty: Film and the Decorative Image* (New York: Columbia University Press, 2011), 15; or a 'Realism of the Senses', which I take from Tiago de Luca, 'Realism of the Senses: A Tendency in Contemporary World Cinema', in *Theorizing World Cinema*, eds Lúcia Nagib, Chris Perriam and Rajinder Dudrah (London: I.B. Tauris, 2013), 183–226.
22 Katy Stewart, 'Establishing the Female Gaze: Narrative Subversion in Lucrecia Martel's *La niña santa* (2004) and *La ciénaga* (2001)', *Tesserae: Journal of Iberian and Latin American Studies* 21, no. 3 (2015): 205–19.
23 Ibid., 206.
24 Mette Hjort and Duncan Petrie (eds), *The Cinema of Small Nations* (Edinburgh: Edinburgh University Press, 2007); Liz, 'Introduction', 4–9.
25 The Faulkner and Liz 2016 interview followed a public screening of *Yvone Kane* at the Institute of Advanced Studies, Senate House, University of London. Cardoso also generously gave a further promotional interview at the 'Mostra: Realizadoras Portuguesas' screening of the film at the University of Lisbon in January 2018, organized by the editors as part of this book project.
26 Faulkner and Liz, 'Portuguese Film'.
27 Ibid.
28 Emma Wilson traced the transnational legibility of the missing child in her *Cinema's Missing Children* (London: Wallflower, 2003).
29 Paul Julian Smith, 'Transnational Co-productions and Female Filmmakers: The Cases of Lucrecia Martel and Isabel Coixet', in *Hispanic and Lusophone Women Filmmakers: Theory, Practice and Difference*, eds Parvati Nair and Julián Daniel Gutiérrez-Albilla (Manchester: Manchester University Press, 2013), 16.
30 Her current plans for a biopic of Angolan revolutionary Sita Valles suggest a possible return to the local and specific.

31 Faulkner and Liz, 'Portuguese Film'.
32 Cardoso, who herself studied photography, revealed in interview (Faulkner and Liz, 'Portuguese Film') that during the shoot of the 2004 film *The Murmuring Coast* she had Ristelhueber's photograph of an abandoned swimming pool and hotel clipped to her notes. She spoke passionately of the inspiration of Ristelhueber for her work, especially the photographer's interest in trauma and its aftermath. The photograph can be found on the site of the page where Ristelhueber exhibited her work in 2005: http://www.transphotographiques.com/2005/officiel/ristelhueber-uk.php3 (accessed 17 March 2019).
33 Lúcia Nagib has noted the significance of the fact that the South Africans are repairing the colonial hotel for the independent nation in an unpublished comment made at the symposium 'Portuguese Film: Colony, Postcolony, Memory', organized by Faulkner and Liz, January 2016.
34 Faulkner and Liz, 'Portuguese Film'.
35 Natália Pinazza, 'Luso-Brazilian Co-productions: Rescue and Expansion', in Liz, *Portugal's Global Cinema*, 252.
36 The Lumière database records just 2,849 admissions overall. By way of comparison, we may note that Cardoso's 2004 *The Murmuring Coast* secured some 12,639 admissions, while Miguel Gomes's *Tabu* (2012), like *Yvone Kane* also set in an unnamed Africa, secured 261,143. See http://lumiere.obs.coe.int/web/search/index.php (accessed 17 February 2019).
37 Audiences might also be forgiven for failing to connect with the clever literary play of Yvone Kane's name. Etymologically, Yvonne derives from 'Yew', the type of wood from which bows were made, thus the name means archer or warrior. Kane, meanwhile, as well as bringing to mind one of cinema history's most famous investigative films, *Citizen Kane* (Orson Welles, 1941), recalls the biblical fraternal conflict of Cain and Abel.
38 Sophie Mayer, '*Gutta cavat lapidem*: The Sonorous Politics of Lucrecia Martel's Swimming Pools', *The Cinema of the Swimming Pool*, eds Christopher Brown and Pam Hirsch (Oxford: Peter Lang, 2014), 191–202.
39 Ibid., 151.
40 Hannah Arendt, *Eichmann in Jerusalem: A Report on the Banality of Evil* (New York: Viking Press, 1963).
41 'Paranoid Hermeneutics as Queer Cinematic Vernacular', Video Essay (2017) https://vimeo.com/channels/222321/42029962 and https://lucreciamartel.blogspot.com/ (accessed 17 February 2019).
42 I would like to offer my sincere thanks to Margarida Cardoso for taking the time to answer follow-up questions from our interviews.

10

Portugal's year zero:
Emergent women directors, 2013–17

Filipa Rosário

Two years after the end of the Portuguese financial crisis (2010–14), Joana Pimenta, Salomé Lamas, Cláudia Varejão and Leonor Teles all directed films that won international critical acclaim.[1] Their films premiered at prestigious film festivals and have subsequently been screened in art-house cinemas and film societies, as well as on television channels and VOD platforms around the world. The films that achieved this are as follows: *Um Campo de Aviação* (*An Aviation Field*; Joana Pimenta, 2016), *Eldorado XXI* (Salomé Lamas, 2016), *Ama-San* (Cláudia Varejão, 2016) and *Balada de um Batráquio* (*Batrachian's Ballad*; Leonor Teles, 2016).[2]

The transnational dimension of these films is not limited to their distribution and critical reception. The individual career trajectories of the filmmakers, the production frameworks of their films and the political interrogations of land and culture that shape their geopoetic outlook on the locations they film, all reflect a transversal cosmopolitanism in contemporary film practice in Portugal. As Paolo Moretti pointed out in 2018, 'One of the common elements of this recent phase in Portuguese film history, is the modernity of the filmmakers' relationship with their nationality, which translates into a natural proximity with the international scene, no matter the "size" of the project.'[3] The international success of these works, which are still circulating in non-commercial networks, attests to their global critical recognition. The radical approaches of these directors to aesthetics and production tend, in fact, to disregard geographical borders. The worlds they document are globalized.

The four films analysed in this chapter premiered after what was known as the 'year zero' of Portuguese cinema.[4] Portugal's Institute of Cinema and Audiovisual (ICA) is a public institution that supports, represents and distributes national cinema. Its budget comes principally from an advertising charge levied from free-to-air television (in 2018, this was 57 per cent) and another service charge from pay-tv (in 2018 this was 38 per cent)[5]. In 2012, ICA did not open a call for funding for artistic projects, film production or distribution. The suspension of this state funding source, on which the vast majority of national cinematographic production depends, was related to the financial crisis that Portugal, as well as Europe in general, had been facing since 2008 following the collapse of the Icelandic banking industry and the Euro-zone debt crisis. Portuguese financial institutions, along with others in the peripheral countries of the EU, such as Italy, Ireland, Greece and Spain, collapsed, in turn giving rise to government debt that would later be renegotiated and paid off with the assistance of other countries. On 17 May 2011, Portugal ratified a Memorandum of Understanding (the Economic Adjustment Programme for Portugal) with the European Commission, the European Central Bank and the International Monetary Fund (from then on identified as 'the Troika') that lasted until 17 May 2014. This period became popularly known as 'the Troika years'. The austerity measures implemented in Portugal during the Troika years led to a tax increase and to very high unemployment, as well as to the bankruptcy of companies and businesses, and a sharp fall in purchasing power among the population more generally.

The stalling of state support for cinema in 2012 was the result of a financially fragile and politically volatile decade in Portugal. In 2002, a centre-right government succeeded a centre-left one, but the centre-left Socialist Party suddenly came back into power after early elections in 2005. A good example of how instability affected cinema was the foundation in 2006 (Decree-Law no. 227/2006) of the *Fundo de Investimento para o Cinema e Audiovisual* (FICA – the Investment Fund for Cinema and Audiovisual Media), which was dedicated to cinematographic, audiovisual and multimedia production and which only lasted until 2009. The fund was managed by a private bank, initially BES (Banco Espírito Santo), and later BANIF (Banco Internacional do Funchal). Three free-to-view Portuguese television channels (RTP, SIC and TVI) were also involved in it, along with a number of other audiovisual partners. The FICA only commenced its activities in 2007, providing funding for projects according to their projected financial revenues, but three years later its continued operation had become uncertain due to the loss of its investment capacity. In 2014, it was dissolved and its accounts were liquidated.

On 12 March 2010, a significant number of film directors and producers joined forces to publish what became known as the 'Manifesto for Portuguese

Cinema' in a Portuguese newspaper.[6] Their objective was to make public their extreme dissatisfaction and concern about the lack of state funding for cinema, which had fallen by 30 per cent over the previous decade. This manifesto was signed by the directors Manoel de Oliveira, Fernando Lopes, Paulo Rocha, João Botelho, Pedro Costa, João Canijo, Teresa Villaverde, Margarida Cardoso, Catarina Alves Costa and João Salaviza, and by the producers Maria João Mayer (Filmes do Tejo), Abel Ribeiro Chaves (OPTEC), Alexandre Oliveira (Ar de Filmes), Joana Ferreira (C.R.I.M.), João Figueiras (Black Maria), João Matos (Terratreme), João Trabulo (Periferia Filmes) and Pedro Borges (Midas Filmes). The manifesto highlights the 'creative vitality' and 'significant international distribution'[7] of Portuguese films, and it speaks out against the FICA, criticizing it as 'a fake exercise which basically legitimized the opportunism of specific individuals'.[8]

The 2000s thus marked a period of rather vague, undefined policies on cinema and audiovisual media.[9] Over the last twenty years, Portuguese cinema – which has always been, and continues to be, defined by conditions of struggle, survival and resistance[10] – has become more receptive to short film genres, alongside commercial cinema characterized by its television aesthetics and narrative simplicity. New production companies emerged that were able to capitalize on various forms of state support. Digital cinema became more prominent, effectively democratizing filmmaking because of its low production costs.[11] The plots and storylines of Portuguese cinema in the 1990s tended towards the inclusion of marginal and disadvantaged characters and life histories. As Tiago Baptista suggests:

> These were the years when the main characters in Portuguese films were young outcasts, teenage mothers or illegal immigrants while the scripts of these films dealt directly with issues such as poverty, illness, unemployment, domestic violence, human trafficking or drug addiction.[12]

The openness that Portuguese filmmakers had demonstrated in the 1990s, with their attempts to use cinema to integrate these forms of 'Otherness' into their world view, was refracted by new structures and new means of production, communicated through narrative forms that were also correspondingly 'new'. Indeed, new 'zero' moments have occurred, and the 'short film generation'[13] is continuing to make disruptive forms of 'cinema committed to experiencing new places and the people who inhabit them, and demonstrating that a new wave of youth is seeking to forge its own identity'.[14]

The sections that follow examine how four documentaries, two full-length and two short films, namely *An Aviation Field*, *Eldorado XXI*, *Ama-San* and *Batrachian's Ballad*, embody diverse, cosmopolitan ways of exploring the world in the context of the financial crisis. These works were launched and became established internationally through the film festival circuit. All of them investigate contemporaneity and the status quo through the power relations between characters and spaces, and they have all been made by directors who are conscious of their own locatedness in the world around them. In this sense, these works transmit very particular visions of the world, embodying the zeitgeist as the same time as they remain conscious of the history of humanity. The four films studied in this chapter focus on the ways in which a universalized capitalist society affects the dynamic relations between culture(s) and genre(s), addressing important contemporary issues for the planet and exposing the worst of human existence, past and present. With this in mind, all of these works contribute to the memory archive of human existence, as well as complicating any attempt to project the future as a world organized around principles of universal connection.

An Aviation Field by Joana Pimenta (b. 1986)

An Aviation Field is an experimental short film; it is a co-production by the Film Study Centre, the Sensory Ethnography Lab (both at Harvard University) and the Portuguese producer Terratreme Filmes, which was created in 2008 by Tiago Hespanha, Luísa Homem, João Matos, Susana Nobre, Leonor Noivo and Pedro Pinho. The Terratreme Filmes collective is a group of directors united by the need for production conditions that can respond to the specificity of each individual project by incorporating the director's artistic vision into the production logic of the film. Over the last ten years, Terratreme Filmes has become one of the largest national film production companies, well represented at major international film festivals and able to attract significant funding, especially for co-productions.

An Aviation Field is a post-apocalyptic fable about marginalized groups. It draws together images of the volcano on Fogo Island, in Cape Verde, and Brasília, the capital city of Brazil. The African archipelago of Cape Verde was one of the most important sites for the trading of enslaved people by the Portuguese from the fifteenth century onwards. Brasília is, in architectural terms, a modernist city that was specifically designed and built in the 1950s to become Brazil's national capital. Brazil, of course, was colonized by Portugal in the sixteenth century, and the Portuguese effectively ruled the territory for over 300 years.

The film's long takes of the volcano disclose a sense of scale, texture, primordial matter and dust, whirled up by two passing figures whose outlines are never quite defined. These are almost abstract shots, slow and at times completely static. Filming at a distance, from both inside and outside the volcanic crater, Pimenta captures the arid, bone-dry, almost lunar geology of the former Portuguese colony. The pace is unhurried, rather in the manner of an observational documentary. In contrast to these shots, there are scenes in the aseptically white, architectonically modelled city of Brasília. These latter scenes take place inside a building with windows, hallways, doors – passages that lead nowhere. The sound of a Brazilian radio station serves to identify the space, and the gaze identified with the 'camera character' is imprisoned in the architecture. The camera is not registering either external space or the city which is totally cut off from it.

The soundscapes of the film, which echo Jana Winderen, combine local ambient sounds with geological audio recordings and recordings from space, provided by the National Oceanic and Atmospheric Agency and NASA, the American national space agency. These give a simultaneously local and global feel to the spaces recorded in the film, as if the planet were being viewed from a distance. *An Aviation Field* is the story of a landscape that is visually expanded by the use of montage to alternate between real spaces that are distant from each other, in such a way that it plays with geography, geology, world history and the history of civilization. The key connection between the primal force of raw nature, embodied by the extinct volcano, and the futuristic aridity that has sculpted and moulded the segregating city of Brasília is provided only at the end of the film by the director herself, whose voiceover narration is heard over a blank screen, making the narrative apparatus of the film even more sensory, indeed almost phenomenological.

The production of *An Aviation Field* echoes Joana Pimenta's own professional trajectory. After she graduated from the Universidade Nova in Lisbon, Portugal, she obtained her PhD in Film and Visual Studies from Harvard University in 2017. While she was at Harvard, she attended a Sensory Ethnography Lab class, taught by the anthropologist and filmmaker Lucien Castaing-Taylor. Pimenta's first short film, *As Figuras Gravadas na Faca com a Seiva das Bananeiras* (*The Figures Carved into the Knife by the Sap of the Banana Trees*, 2014), was the result of an experiment in the Sensory Ethnography Lab. Shot on the Island of Madeira and in the former Portuguese colony of Mozambique, the film reconstructs a colonial memory from which people are absent.

In a statement made in September 2018, Pimenta claimed that she was deeply influenced by the idea of spatial awareness and the filming of space, incorporating random elements into the process, and structuring her film by simply allowing the land and buildings to reveal themselves to the camera. As Pimenta herself explains, the approach she adopted in *An Aviation Field* was substantially influenced by the English visual artist Tacita Dean, with whom Pimenta lived during an artistic residency at the Botín Foundation in Spain in 2013.

After she finished *The Figures Carved into the Knife by the Sap of the Banana Trees*, Pimenta travelled solo to Chã das Caldeiras, on Fogo Island, Cape Verde, financially supported by Sensory Ethnography Lab and Film Study Centre scholarships to devote more time to sound and image recording. In Argentina, Pimenta subsequently met Adirley Queirós, one of Brazil's most provocative contemporary filmmakers. Queirós works on recording the complexities of Brasília and its official history, with a particular focus on the dystopian social effects of its construction as a purpose-built national capital at the end of the 1950s. Queirós, who has won numerous awards for his low-budget political films, specializes in science fiction documentaries. Pimenta began collaborating with him in 2015, doing the photography for the film *Era Uma Vez Brasília* (*Once There Was Brasilia*, Adirley Queirós, 2017).

While she was doing the preparatory work for *Once There Was Brasilia*, Joana Pimenta became closely acquainted with the Brazilian capital, where she spent a week shooting solo. She has described the city as 'white, phallic, modernist'.[15] Following this experience, she returned to Harvard where she built and filmed the scale models for *An Aviation Field* (see Figure 10.1). She also conducted research in the sound archives of NASA and the National Oceanic and Atmospheric Agency, and that was when she realized what it was that she wanted to achieve with her own film, structuring it around her own ethnographic experience and adding some sophisticated touches of science fiction. It is because the science fiction genre can incorporate elements of strangeness that do not look out of place, that *An Aviation Field* feels simultaneously alien yet familiar. The editing process began in the United States, but the film was finished in Portugal, and the post-production and distribution were undertaken by Terratreme Filmes. In the two years after its release, the film was screened at over forty film festivals and galleries around the world, including Locarno, Toronto, New York, Rotterdam, Mar del Plata and IndieLisboa, as well as the Zinebi – Bilbao International Festival where it won the 2016 Grand Award.

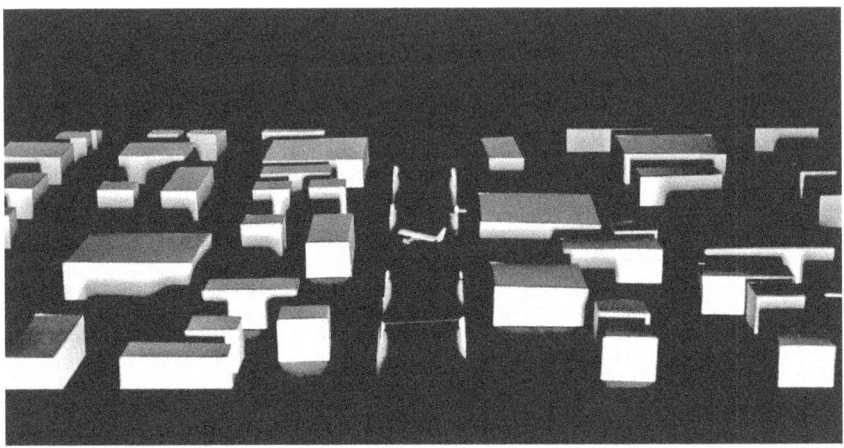

Figure 10.1 A city scale model in *An Aviation Field* (Joana Pimenta, 2016).

Academic experience shaped Joana Pimenta's work and perspective as well as influencing the conceptual and theoretical development of *An Aviation Field* and enabling her to secure financing for most of the film's budget. The cosmopolitanism of Pimenta's career trajectory as a film director resulted in a transnational production that reinforced her trans-genre approach, mixing experimentalism, ethnography and science fiction. Where Joana Pimenta used montage to construct her diegetic world in *An Aviation Field*, Salomé Lamas, as we will now discuss, seems rather to adapt her vision to fit the reality that she witnesses and portrays in *Eldorado XXI*.

Eldorado XXI by Salomé Lamas (b. 1987)

Eldorado XXI was co-produced by O Som e a Fúria (Portugal) and Shellac Sud (France) and partly funded by ICA. Lamas also secured the support of the Ministry for Foreign Affairs and International Development – Institut Français, EURIMAGES – Council of Europe, and the Provence-Alpes-Côte d'Azur Region in cooperation with the French National Centre for Cinema and Moving Image (Centre National du Cinéma et de l'Image Animée – CNC). O Som e a Fúria is a Portuguese production company headed by Luís Urbano and Sandro Aguilar that was set up in 1998. The company tends to produce films with a specific, select group of directors that includes Miguel Gomes, Sandro Aguilar, Manuel Mozos, Salomé Lamas and João Nicolau. Other well-known names, such as Manoel de Oliveira, Lucrecia Martel, Ira Sachs, Eugène Green and Alberto Seixas Santos also work, or have worked, with the company. Luís Urbano is the person in charge of management and production policy at O Som e a Fúria. He is closely, personally involved with all the films under development there, which is why they limit the number of projects they take on at any one time.

During the development phase of *Eldorado XXI*, Salomé Lamas was able to draw on various sources of support. She was awarded the project development prize at the 2013 FIDLab (the discussion and pitching forum for FIDMarseille – Marseille International Film Festival). Her project was also selected for the 2014 Berlinale Talents – Doc Station. During this period, Lamas was artist-in-residence for the Rockefeller Foundation–Bellagio Center, the MacDowell Colony, the Yaddo Community, the Bogliasco Foundation and the DAAD Berliner Künstlerprogramm.

Eldorado XXI takes a very distinctive view of the lives and work patterns of the inhabitants of La Rinconada y Cerro Lunar. La Rinconada is the highest settlement in the world, located in the Peruvian Andes, at 5,100 metres (16,700 foot) above sea level. Some of the world's poorest and most desperate people head there to dig for gold. Approximately 30,000 miners live in La Rinconada in extreme poverty. In the first half of the film, the workers' ceaseless movement up and down the mountain is captured and sustained by a static low-angle shot that is powerful and austere. At the same time, the audience hears statements from local residents about poverty, famine and unemployment alongside excerpts from a programme on La Rinconada's radio station, which introduces other tragic life stories. This incredibly long take, which lasts for about an hour, inserts the viewer into a hellish, never-ending landscape, establishing direct contact with its reality, and forcing the viewer to become conscious of these dehumanizing stories. Through the fact of its sheer persistence, the image created here evokes the history of all of human civilization with its tales of endurance, illusion, injustice, powerlessness and condemnation. In this respect, *Eldorado XXI* manages to remain local and contemporary while also conveying a sense of the timeless and the universal, even in the second half of the film depicting the social dynamics and iconographies which enliven this post-apocalyptic landscape in the form of elections, masked rituals, festivals, processions, planning meetings and women chatting (see Figure 10.2). The combined sound and photographic effects of the film convey a place at the world's end, which is somehow real, sublime and allegorical at the same time.

Figure 10.2 A religious ceremony in *Eldorado XXI* (O Som e A Fúria, Shellac Sud, 2016).

The idea of filming in La Rinconada first occurred to the director at Christmas in 2012, in the notorious 'year zero' of Portuguese cinema. According to Lamas's own recollections in October 2018, a lack of available funding led her to rethink her development and production plans for the project she was working on at the time.[16] In this context, a major turning point for her was O Som e a Fúria's decision to invest in that project, which was a low-budget documentary about a Portuguese colonial mercenary. The partnership was successful, and *Terra de Ninguém* (*No Man's Land*, 2012) premiered at the Berlinale with Shellac Sud expressing an interest in supporting Lamas's future work. Since then, O Som e a Fúria has produced all of the director's work to date, allowing Lamas to control the various stages of production and distribution for her films, which is how the company operates. Lamas's standing in the field of visual arts, as well as now in cinema, gives her the added advantage of having access to a wider network of venues interested in exhibiting her work.

When Lamas directed *Eldorado XXI*, she was already a well-known visual artist. *No Man's Land* had premiered commercially in Portugal, France and Spain, and she had shown various video installations and short films at galleries, museums and international film festivals. Lamas's work as an artist, underpinned by an undergraduate degree in Cinema and a Masters in Art, is consistently well defined thematically as well as being conceptually well developed, even if the final shape of the piece sometimes emerges only at the editing stage, when the key issues that she has transposed onto film, are finally integrated. Taken as a whole, her works signal a wider interest in the communicative potential of moving image-related media, a potential which is tested to the full by her own works in practice. On this topic, she has claimed, 'I'm always seeking the limits of the forms themselves, whether of non-fiction cinema or of presentation, showing the same work in different contexts.'[17] An example of this would be the screening of *No Man's Land* as a video installation at the Serralves Foundation in Portugal.

Lamas's obsession with limit-spaces and marginal characters, with angels and demons as well as territories that resist easy framing, has led her to travel extensively, as she notes in the above quotation. Lawrence Weschler observes that she is

> still in her twenties though already the veteran of film projects that range from the Azores to the Netherlands to Moldovan Transnistria, focusing on everything from the confessions of former French Foreign legionaries and Portuguese colonial mercenaries to the midnight exertions of North Sea fishermen and the borderland perambulations of Post-Soviet nowhere men.[18]

This frantic, sometimes ethnographic, interest in the heterotopias of the world and its inhabitants, along with her own high levels of productivity and artistic virtuosity, have made Lamas an inveterate traveller. This in turn has brought a transnational, transcultural and cosmopolitan dimension to her creative vision. *Eldorado XXI* premiered at the Berlinale and has since been screened in over fifty film theatres, film clubs, international festivals, galleries and museums. Her work is available on the VOD MUBI platform, and according to a September 2018 statement by Fabianne Martinot, who is in charge of festivals and sales at O Som e a Fúria, *Eldorado XXI* has the company's second highest viewing figures.[19]

Viewed from a slightly different angle, *Eldorado XXI* also deepens and expands the ethnographic impulse that lies at the core of *An Aviation Field*. Both films may be understood as creative studies in the power of sound and image. Aside from the fact that Lamas and Pimenta have both produced critical, at times, militant work engaging with different landscapes, times and communities, they also share an active commitment to exploring the expressive capacities of the medium itself. Cláudia Varejão's film, *Ama-San*, on the other hand, is focused on paying tribute to a positive universe grounded in the resilience of women.

Ama-San by Cláudia Varejão (b. 1980)

Ama-San was funded by ICA and was produced by Terratreme Filmes (the same production company that worked on *An Aviation Field*) along with Swiss Mira

Film, and co-produced by the Japanese company Flying Pillow Films and SRF – Swiss Radio and Television. *Ama-San* is about the life and work of Japanese pearl divers who still practice the age-old, almost extinct, practice of diving without oxygen tanks for oysters, molluscs and abalones to sell (see Figure 10.3). In Japanese, *ama-san* literally means 'women of the sea'. The women's common everyday activities are shown in the film, as they cook, do laundry, go to the hairdresser, sing karaoke at a bar, bathe grandchildren, eat their dinner and watch television. The rest of their daily activities, however, relate to their work. We see the *amas* getting ready for the dive, fishing and talking among themselves, as we follow their rituals and routines.

The photography and sound effects, particularly in the scenes shot at sea, add a mythical dimension to the film, which is already intimated at the beginning by the words spoken off-screen, although the narrative resists the temptation to over-concentrate on the magical effects of being underwater. The divers (whose ages range from thirty-eight to eighty-three) are presented as human women who live everyday lives but are also simultaneously 'fish in female form' endowed with superhuman resilience. They fish every working day, for two hours in the morning and two in the afternoon, from March to September. Their dives reach depths of up to 20 metres in two minutes.

The universe of *Ama-San* is presented as a world inhabited almost exclusively by brave, independent women, whose lives are still nonetheless constrained by Japan's strictly patriarchal social hierarchy.[20] The division of their time

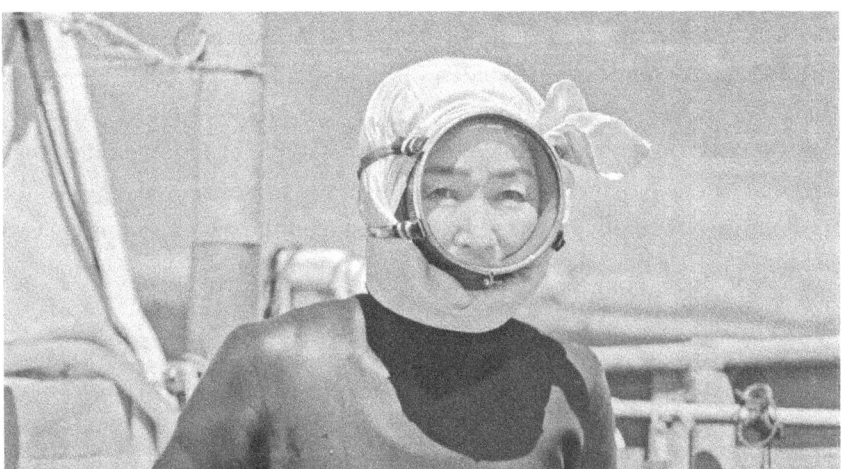

Figure 10.3 A diver in *Ama-San* (Cláudia Varejão, 2016).

between domesticity and work is what gives them a mythical aura.[21] They are shown taking responsibility for their families and household chores, in addition to their working lives, and they invest equally in both with a powerful sense of duty and no sign of self-congratulation. The film that results is focused on Varejão's fascination with these women and with their unique 2000-year-old fishing tradition. In a statement in November 2018, Varejão claims that 'the film is not ethnographic, it depicts an experience of encounter'.[22] Varejão's feminist approach to this film, which celebrates and mythologizes the divers, focuses on the age-old connection that binds Japanese women to the sea and to a primordial vision of nature, linking them to a distant, mythical time in the history of the world, a temporality that seems almost timeless, illustrated by the breathtakingly beautiful scenes filmed at the bottom of the sea.

Varejão studied cinema through the Creativity and Artistic Creation Programme at the Calouste Gulbenkian Foundation in partnership with the German Film und Fernsehakademie Berlin. She also studied at São Paulo's International Cinema Academy (Brazil), and she took a photography course at AR.CO in Lisbon. The advent of Portugal's 'year zero' for film funding forced Varejão to take a break from cinematography which coincided with a period of research on the *ama-san*. Before that, she had worked with Filmes do Tejo/Filmes do Tejo II to produce a documentary entitled *Falta-me* (*Wanting*, 2005) and the trilogy of short fiction films that preceded *Ama-San*: *Fim de Semana* (*Weekend*, 2007), *Um Dia Frio* (*Cold Day*, 2009) and *Luz da Manhã* (*Morning Light*, 2012).

Filmes do Tejo is the commonly used name for the Filmes do Tejo II (as it appears in ICA documentation) and Maria & Mayer, Lda companies. Set up twenty-one years ago by Maria João Mayer, Filmes do Tejo was responsible for various films that won prestigious international festival awards. The company's successive periods of bankruptcy since then have given way to new production, distribution and audiovisual screening projects with different names and a re-distribution of functions. The production company is now marketed simply under the name Filmes do Tejo, effectively consolidating and capitalizing on its existing productivity and prestige. The company now works primarily in advertising. When Filmes do Tejo got into debt and filed for bankruptcy in 2012, their collaboration with Varejão came to an end. Varejão's other projects which were filmed before and during *Ama-San* were commissions which had access to other sources of funding.[23]

Varejão's first trip to Japan was funded by a scholarship from the Fundação Oriente. The trip resulted in a photography exhibition and a self-published photobook about the *amas*' traditions. The trip also worked as a *repérage* for the film, which was still at an embryonic stage at the time. In 2012, Terratreme Filmes agreed to support the project. This was possible because Terratreme had, from its inception, avoided reliance on state funding. Consequently, it was not so heavily affected by the financial crisis, as João Matos noted in September 2018.[24] The film was shot in Japan in May 2014, with the support of ICA. In addition to the technical crew and the local production crew, Varejão was joined by Aya Koretzky and Takashi Sugimoto. Koretzky is a film director of Japanese descent who worked on *Ama-San* as translator and assistant to the director, and Sugimoto, who is a Japanese photographer and film director, was responsible for sound.[25] The financial support from the Swiss production company Mira Film and from the SRF public television channel came about as the result of a successful pitch at the 2015 Swiss festival, Visions du Réel. The funding still fell short however, so Terratreme Filmes ended up investing about 30,000 euros in the film. Their investment was fully recouped in October 2018 with the revenues from the film's commercial distribution and sales to television. To date, *Ama-San* has been selected for seventy international festivals and has won awards at fourteen of them.

In the context of the present analysis, *Ama-San*'s celebration of gender contrasts with the mood of outrage fuelling Lamas's documentary. Where *Ama-San* spins a luminous world of myth, *Eldorado XXI* is sombre, dark and indignant. *An Aviation Field* is even more different from *Ama-San*, partly on account of its sophisticated plot structure, but also because its characters are physically absent, their presence implied only through the film's soundtrack and POV shots. Nevertheless, all three films do possess clear political agendas. In this respect, our fourth film, Leonor Teles's *Batrachian's Ballad*, contributes not only to the aesthetic heterogeneity of this body of work but also to the common ethical positioning that they share.

Batrachian's Ballad by Leonor Teles (b. 1992)

Batrachian's Ballad was funded by the Calouste Gulbenkian Foundation Programme for Portuguese Language and Film, and by ICA, and produced by Uma Pedra no Sapato. The film is about empowering (one member of) the Roma community, who are targeted by racism and cultural discrimination in Portugal. The film is centred on a personal, political (in this case, *punk*) act of resistance to segregation and xenophobia, undertaken by the director herself, who is the daughter of a Roma father. While the audience watches a sequence of home movies showing family parties being thrown by a Roma community, the narrator tells a fable in voice-off about the dawn of time, which is then more fully illustrated with images of a garden and toads sitting by a pond. In this fable, the toad is marginalized and maltreated so he takes his posthumous revenge by spreading poison in the world, forcing the flowers to remain rooted in the earth and permanently imprisoning the fish in their element, effectively altering the order of the world forever. We then encounter two young people – the film director and her sound assistant – who are seen breaking ceramic toads in shop windows and on shop counters. A little-known social custom is explained by a voiceover: Portuguese shopkeepers have traditionally placed toads where passers-by can see them in order to ward off the Roma who have a superstitious fear of frogs and toads (see Figure 10.4).

Batrachian's Ballad puts this practice on record and speaks out against it, effectively intervening in historical reality through a series of episodes which register real and symbolic protest, and also provide some comic relief. Taking advantage of the unpredictability and immediacy entailed in stealing and smashing the grinning toads, Teles exposes racial prejudice and avenges her own community, one shop at a time. The film ends as it began, with amateur images of a family party at which a little girl named Leonor (the director herself) hears her now dead father calling her name. Teles's film is both a politically engaged

Figure 10.4 Toads in *Batrachian's Ballad* (Leonor Teles, 2016).

documentary and a powerfully emotional melodrama in the way that it appeals to both collective and individual memory.

This radical demand for justice combined with narrative economy and innovation, and a clear sense of humour in the way it deals with veiled xenophobia, made *Batrachian's Ballad* a rare piece of cinema which struck a chord with international audiences. The film is Teles's second short. Her first short film, *Rhoma Acans* (2013), was made as a course assignment at the Lisbon Film School, and focuses on the lives of young teenagers in the Roma community of Casal dos Estanques, Vialonga, Portugal. The film earned a special mention at the 2013 IndieLisboa, Lisbon's Film Festival of Independent Cinema, and the money from the award allowed Teles to start filming *Batrachian's Ballad*. She then went on to become, at the age of twenty-four, the youngest filmmaker to win a Golden Bear at the Berlin Film Festival, in 2016. Winning this award at one of the most prestigious film festivals in the world boosted the film's popularity. *Batrachian's Ballad* was selected for approximately 100 more festivals, making it possibly the most widely viewed Portuguese short film ever.[26] The extraordinary international reach of this film is also down to the work of Portugal Film, an agency for the international sale and promotion of Portuguese films, which was set up in 2015 by IndieLisboa – Cultural Association, a non-profit institution which runs the annual IndieLisboa – International Film Festival, established in Lisbon in 2004.

Teles directed her first feature film in 2018. *Terra Franca* (*Ashore*) is a documentary about a fisherman who lives in a fishing community in Vila Franca de Xira, not far from Lisbon. The film premiered commercially in France and Portugal. By January 2019, it had been selected by twenty-one festivals and had won awards at six of them, including the SCAM International Award at the Cinéma du Réel – Festival International de Films Documentaires (France), the Schools Award – ETIC prize for best Portuguese film at DocLisboa – International Film Festival (Portugal) and the Young Critics Award – Best International First Film at the Mar del Plata International Film Festival (Argentina). *Ashore* has continued Teles's work on the relationship between space and identity, establishing her place on the international film festival circuit as well as her leading role in the regeneration of Portuguese cinema.[27]

The difference between *Batrachian's Ballad* and the other films discussed in this chapter is even more evident when we take *Ashore* into account. *Ashore* documents and reconstructs a specific period in the life of a fisherman, Albertino and his family. It is light in tone, even at times humorous. The family is central to both of Teles's films, particularly the figure of the father who discloses the inner workings of the stories. In *Ashore*, family life is depicted as joyful and funny, with celebration as a constant feature. Even in a clearly condemnatory film which endeavours to expose and denounce a harsh reality, as is the case with *Batrachian's Ballad*, Leonor Teles also sets out to entertain us, and this makes her short film an even more appealing and unusual work, particularly in the context of Portuguese national cinema.

Encounters in space

The films analysed in this chapter find various ways of addressing conflicts and clashes between cultures. *An Aviation Field* brings specific geographical spaces and their histories together in diegetic time. *Eldorado XXI* evokes the history of civilization by portraying a wretchedly poor community living and working at the highest inhabited point in the world. *Ama-San* documents an age-old tradition that demonstrates female resilience in Japan. *Batrachian's Ballad* depicts social struggles in the interracial and intercultural dynamics of contemporary Portugal. The geopolitics of those on the margins is a key theme in *An Aviation Field*; unrestrained capitalism is a focus in *Eldorado XXI*; gender equality is a crucial feature of *Ama-San*; and xenophobia is confronted in *Batrachian's Ballad*. By addressing these specific themes, the films collectively represent and discuss the effects of globalization and the transnational issues that result from it, in order to highlight matters of major international concern.

Regardless of the different circumstances that led to the production of these four films, all of them had relatively small technical crews. In the case of *An Aviation Field*, the crew was effectively Joana Pimenta. Salomé Lamas shot her film in La Rinconada with just three crew members, who did sound, cinematography and production. *Ama-San*'s crew was about the same size. *Batrachian's Ballad* was smaller still. Leonor Teles shot, cut and edited the film, while Bernardo Theriaga was responsible for sound. However, the minimal size of the crews on set actually gave these projects greater freedom as well as logistical and creative control, which in turn allowed them to gain access to the locations where they were shooting without interfering in their internal dynamics. The exception is *Batrachian's Ballad*, of course, but the intention there always was to disrupt the racist discourses that were governing those spaces in the first place, and the fact that the crew was so small was what made this violent intervention possible.

All of these films narrate the encounter between a film director and a specific, real space to which she does not belong. This is even the case for Teles, as she never actually lived in a Roma community. *An Aviation Field*, *Eldorado XXI*, *Ama-San* and *Batrachian's Ballad* all undertake cultural, political and ideological investigations which translate and mobilize concepts of space into ideas of territory. Territory is conceived by these directors not in nationalistic terms, nor in terms of the nation-state, but rather in terms of the cosmopolitan. The historical world of the Cape Verdean volcano, Brazil's federal capital, the Peruvian mountain, the Japanese villages by the sea and the Portuguese city is one and the same, a globalized, capitalist, neoliberal world. All of these films are political, therefore, in the sense that their directors are motivated by scenes of social injustice to show us the specific histories of these places in the world system, at the same time as they set out to address universal problems.

The career trajectories of Joana Pimenta, Salomé Lamas, Cláudia Varejão and Leonor Teles all began and have since progressed in a globalized world characterized by constant economic and political crisis. The sophisticated views they hold about the world and about cinema, as well as the political choices they make are profoundly influenced by this fact. In this sense, the fact that Pimenta and Lamas are also visual artists, experimenting and working with different media, means that their films have access to more varied circulation networks and can get screenings both in film theatres and in international art spaces across the world. The production frameworks that brought these films into existence is evidence of a highly effective strategic vision, ultimately realized by the filmmakers' own determination to thrive in a fragile scenario that was financially and institutionally unstable. Viewed in this light, the Portuguese financial crisis actually worked as a driving force for change in the way Portuguese film production operated. Indeed, the fact that these four films were so successful in terms of their international circulation and reception, at a time when the main source of national film funding was frozen, can only reinforce Portugal's integration into the world cinema system.

Notes

1 The translation of this chapter into English was completed by Ana Rita Martins, Rhian Atkin and Hilary Owen.
2 For this study, other short and feature-length films could also have been considered, such as *Tudo o que Imagino* (*All I Imagine*; Leonor Noivo, 2017), *Farpões, Baldios*

(*Barbs, Wastelands*; Marta Mateus, 2017), *Água Mole (Drop by Drop*; Alexandra Ramires and Laura Gonçalves, 2017), *No Trilho dos Naturalistas* (*Tracking the Naturalists*; Luísa Homem and Tiago Hespanha, 2016), *Provas, Exorcismo* (*Trials, Exorcism*; Susana Nobre, 2015), *Rampa* (*Slope*; Margarida Lucas, 2015), *Água Forte* (*Strong Waters*; Mónica Baptista, 2018), among others. However, the films selected here are of particular interest for this study of cosmopolitanism.

3 Paolo Moretti, 'Composing an Image, Connecting the Dots', in *Gulbenkian and the Portuguese Cinema I. Territories of Passage – Cinema in Six Movements*, ed. MiguelValverde (Lisbon: Fundação Calouste Gulbenkian, 2018), 14.
4 See Olga Kourelou, Mariana Liz and Belén Vidal, 'Crisis and Creativity: The New Cinemas of Portugal, Greece and Spain', *New Cinemas*, 12, nos 1+2 (2014): 133–51.
5 ICA, 'Orçamento 2018', http://ica-ip.pt/fotos/downloads/orcamento2018_51045ac3 58a57a45c.pdf (accessed 5 July 2019).
6 Manoel de Oliveira et al., 'Manifesto pelo Cinema Português', *Público*, 12 March 2010, https://www.publico.pt/2010/03/12/jornal/manifesto-pelo-cinema-portugu es-18976210 (accessed 5 July 2019).
7 Ibid.
8 Ibid.
9 Daniel Ribas, '2000–2009: O Cinema do Futuro', in *Cinema Português: Um Guia Essencial*, eds Michelle Salles and Paulo Cunha (São Paulo: SESI-SP, 2013), 272.
10 Mariana Liz, 'Introduction: Framing the Global Appeal of Contemporary Portuguese Cinema', in *Portugal's Global Cinema: Industry, History and Culture*, ed. Mariana Liz (London and New York: I.B. Tauris, 2018), 4.
11 Ribas, '2000–2009: O Cinema do Futuro', 285–90.
12 Tiago Baptista, 'Nacionalmente correcto: A invenção do cinema português', *Revista Estudos do Século XX*, no. 9 (2009): 320.
13 Augusto M. Seabra, 'Saudação às "gerações curtas"', *Público*, 31 October 1999, https://www.publico.pt/1999/10/31/jornal/saudacao-as-geracoes-curtas-125735 (accessed 30 December 2018).
14 Daniel Ribas, 'Filmes Zero', *Público*, 11 January 2019, https://www.publico.pt/20 19/01/11/culturaipsilon/cronica/filmes-zero-1857162 (accessed 11 January 2019).
15 Personal interview with the author, 9 September 2018.
16 Personal interview with the author, 28 October 2018.
17 Jorge Mourinha, 'To the Ends of the Earth: An Interview with Salomé Lamas', *MUBI Notebook*, 21 March 2016, https://mubi.com/pt/notebook/posts/to-the-end s-of-the-earth-an-interview-with-salome-lamas (accessed 30 December 2018).
18 Lawrence Weschler, 'On Salomé Lamas's ELDORADO XXI', *Eldorado XXI Press Kit*, 2016, http://lawrenceweschler.com/static/images/uploads/Lamas_ELDORADOX XI_edited_copy.pdf (accessed 30 December 2018).
19 Personal interview with the author, 13 September 2018.

20 Francisca Gorjão Henriques, 'Meninas do Mar', *Público*, 28 June 2015, https://www.publico.pt/2015/06/28/culturaipsilon/noticia/meninas-do-mar-1700187 (accessed 30 December 2018).

21 Raquel Morais, 'Ama-San (2016) de Cláudia Varejão', *À Pala de Walsh*, 2 February 2017, http://www.apaladewalsh.com/2017/02/ama-san-2016-de-claudia-varejao (accessed 30 December 2018).

22 Personal interview with the author, 6 November 2018.

23 Ricardo Vieira Lisboa, 'Cláudia Varejão: "O meu cinema não se fecha sobre si mesmo"', *À Pala de Walsh*, 13 January 2016, http://www.apaladewalsh.com/2016/01/claudia-varejao-o-meu-cinema-nao-se-fecha-sobre-si-mesmo/ (accessed 30 December 2018).

24 Personal interview with the author, 12 September 2018.

25 Both Koretzky and Sugimoto have since then settled in Portugal.

26 Miguel Valverde, 'Batrachian's Ballad', in Valverde, *Gulbenkian and the Portuguese Cinema* I, 173–5.

27 Ribas, 'Filmes Zero'.

Bibliography

Allina-Pisano, Eric. 'Kuxa-Kanema – The Birth of Cinema'. *The International Journal of African Historical Studies* 38, no. 2 (2005): 393–95.
Almeida, Miguel Vale de. 'Tripping over History: Same-Sex Marriage in Portugal'. *Anthropology Today* 28, no. 3 (2012): 24–7.
Alpen, Ernst van. *Staging the Archive: Art and Photography in the Age of New Media*. London: Reaktion, 2014.
Alter, Nora M. 'Translating the Essay into Film and Installation'. *Journal of Visual Culture* 6, no. 1 (2007): 44–57.
Alter, Nora M. and Timothy Corrigan. 'Introduction'. In *Essays on the Essay Film*, edited by Nora M. Alter and Timothy Corrigan, 1–20. New York: Columbia University Press, 2017.
Alvão, Luísa. 'Noémia Delgado'. Special issue of *Revista Enquadramento*, Cineclube de Guimarães, no. 15 (2018). https://issuu.com/enquadramento/docs/enquadramento-15 (accessed 25 June 2019).
Álvarez López, Cristina and Adrian Martin. 'Broken Links: The Cinema of Teresa Villaverde'. In *Portugal's Global Cinema: Industry, History and Culture*, edited by Mariana Liz, 151–66. London: I.B. Tauris, 2018.
Amad, Paula. *Counter-Archive: Film, the Everyday, and Albert Kahn's Archives de la Planète*. New York: Columbia University Press, 2010.
Andersson, Johan and Lawrence Webb. 'Introduction: Decentring the Cinematic City – Film and Media in the Digital Age'. In *Global Cinematic Cities: New Landscapes of Film and Media*, edited by Johan Andersson and Lawrence Webb, 1–17. London and New York: Wallflower, 2016.
Anon. *Panorama do Cinema Português*. Lisbon: Cinemateca Portuguesa, 1980.
Anon. 'Cinema português – cinco filmes para subsidiar'. *Jornal de Letras, Artes e Ideias* (17 to 23 April 1984): 13.
Anon. 'Cinema português, júris e projetos para 85'. *Jornal de Letras, Artes e Ideias* (15 to 21 January 1985): 12.
Areal, Leonor. 'Estética da escola portuguesa de cinema: contributos para uma definição'. In *Cinema em Português: IV Jornadas*, edited by Frederico Lopes, 97–130. Covilhã: UBI, Livros Labcom, 2012. http://labcom-ifp.ubi.pt/book/87 (accessed 25 June 2019).
Arendt, Hannah. *Eichmann in Jerusalem: A Report on the Banality of Evil*. New York: Viking Press, 1963.
Arthur, Paul. 'Essay Questions: From Alain Resnais to Michael Moore'. *Film Comment* 39, no. 1 (2003): 58–62.

Aufderheide, Patricia. *Documentary Film: A Very Short Introduction*. Oxford: Oxford University Press, 2007.
Ballard, J. G. *Low-Flying Aircraft*. London: Flamingo, 1992 [1976].
Bandeira, José Gomes. 'Quem foste Alvarez?'. In *Catálogo Festfigueira* (1990): 313–4.
Baptista, Tiago. 'Nacionalmente correcto: A invenção do cinema português'. *Revista Estudos do Século XX*, no. 9 (2009): 307–23.
Baptista, Tiago. 'Nationally Correct: The Invention Of Portuguese Cinema'. *P: Portuguese Cultural Studies* 3 (2010): 3–18.
Baron, Jaimie. *The Archival Effect: Found Footage and the Audiovisual Experience of History*. London: Routledge, 2014.
Barreno, Maria Isabel, Maria Teresa Horta and Maria Velho da Costa. *New Portuguese Letters*. London: Readers International, 1994.
Barreno, Maria Isabel, Maria Teresa Horta and Maria Velho da Costa. *Novas Cartas Portuguesas*, edited by Ana Luísa Amaral. Lisbon: Dom Quixote, 2010.
Bennett, Jill. *Empathic Vision: Affect, Trauma, and Contemporary Art*. Stanford, CA.: Stanford University Press, 2005.
Benthien, Claudia. *Skin: On the Cultural Border Between Self and the World*. New York: Columbia University Press, 2002.
Bittencourt, Ela. '"One day, the swan sang this with its wings": An interview with Teresa Villaverde'. *Senses of Cinema* 65 (December 2012). http://sensesofcinema.com/2012/feature-articles/one-day-the-swan-sang-this-with-its-wings-an-interview-with-teresa-villaverde/ (accessed 7 July 2015).
Blankenship, Janelle and Tobias Nagl. 'Introduction: Towards a Politics of Scale'. In *European Visions: Small Cinemas in Transition*, edited by Janelle Blankenship and Tobias Nagl, 15–48. Bielefeld: Transcript Verlag, 2015.
Blümlinger, Christa and Harun Farocki. *Christa Blümlinger/Harun Farocki: The ABCs of the Essay Film*. Berlin: Harun Farocki Institut & Motto Books, 2017.
Bordwell, David. 'The Art Cinema as Mode of Practice'. *Film Criticism* 4, no. 1 (1979): 56–64.
Bozak, Nadia. *The Cinematic Footprint: Lights, Camera, Natural Resources*. New Brunswick, NJ and London: Rutgers University Press, 2012.
Braidotti, Rosi. *Nomadic Subjects: Embodiment and Sexual Difference in Contemporary Feminist Theory*. New York: Columbia University Press, 1994.
Braidotti, Rosi, *The Posthuman*. London: Polity Press, 2013.
Branco, Sofia. 'Agustina e Lídia Jorge apoiam movimento pela despenalização. Médicos pela Escolha prosseguem formações sobre o aborto'. *Público*, 13 November 2006. https://www.publico.pt/2006/11/13/politica/noticia/agustina-e-lidia-jorge-apoiam-movimento-pela-despenalizacao-1276400 (accessed 12 August 2017).
Brereton, Pat. *Environmental Ethics and Film*. London and New York: Routledge, 2016.

Bruno, Cátia. 'Inês de Medeiros: A vida e as polémicas da mulher que tirou Almada ao PCP'. *Observador*, 5 October 2017. https://observador.pt/especiais/ines-de-medeiros-a-vida-e-as-polemicas-da-mulher-que-tirou-almada-ao-pcp/ (accessed 12 July 2019).

Brunsdon, Charlotte. 'The Attractions of the Cinematic City'. *Screen* 53, no. 3 (2012): 209–27.

Butler, Alison. *Women's Cinema: The Contested Screen*. London: Wallflower, 2002.

Castro, Ilda. 'Entrevista com Noémia Delgado'. In *Cineastas Portuguesas 1874–1956*, edited by António Cunha, 30–74. Lisbon: Câmara Municipal de Lisboa, 2000.

Coelho, Maria Luísa and Cláudia Pazos Alonso (eds). Special issue on 'Portuguese Transnational Women Artists and Writers.' *Portuguese Studies* 35, no. 2. (2019), forthcoming.

Cohen, Jeffrey Jerome. 'Posthuman Environs'. In *Environmental Humanities: Voices from the Anthropocene*, edited by Serpil Oppermann and Serenella Iovinio, 25–44. London and New York: Rowman and Littlefield.

Cordero Hoyo, Elena and Begoña Soto-Vázquez (eds). *Women in Iberian Cinemas: A Feminist Approach to Portuguese and Spanish Filmic Culture*. London: Intellect, forthcoming.

Corrigan, Timothy (ed.). *Film and Literature: An Introduction and Reader*. Milton Park, Abingdon, Oxon; New York: Routledge, 2011.

Corrigan, Timothy. *The Essay Film: From Montaigne, After Marker*. New York: Oxford University Press, 2011.

Costa, Alves. 'Dois dedos de conversa com Noémia Delgado'. *Cinema Novo* (1981): 16–19.

Costa, Alves. 'Para Noémia Delgado (sem subsídios) "O cinema é uma forma de sonhar"'. *Jornal de Notícias* 96, no. 282 (20 March 1984): 20–4.

Costa, Catarina Alves. 'Camponeses do cinema: a representação da cultura popular no cinema português entre 1960 e 1970'. PhD diss., Universidade Nova de Lisboa, 2012.

Costa, João Bénard da. 'Breve história mal contada de um cinema mal visto'. In *Portugal 45–95 nas Artes, nas Letras e nas Ideias*, edited by Vítor Vladimiro Ferreira, 45–83. Lisbon: Centro Nacional de Cultura, 1998.

Cova, Anne and António Costa Pinto. 'Women Under Salazar's Dictatorship'. *Portuguese Journal of Social Science* 2 (2002): 129–46.

Cox, Christoph. 'Beyond Representation and Signification: Toward a Sonic Materialism'. *Journal of Visual Culture* 10, no. 2 (2011): 145–61.

Creed, Barbara. *The Monstrous-Feminine: Film, feminism and psychoanalysis*. London and New York: Routledge, 1993.

Cunha, António (ed.). *Cineastas Portuguesas 1874–1956*. Lisbon: Câmara Municipal de Lisboa, 2000.

Cunha, Paulo. 'Genealogias, filiações e afinidades no cinema português: Do Novo Cinema ao cinema português contemporâneo'. In *Filmes Falados, Cinema em Português V Jornadas*, edited by Frederico Lopes and Ana Catarina Pereira, 177–90. Covilhã: LabCom, Universidade da Beira Interior, 2013.

Cunha, Paulo. 'O novo cinema português. Políticas públicas e modos de produção (1949–80)'. PhD diss., University of Coimbra, 2014.

Cunha, Paulo. 'Cinema de Garagem: Distribuição e Exibição de Cinema em Portugal'. In *Cinema em Português – VII Jornadas*, edited by Frederico Lopes, Paulo Cunha and Manuela Penafria, 117–37. Covilhã: LabCom, Universidade da Beira Interior, 2016.

Cunha, Paulo. *Uma nova história do novo cinema português*. Lisbon: Outro Modo Cooperativa Cultural, 2018.

Davis, Natalie Zemon. *Fiction in the Archives: Pardon Tales and Their Tellers in Sixteenth-Century France*. Stanford: Stanford University Press, 1987.

De Baecque, Antoine. *La cinéphilie: Invention d'un regard, histoire d'une culture. 1944–1968*. Paris: Fayard, 2003.

Delgado, Noémia. 'Gente de cinema em panorâmica: o realizador António de Macedo. Entrevista'. *Jornal de Letras e Artes* (1965): 4.

Delgado, Noémia. 'M. G. Faria de Almeida – realizador e produtor de cinema. Entrevista'. *Jornal de Letras e Artes* (1965): 7.

De Luca, Tiago. 'Realism of the Senses: A Tendency in Contemporary World Cinema'. In *Theorizing World Cinema*, edited by Lúcia Nagib, Chris Perriam and Rajinder Dudrah, 183–206. London: I.B. Tauris, 2013.

D'Lugo, Marvin. 'Auteurism and Spain'. In *A Companion to Spanish Cinema*, edited by Jo Labanyi and Tatjana Pavlović, 113–9. Malden/Oxford/Chichester: Wiley-Blackwell, 2013.

Didi-Huberman, Georges. *Devant le temps: histoire de l'art et anachronisme des images*. Paris: Minuit, 2000.

Elsaesser, Thomas. *Harun Farocki: Working on the Sightlines*. Amsterdam: Amsterdam University Press, 2004.

Elsaesser, Thomas. 'Cinephilia or the Uses of Disenchantment'. In *Cinephilia: Movies, Love and Memory*, edited by Marijke de Valck and Malte Hagener, 27–43. Amsterdam: Amsterdam University Press, 2005.

'Entrevista com Margarida Gil, realizadora de "Paixão" @ Canal 180', 20 February 2012. https://www.youtube.com/watch?v=IVUvOzzCFWY (accessed 8 July 2019).

European Audiovisual Observatory. 'Film Production in Europe Report', November 2017. https://rm.coe.int/filmproductionineurope-2017-j-talavera-pdf/1680788952 (accessed 9 July 2019).

Faulkner, Sally. 'Cinephilia and the Unrepresentable in Miguel Gomes's *Tabu* (2012)'. *Bulletin of Spanish Studies* 92, no. 3 (2015): 341–60.

Faulkner, Sally and Mariana Liz. 'Portuguese Film: Colony, Postcolony, Memory – Q&A with Margarida Cardoso', 14 January 2016. https://www.youtube.com/watch?v=xO8pFfoDqwA (accessed 16 March 2019).

Faulkner, Sally and Mariana Liz (eds). 'Portuguese Film: Colony, Postcolony, Memory'. Special issue of *Journal of Romance Studies* 16, no. 2 (2016): 1–120.

Ferreira, Ana Paula. 'Home Bound: The Construction of Femininity in the *Estado Novo*'. *Portuguese Studies* 12 (1996): 133–44.

Ferreira, Ana Paula. 'Loving in the Lands of Portugal: Sex in Women's Fictions and the National Order'. In *Lusosex: Gender and Sexuality in the Portuguese-Speaking World*, edited by Susan Canty Quinlan and Fernando Arenas, 107–29. Minneapolis: University of Minnesota Press, 2002.

Ferreira, Caroline Overhoff. *Identity and Difference: Postcoloniality and Transnationality in Lusophone Films*. Münster: LIT Verlag, 2012.

Ferreira, Virgínia. 'Engendering Portugal: Social Change, State Politics, and Women's Social Mobilization'. In *Modern Portugal*, edited by António Costa Pinto, 162–88. Palo Alto: The Society for the Promotion of Science and Scholarship, 1998.

Fischer, Lucy. *Cinematernity: Film, Motherhood and Genre*. Princeton, NJ: Princeton University Press, 1996.

Fischer, Lucy. 'Feminist Forms of Address: Mai Zetterling's *Loving Couples*'. In *The Routledge Companion to Cinema and Gender*, edited by Kristin Lené Hole, Dijana Jelača, E. Ann Kaplan and Patrice Petro, 36–46. London and New York: Routledge, 2018.

Galt, Rosalind and Karl Schoonover. *Global Art Cinema: New Theories and Histories*. Oxford: Oxford University Press, 2010.

Galt, Rosalind. *Pretty: Film and the Decorative Image*. New York: Columbia University Press, 2011.

Gil, Margarida. 'Conversa' [interview with Ilda Castro]. In *Cineastas Portuguesas 1874–1956*, edited by António Cunha, 209–40. Lisbon: Câmara Municipal de Lisboa, 2000.

Gil, Margarida. 'Relato de Paixões'. In *Cineastas Portuguesas 1874–1956*, edited by António Cunha, 204–7. Lisbon: Câmara Municipal de Lisboa, 2000.

Gil, Margarida. 'Statements'. In *Pour João César Monteiro: Contre tous les feux, le feu, mon feu*, edited by Fabrice Revault Allonnes, 95–106. Crisnée: Yellow Now – Cotê Cinèma, 2004.

Gil, Margarida. 'O produtor não põe um cêntimo no filme' [interview to Vanessa Sousa Dias]. In *Novas & Velhas Tendências no Cinema Português Contemporâneo*, edited by João Maria Mendes, 53–8. Faro: CIAC – Centro de Investigação em Artes e Comunicação, 2010.

Gomes, Hugo 'Susana Nobre: "Um realizador não se faz de um filme"'. *c7nema*, 27 April 2018. http://www.c7nema.net/entrevista/item/48038-susana-nobre-um-realizador-nao-se-faz-de-um-filme.html (accessed 8 August 2018).

Gomes, Rui Telmo, Teresa Duarte Martinho and Vanda Lourenço. *Carreiras Profissionais Segundo o Género na Produção de Cinema: Diferentes Contextos e Gerações*. Lisbon: Observatório das Actividades Culturais, 2005.

Gorin, Jean-Pierre. 'Proposal for a Tussle'. In *Essays on the Essay Film*, edited by Nora M. Alter and Timothy Corrigan, 269–75. New York: Columbia University Press, 2017.

Graham, Elaine. *Representations of the Post/Human: Monsters, Aliens and Others in Popular Culture*. New Brunswick: Rutgers University Press, 2002.

Grant, Catherine. 'Paranoid Hermeneutics as Queer Cinematic Vernacular', Video Essay (2017) https://vimeo.com/channels/222321/42029962 and https://lucreciamartel.blogspot.com (accessed 17 February 2019).

Grant, Catherine. 'www.auteur.com?'. *Screen* 41, no. 1 (2000): 101–8.

Grant, Catherine. 'Secret Agents: Feminist Theories of Women's Film Authorship'. *Feminist Theory* 2, no. 1 (2001): 113–30.

Halberstam, Judith. *Skin Shows: Gothic Horror and the Technology of Monsters*. Durham: Duke University Press, 1995.

Haraway, Donna. 'A Cyborg Manifesto: Science, Technology and Socialist-Feminism in the late Twentieth-century'. In *The Cybercultures Reader*, edited by David Bell and Barbara M. Kennedy, 291–324. London and New York: Routledge, 2000.

Henrique, Francisca Gorjão, 'Meninas do Mar'. *Público*, 28 June 2015. https://www.publico.pt/2015/06/28/culturaipsilon/noticia/meninas-do-mar-1700187 (accessed 30 December 2018).

Hjort, Mette and Duncan Petrie (eds). *The Cinema of Small Nations*. Edinburgh: Edinburgh University Press, 2007.

Hjort, Mette. 'The Risk Environment of Small-Nation Filmmaking'. In *European Visions: Small Cinemas in Transition*, edited by Janelle Blankenship and Tobias Nagl, 49–64. Bielefeld: Transcript Verlag, 2015.

Holanda, Karla and Marina Cavalcanti Tedesco (eds). *Feminino e Plural: Mulheres no Cinema Brasileiro*. São Paulo: Editora Papirus, 2017.

Horta, Maria Teresa, Célia Metrass and Helena Sá de Medeiros. *Aborto: Direito ao nosso Corpo*. Lisbon: Futura, 1975.

ICA. 'Cinema/Audiovisual from Portugal 2019'. https://ica-ip.pt/fotos/editor2/catalogo 2019/ICA_CATALOGO_2019.pdf (accessed 9 July 2019).

ICA. 'Orçamento 2018'. http://ica-ip.pt/fotos/downloads/orcamento2018_51045ac3 58a57a45c.pdf (accessed 5 July 2019).

Ince, Kate. *The Body and the Screen: Female Subjectivities in Contemporary Women's Cinema*. New York: Bloomsbury, 2017.

Ingram, David. 'The Aesthetics and Ethics of Eco-Film Criticism'. In *Ecocinema Theory and Practice*, edited by Stephen Rust, Salma Monani and Sean Cubitt, 43–61. New York and London: Routledge, 2013.

Ivakhiv, Adrian. 'Green Film Criticism and Its Futures'. *Interdisciplinary Studies in Literature and Environment* 15, no. 2 (Summer 2008): 1–28.

Jäckel, Anne. 'Changing the Image of Europe? The Role of European Co-productions, Funds and Film Awards'. In *The Europeanness of European Cinema. Identity, Meaning, Globalization*, edited by Mary Harrod, Mariana Liz and Alissa Timoshkina, 59–71. London: I.B. Tauris, 2015.

Jackson, Emma. 'The Eyes of Agnès Varda: Portraiture, Cinécriture and the Filmic Ethnographic Eye'. *Feminist Review* 96, no. 1 (2010): 122–26.

Jenkins, Janis Hunter. 'The State Construction of Affect: Political Ethos and Mental Health Among Salvadoran Refugees'. *Culture, Medicine and Psychiatry* 15 (1991): 139–65.

Johnston, Claire. 'Women's Cinema as Counter-Cinema'. In *Notes on Women's Cinema*, edited by Claire Johnston, 24–31. London: Society for Education in Film and Television, 1973.

Kääpä, Pietari. 'Transnational Approaches to Ecocinema: Charting an Expansive Field.' In *Transnational Ecocinema: Film Cuture in an Era of Ecological Transformation*, edited by Pietari Kääpä and Tommy Gustafsson, 21–44. Bristol, UK and Chicago, US: University of Chicago Press, 2013.

Kaplan, E. Ann. *Motherhood and Representation: The Mother in Popular Culture and Melodrama*. London and New York: Routledge, 1992.

Kaplan, E. Ann. 'Visualizing Climate Trauma: The Cultural Work of Films Anticipating the Future'. In *The Routledge Companion to Cinema and Gender*, edited by Kristin Lené Hole, Dijana Jelača, E. Ann Kaplan and Patrice Petro, 407–16. London and New York: Routledge, 2017.

Klobucka, M. Anna and Hilary Owen . 'Introduction'. In *Gender, Empire and Postcolony. Luso-Afro-Brazilian Intersections,* edited by Hilary Owen and Anna M. Klobucka, 1–16. New York: Palgrave Macmillan, 2014.

Kourelou, Olga, Mariana Liz and Belén Vidal. 'Crisis and Creativity: The New Cinemas of Portugal, Greece and Spain'. *New Cinemas* 12, nos 1+2 (2014): 133–51.

Lázaro Reboll, Antonio, Steven Marsh, Susan Martin-Márquez and Santos Zunzunegui. 'Strategic Auteurism'. In *A Companion to Spanish Cinema*, edited by Jo Labanyi and Tatjana Pavlović, 152–90. Malden/Oxford/Chichester: Wiley-Blackwell, 2013.

Lefebvre, Martin. 'Between Setting and Landscape in the Cinema'. In *Landscape and Film*, edited by Martin Lefebvre, 19–59. New York and London: Routledge, 2006.

Liandrat-Guigues, Suzanne and Murielle Gagnebin. *L'Essai et Le Cinéma*. Seyssel: Éditions Champ Vallon, 2004.

Lisboa, Maria Manuel. 'An Interesting Condition. The Abortion Pastels of Paula Rego'. *Luso-Brazilian Review* 39, no. 2 (1992): 125–49.

Lisboa, Ricardo Vieira. 'Cláudia Varejão: "O meu cinema não se fecha sobre si mesmo"'. *À Pala de Walsh*, 13 January 2016. http://www.apaladewalsh.com/20 16/01/claudia-varejao-o-meu-cinema-nao-se-fecha-sobre-si-mesmo/ (accessed 30 December 2018).

Liz, Mariana. 'Introduction: Framing the Global Appeal of Contemporary Portuguese Cinema'. In *Portugal's Global Cinema: Industry, History and Culture*, edited by Mariana Liz, 1–14. London: I.B. Tauris, 2018.

Liz, Mariana (ed.). *Portugal's Global Cinema: Industry, History and Culture*. London: I.B. Tauris, 2018.

Lopate, Phillip. *Totally, Tenderly, Tragically: Essays and Criticism from a Lifelong Love Affair with the Movies*. New York: Anchor, 1998.

MacDonald, Scott. 'Toward an Eco-Cinema'. *Interdisciplinary Studies in Literature and Environment* 11, no. 2 (2004): 107–32.
MacDonald, Scott. 'The Ecocinema Experience'. In *Ecocinema Theory and Practice*, edited by Stephen Rust, Salma Monani and Sean Cubitt, 17–41. New York and London: Routledge, 2013.
MacDonald, Scott. 'Susana de Sousa Dias'. *Avant-Doc: Intersections of Documentary and Avant-Garde Cinema*. New York: Oxford University Press, 2014.
Magalhães, Maria José. *Movimento Feminista e Educação, Portugal décadas de 70 e 80*. Oeiras: Celta, 1998.
Maly, Ico and Piia Varis. 'The 21st-Century Hipster: On Micro-Populations in Times of Superdiversity'. *European Journal of Cultural Studies* 19, no. 6 (2016): 637–53.
Manuel, Paul Christopher and Maurya N. Tollefsen. 'Roman Catholicism, Secularization, and the Recovery of Traditional Communal Values: The 1998 and 2007 Referenda on Abortion in Portugal'. *South European Society and Politics* 13, no. 1 (2008): 117–219.
Marks, Laura U. *The Skin of the Film: Intercultural Cinema, Embodiment, and the Senses*. Durham and London: Duke University Press, 2000.
Massey, Doreen. *Space, Place and Gender*. Minneapolis: University of Minnesota Press, 1994.
Mayer, Sophie. '*Gutta cavat lapidem*: The Sonorous Politics of Lucrecia Martel's Swimming Pools'. In *The Cinema of the Swimming Pool*, edited by Christopher Brown and Pam Hirsch, 191–202. Oxford: Peter Lang, 2014.
Mayer, Sophie. *Political Animals: The New Feminist Cinema*. London: I.B. Tauris, 2016.
McDowell, Linda. *Gender, Identity and Place: Understanding Feminist Geographies*. Minneapolis: University of Minnesota Press, 1999.
McDowell, Linda. 'Spaces of the Home'. *Home Cultures* 4, no. 2 (2007): 129–46.
Melo, Daniela. 'The European Union, Executive Politics, and the Women's Movement in Portugal: The Consequences of Europeanization, 1986 to the Present'. In *The Gendered Executive: A Comparative Analysis of Presidents, Prime Ministers, and Chief Executives*, edited by Janet E. Martin and MaryAnne Borrelli, 165–84. Philadelphia: Temple University Press, 2016.
Melo, Daniela. 'Women's Movements in Portugal and Spain: Democratic Processes and Policy Outcomes'. *Journal of Women, Politics and Policy* 38, no. 3 (2017): 251–75.
Mendes, Luís. 'What Can Be Done to Resist or Mitigate Tourism Gentrification in Lisbon? Some Policy Findings & Recommendations'. In *City Making and Tourism Gentrification*, edited by Marc Glaudemans and Igor Marko, 35–42. Tilburg: Stadslab, 2016.
Merchant, Carolyn. *The Death of Nature: Women, Ecology and the Scientific Revolution*. New York: HarperOne, 1989.
Mira, Alberto (ed.). *The Cinema of Spain and Portugal*. London: Wallflower, 2005.
Miranda, Ana (ed.). *Catálogo Olhadelas*. Porto: Confederação, 2010.

Monteiro, Rosa. 'A descriminalização do aborto em Portugal: Estado, movimentos de mulheres e partidos políticos'. *Análise Social* 204, no. 47 (2012): 586–605.

Montero, David. *Thinking Images: The Essay Film as a Dialogic Form in European Cinema*. Bern: Peter Lang, 2012.

Moore, Ellen E. *Landscape and the Environment in Hollywood Film: The Green Machine*. New York: Palgrave Macmillan, 2017.

Morais, Raquel. 'Ama-San (2016) de Cláudia Varejão'. *À Pala de Walsh*, 2 February 2017. http://www.apaladewalsh.com/2017/02/ama-san-2016-de-claudia-varejao (accessed 30 December 2018).

Moretti, Paolo. 'Composing an Image, Connecting the Dots'. In *Gulbenkian and the Portuguese Cinema I. Territories of Passage – Cinema in Six Movements +2*, edited by Miguel Valverde, 13–19. Lisbon: Fundação Calouste Gulbenkian, 2018.

Moure, José. 'Essai de Définition de l'essai Au Cinéma'. In *L'Essai et Le Cinéma*, edited by Suzanne Liandrat-Guigues and Murielle Gagnebin, 25–40. Seyssel: Éditions Champ Vallon, 2004.

Mourinha, Jorge. 'To the Ends of the Earth: An Interview with Salomé Lamas'. *MUBI Notebook*, 21 March 2016. https://mubi.com/pt/notebook/posts/to-the-ends-of-the-e arth-an-interview-with-salome-lamas (accessed 30 December 2018).

Mourinha, Jorge. 'Cinema. Sophia e Jorge de Sena Vão a Locarno Com Rita Azevedo Gomes'. *Público*, 3 August 2016. https://www.publico.pt/2016/08/03/culturaipsi lon/noticia/-rita-azevedo-gomes-leva-sophia-e-jorge-de-sena-a-locarno-1740074 (accessed 3 July 2019).

Mourinha, Jorge. 'Connections in Invisible Ink: A Look Back at Locarno 69 on Notebook'. *MUBI* (blog), 25 August 2016. https://mubi.com/notebook/posts/con nections-in-invisible-ink-a-look-back-at-locarno-69 (accessed 3 July 2019).

Mourinha, Jorge. 'Um retrato de mulher à sombra de Oliveira iluminou a Berlinale'. *Público* (blog), 7 February 2019. https://www.publico.pt/2019/02/07/culturaipsilon/n oticia/retrato-mulher-sombra-oliveira-1861100 (accessed 3 July 2019).

Mulvey, Laura. 'Visual Pleasure and Narrative Cinema'. *Screen* 16, no. 3 (1975): 6–18.

Muñoz Fernández, Horacio and Iván Villarmea Álvarez (eds). *Jugar con la Memoria: el cine portugués en el siglo XXI*. Shangrila/a cuarta parede: Santander, 2014.

Muñoz Fernández, Horacio and Iván Villarmea Álvarez. 'Aesthetic Tendencies in Contemporary Portuguese Cinema'. *Comparative Cinema* 6 (2015): 39–45.

Nagib, Lúcia. 'Towards a Positive Definition of World Cinema'. In *Remapping World Cinema: Identity, Culture and Politics in Film*, edited by Stephanie Dennison and Song Hwee Lim, 30–7. London: Wallflower Press, 2006.

Nair, Parvati and Julián Daniel Gutiérrez-Albilla (eds). *Hispanic and Lusophone Women Filmmakers: Theory, Practice and Difference*. Manchester: Manchester University Press, 2013.

Nichols, Bill. *Speaking Truths with Film: Evidence, Ethics, Politics in Documentary*. Oakland, CA.: University of California Press, 2016.

Nichols, Bill. *Introduction to Documentary*, Third Edition. Bloomington: Indiana University Press, 2017.

Oliveira Junior, Luiz Carlos. 'Retratos em movimento'. *Revista Ars* 15, no. 31 (2017): 183–208. http://www.revistas.usp.br/ars/article/view/141282 (accessed 25 June 2019).

Oliveira, Manoel et al. 'Manifesto pelo Cinema Português'. *Público*, 12 March 2010. https://www.publico.pt/2010/03/12/jornal/manifesto-pelo-cinema-portugues-18976210 (accessed 30 December 2018).

Owen, Hilary and Anna M. Klobucka (eds). *Gender, Empire, and Postcolony: Luso-Afro-Brazilian Intersections*. New York: Palgrave Macmillan, 2014.

Pasley, Victoria. '*Kuxa Kanema*: Third Cinema and Its Transatlantic Crossings'. In *Rethinking Third Cinema: The Role of Anti-colonial Media and Aesthetics in Postmodernity*, edited by Frieda Ekotto and Adeline Koh, 107–23. Münster: LIT Verlag, 2009.

Paszkiewicz, Katarzyna. *Genre, Authorship and Contemporary Women Filmmakers*. Edinburgh: Edinburgh University Press, 2017.

Penafria, Manuela. *O Paradigma do Documentário: António Campos, Cineasta*. Livros LabCom, 2009.

Penafria, Manuela, Eduardo Tulio Baggio, André Rui Graça and Denize Correa Araújo (eds). *Ver, Ouvir e Ler os Cineastas – Teoria dos cineastas, vol. 1*. Covilhã: UBI, Labcom.IFP, 2016.

Pereira, Ana Catarina. *A Mulher-Cineasta: Da arte pela arte à uma estética da diferenciação*. Covilhã: LABCOM.IFP, Universidade da Beira Interior, 2016.

Pereira, Maria do Mar. 'The Importance of Being "Modern" and Foreign: Feminist Scholarship and the Epistemic Status of Nations'. *Signs* 39, no. 3 (2014): 627–57.

Pinazza, Natália. 'Luso-Brazilian Co-Productions: Rescue and Expansion'. In *Portugal's Global Cinema: Industry, History and Culture*, edited by Mariana Liz, 239–55. London: I.B. Tauris, 2018.

Plumwood, Val. *Feminism and the Mastery of Nature*. London and New York: Routledge, 1997.

Portugal, Paulo. 'Rita Azevedo Gomes: "Sinceramente, Nunca Pensei Que Estava a Fazer Um Filme Feminista"'. *Jornal i*, 2 February 2019. https://ionline.sapo.pt/646146 (accessed 3 July 2019).

Prata, Ana Filipa. 'Transdifference and Abjection in Maria Velho da Costa's *Myra* and Teresa Villaverde's *Transe*'. *Portuguese Studies* 33, no. 2 (2017): 202–18.

Rabinowitz, Paula. *They Must Be Represented: The Politics of Documentary*. New York: Verso, 1994.

Ramos, Jorge Leitão. *Dicionário do Cinema Português 1989–2003*. Lisbon: Caminho, 2005.

Rascaroli, Laura. 'The Essay Film: Problems, Definitions, Textual Commitments'. *Framework: The Journal of Cinema and Media* 49, no. 2 (2008): 24–47.

Rascaroli, Laura. *How the Essay Film Thinks*. New York: Oxford University Press, 2017.
Reis, Marta F. 'Manuela Tavares sobre a despenalização do aborto: "Para nós, Guterres ficou sempre marcado": Interview with Manuela Tavares'. *Jornal i*, 10 February 2017. https://ionline.sapo.pt/548255 (accessed 12 August 2017).
Ribas, Daniel. '2000–2009: O Cinema do Futuro'. In *Cinema Português: Um Guia Essencial*, edited by Michelle Salles and Paulo Cunha, 268–99. São Paulo: SESI-SP, 2013.
Ribas, Daniel. 'Filmes Zero'. *Público*, 11 January 2019. https://www.publico.pt/2019/01/11/culturaipsilon/cronica/filmes-zero-1857162 (accessed 11 January 2019).
Ribeiro de Meneses, Filipe. *Salazar: A Political Biography*. New York: Enigma, 2009.
Ribeiro de Menezes, Alison. 'The Enchantment and Disenchantment of the Archival Image: Politics and Affect in Contemporary Portuguese Cultural Memories'. In *Film, History and Memory*, edited by Jennie M. Carlston and Fearghal McGarry, 66–82. Basingstoke: Palgrave Macmillan, 2015.
Rust, Stephen and Salma Monani. 'Introduction – Cuts to Dissolves: Defining and Situating Ecocinema Studies'. In *Ecocinema Theory and Practice*, edited by Stephen Rust, Salma Monani and Sean Cubitt, 1–13. New York and London: Routledge, 2013.
Rust, Stephen, Salma Monani and Sean Cubitt (eds). *Ecocinema Theory and Practice*. New York and London: Routledge, 2013.
Schatz, Thomas. *Hollywood Genres: Formulas, Filmmaking, and The Studio System*. New York: Random House, 1981.
Scholz, Annette and Marta Álvarez (eds). *Cineastas Emergentes: Mujeres en el cine del siglo XXI*. Madrid: Iberoamericana, 2018.
Seabra, Augusto M. 'Saudação às "gerações curtas"'. *Público*, 31 October 1999. https://www.publico.pt/1999/10/31/jornal/saudacao-as-geracoes-curtas-125735 (accessed 30 December 2018).
Sellier, Geneviève. *La nouvelle vague, un cinéma au masculin singulier*. Paris: CNRS, 2005.
Sena, Jorge de. *Antigas e novas andanças do demónio*. Lisbon: Edições 70, 1984.
Silverman, Kaja. *The Subject of Semiotics*. New York: Oxford University Press, 1984.
Silverman, Kaja. *The Threshold of the Visible World*. New York and London: Routledge, 1996.
Smith, Paul Julian. 'Transnational Co-Productions and Female Filmmakers: The Cases of Lucrecia Martel and Isabel Coixet'. In *Hispanic and Lusophone Women Filmmakers: Theory, Practice and Difference*, edited by Parvati Nair and Julián Daniel Gutiérrez-Albilla, 12–24. Manchester: Manchester University Press, 2013.
Sousa Dias, Susana de. '(In)visible Evidence: The Representability of Torture'. In *A Companion to Documentary Film*, edited by Alexandra Juhasz and Alisa Lebow, 482–505. Oxford: Wiley-Blackwell, 2015.
Sousa Dias, Susana de. '*Natureza Morta*'. *Lumière*. http://www.elumiere.net/exclusivo_web/reel12/sousa_01.php (accessed 5 July 2019).

Sousa Santos, Boaventura de. 'State and Society in Portugal'. In *After the Revolution. Twenty Years of Portuguese Literature, 1974–1994*, edited by Helena Kaufman and Anna Klobucka, 31–72. Lewisburg: Bucknell University Press, 1997.

Souto, Mariana. 'Susana de Sousa Dias and the Ghosts of the Portuguese Dictatorship'. *Comparative Cinema* 6. http://www.ocec.eu/cinemacomparativecinema/index.php/en/27-n-1-portuguese-cinema/298-susana-de-sousa-dias-and-the-ghosts-of-the-portuguese-dictatorship (accessed 29 August 2018).

Steedman, Carolyn. *Dust: The Archive and Cultural History*. Manchester: Manchester University Press, 2001.

Steven, Mark. 'Dark, Satanic'. *Sight and Sound* 27, no. 10 (2017): 21.

Stewart, Katy. 'Establishing the Female Gaze: Narrative Subversion in Lucrecia Martel's *La niña santa* (2004) and *La ciénaga* (2001)'. *Tesserae: Journal of Iberian and Latin American Studies* 21, no. 3 (2015): 205–19.

Stock, Robert. 'Archival Images and Audiovisual Testimony – Negotiating the End of Empire in the Documentary Films Guerra Colonial. Histórias de Campanha em Moçambique (1998) and Natal 71 (1999)'. *International Journal of Iberian Studies* 27, nos 2–3 (2014): 183–201.

Stock, Robert. 'Cinema and Conflict in Postcolonial Mozambique: Archival Images as Illustration and Evidence in *Estas são as armas* (1978)'. In *Mediations of Disruption in Post-conflict Cinema*, edited by Adriana Martins, Alexandra Lopes and Mónica Dias, 75–91. London: Palgrave Macmillan, 2016.

Stoler, Ann Laura. *Along the Archival Grain: Epistemic Anxieties and Colonial Common Sense*. Princeton: Princeton University Press, 2009.

Sturgeon, Noël. *Environmentalism in Popular Culture: Gender, Race, Sexuality and the Politics of the Natural*. Tucson: University of Arizona Press, 2009.

Tavares, Manuela. 'Feminismos em Portugal (1947–2007)'. PhD diss., Universidade Aberta, 2008.

Tavares, Manuela. *Movimentos de Mulheres em Portugal: Décadas de 70 e 80*. Lisbon: Livros Horizonte, 2000.

'Teresa Villaverde, Director'. Interview in *Cineuropa* (February 2017). https://cineuropa.org/en/video/323517/ (accessed 1 March 2019).

Thornham, Sue. *Spaces of Women's Cinema: Space, Place and Genre in Contemporary Women's Filmmaking*. New York: Bloomsbury/BFI, 2019.

Torres, Anália. 'Women, Gender, and Work: The Portuguese Case in the Context of the European Union'. *International Journal of Sociology* 38, no. 4 (2008): 36–56.

Torres, Anália (ed.). *Igualdade de Género Ao Longo Da Vida: Portugal no Contexto Europeu*. Lisbon: Fundação Francisco Manuel dos Santos, 2018.

Torres, Anália, Bernardo Coelho and Miguel Cabrita. 'Bridge over Troubled Waters'. *European Societies* 15, no. 4 (2013): 535–56.

Tracy, Andrew, Ginette Vincendeau, Katy McGahan, Chris Darke, Geoff Andrew, Olaf Möller, Sergio Wolf, Nina Power, and Nick Bradshaw. 'The Essay Film'. *Sight &*

Sound, 5 August 2015. https://www.bfi.org.uk/news-opinion/sight-sound-magazine/features/deep-focus/essay-film (accessed 7 November 2019).

Triana-Toribio, Núria. 'Auteurism and Commerce in Contemporary Spanish Cinema: *directores mediáticos*'. *Screen* 49, no. 3 (2008): 259–76.

Valverde, Miguel. 'Batrachian's Ballad'. In *Gulbenkian and the Portuguese Cinema I. Territories of Passage – Cinema in Six Movements +2*, edited by Miguel Valverde, 170–5. Lisbon: Fundação Calouste Gulbenkian, 2018.

Van Cleaf, Kara. 'Mothering Through Precarity: Women's Work and Digital Media; Interrogating Motherhood'. *Feminist Media Studies* 18, no. 3 (2018): 509–12.

Vaz de Castro, Bernardo. 'Correspondências (2016) de Rita Azevedo Gomes'. *À pala de Walsh*, 12 March 2018. http://www.apaladewalsh.com/2018/03/correspondencias-2016-de-rita-azevedo-gomes/ (accessed 3 July 2019).

Verstraete, Ginette. 'Women's Resistance Strategies in a High-Tech Multicultural Europe'. In *Transnational Feminism in Film and Media*, edited by Katarzyna Marciniak, Anikó Imre and Áine O'Healy, 111–28. New York: Palgrave Macmillan, 2007.

Vieira, Alice. 'Noémia Delgado realizadora: não faço as coisas com os pés…'. *Diário de Lisboa* (3 September 1983): 18.

Vieira, Patrícia. 'Filming Women in the Colonies: Gender Roles in New State Cinema About the Empire'. In *Gender, Empire and Postcolony: Luso-Afro-Brazilian Intersections*, edited by Hilary Owen and Anna M. Klobucka, 71–85. New York: Palgrave Macmillan, 2014.

Vincendeau, Ginette. 'Women's Cinema, Film Theory and Feminism in France'. *Screen* 28, no. 4 (1986): 4–18.

Waldman, Diane and Janet Walker (eds). *Feminism and Documentary*. Minneapolis: University of Minnesota Press, 1999.

Weschler, Lawrence. 'On Salomé Lamas's ELDORADO XXI', *Eldorado XXI Press Kit*, 2016. http://lawrenceweschler.com/static/images/uploads/Lamas_ELDORADOXXI_edited_copy.pdf (accessed 30 December 2018).

Wheeler, Duncan. 'The (Post-)Feminist Condition: Women Filmmakers in Spain'. *Feminist Media Studies* 16, no. 6 (2016): 1057–77.

White, Patricia. *Women's Cinema, World Cinema: Projecting Contemporary Feminisms*. Durham: Duke University Press, 2015.

Wieviorka, Annette. *The Era of the Witness*. Translated by Jared Stark. Ithaca NY: Cornell University Press, 2006.

Williamson, Milly. *The Lure of the Vampire: Gender, Fiction and Fandom from Bram Stoker to Buffy*. New York: Wallflower Press, 2005.

Willoquet-Maricondi, Paula. 'Shifting Paradigms: From Environmentalist Film to Ecocinema'. In *Framing the World: Explorations in Ecocriticism and Film*, edited by Paula Willoquet-Maricondi, 43–61. Charlottesville and London: University of Virginia Press, 2010.

Wilson, Emma. *Cinema's Missing Children*. London: Wallflower, 2003.

Woodward, Alison E., Mercè Renom and Jean-Michel Bonvin (eds). *Transforming Gendered Well-Being in Europe: The Impact of Social Movements*. Farnham and Burlington: Ashgate, 2011.

Xavier, Flávio Scotellaro, Jr. 'Margarida sobre Margarida: escrita e reescrita da vida de Soror Clara do Santíssimo Sacramento'. MA diss., Faculdade de Letras da Universidade do Porto, 2018. https://sigarra.up.pt/flup/en/pub_geral.show:file?pi_doc_id=181112 (accessed 5 July 2019).

Index

11th Hour, The 108
16 mm 29, 30
25 April 1974 10, 25, 45, 72, 121, 133, 158, 186
35 mm 24, 136, 138
48 12, 15, 129, 141, 143, 144, 146–8, 152, 153, 159–65

abortion 5, 11, 13, 14, 45, 65–70, 75–9, 83
adaptation(s) 12, 24, 31, 32, 38, 46, 47–9, 67, 79, 133, 203
Adriana 12, 13, 43, 44, 56, 57
affect 150, 154, 157, 163, 164
Afonso, Zeca 72
Africa 5, 38, 133, 192, 196, 204
African Independence 15
Agamben, Giorgio 120
ageing 16, 161
Aguilar, Sandro 218
Airosa, José 58
Alce Filmes 90
Alegre, Manuel 77
Alentejo 95, 98
Almeida, Acácio de 45, 58
Altar 171
Alves Costa, Catarina 27, 47, 48, 214
Ama-San 16, 90, 212, 215, 221–4, 227, 228
Andala, Mina 191, 205
Andresen, Sophia de Mello Breyner 15, 169–71, 173, 176–8, 180, 182, 183
Angola 23, 205
ANIM 11
anthropocentrism 109
anticinema 131
Antigone 52, 53
Aparelho Voador a Baixa Altitude 14, 67
AR.CO 223

archive 5, 7, 11, 12, 15, 40, 129, 134, 141, 147, 148, 150–5, 158, 160, 164, 198, 204, 215, 217
archival footage 15, 131, 133, 139, 140
archival turn 150
archive effect 130
Ar de Filmes 214
Argentina 192, 203, 207, 217, 226
art cinema 3, 4, 40, 43, 60
art-house 8, 13, 16, 192, 195, 212
Ashore (Terra Franca) 226–7
austerity 14, 88, 93, 101–3, 213
Austria 152
auteur(s) 2, 3, 6, 38, 192–6
auteurism 6, 7, 13, 193–5, 203
authorship 6, 183, 192
Aviation Field, An (Um Campo de Aviação) 16, 212, 215–18, 221, 224, 227, 228
Azevedo Gomes, Rita 1, 12, 15, 169–71, 174–84

backwardness 3, 89, 93, 104
BAFICI (Buenos Aires International Festival of Independent Cinema) 170
Bairro das Colónias 91, 92
Ballard, J. G. 67, 78–81
Batarda, Beatriz 97, 191, 204
Batrachian's Ballad (Balada de um Batráquio) 12, 16, 90, 212, 215, 224–8
Bazin, André 172
Bénard da Costa, João 40, 43
Benilde ou a Virgem Mãe 49
Benis, Rita 59
Berlin (film festival) 90, 170, 226
Berlinale 219–21

Bessa-Luís, Agustina   50, 66
biography   30, 47, 133, 196, 200, 202
   autobiography   46, 169, 175
   biographies   29, 30, 142, 178
Birth of a Nation, The   134
black and white   24, 30, 38, 171
Black Maria   214
Black Rose   13, 44, 50–2, 55, 57
Borges, Pedro   214
Botelho, João   214
Branco, David   198
Brandão, Ana   59
Brasília   215–17
Bravo, Bruno   57
Brazil   5, 169, 177, 204, 215–17, 223, 228
Buenos Aires International Festival of Independent Cinema (also BAFICI)   16, 70
Buñuel, Luis   73, 115

Cabrita Reis, Pedro   59, 60
Cahiers du Cinéma   193
Calle, Mónica   136
Calouste Gulbenkian Foundation   7, 31, 223, 224
Campos, António   27, 131
Canijo, João   51, 214
Cannes (film festival)   195, 207, 208
Cape Verde   215, 217
Cape Verdean   68, 228
capitalism   117, 227
Cardoso, Margarida   1, 8, 10, 12, 15, 16, 129–32, 134, 136–46, 191, 192, 195–200, 203–8, 214
Carmo, Dalila   53–55
Carnation Revolution   25, 50, 112, 116, 133, 141; *see also* 25 April 1974
Carnival   26, 27, 114
Carvalhal, Álvaro   31
Castaing-Taylor, Lucien   216
Catembe   37, 38
César, Filipa   8
Chien Andalou, Un   115
Christmas   26, 98, 220
Christmas 71 (*Natal 71*)   132, 203
cinécriture   174
cinéma du réel   171
Cinemagazine   24

Cinema Novo (also Portuguese New Cinema)   24, 31, 193
cinephilia   193, 194
class   10, 77, 83, 156
close-up(s)   27, 30, 49, 51, 71, 72, 76, 113, 115, 144, 145, 153, 155, 198, 200
Coimbra   66, 73–8
Cold Day (*Um Dia Frio*)   223
Cold War   140
Colo   14, 88–99, 101, 102, 104
colonialism   204
Colonial War   15, 33, 132, 162
colonies   4, 5, 133, 137
colonizer   10
colony   8, 216, 217
co-production(s)   2, 90, 133, 204, 215
Cordeiro, Margarida   11, 25, 108, 113, 131
Correia de Oliveira, Adriano   77
Correspondences (*Correspondências*)   12, 15, 169–84
cosmopolitan   16, 89, 91, 215, 221, 228
Costa, João Bénard da   40, 43
Costa, José Filipe   90
Costa, Pedro   2, 3, 8, 195, 214
Costa e Silva, Manuel   27
Cotta, Carloto   59
CPC (Centro Português de Cinema)   31, 39
C.R.I.M.   214
crisis   4, 5, 14, 16, 88, 91, 101, 102, 212, 213, 215, 224, 228
Cuba   133
cyborg   80, 83

Danford, Susan   198
Dean, Tacita   217
Deleuze, Gilles   3
Delgado, Humberto   152
Delgado, Noémia   1, 7, 12–14, 23, 24, 107, 111, 113, 131
Derrida, Jacques   150
Deus, Pátria e Família (God, Fatherland and Family)   157
Deus, Pátria, Autoridade   25
Diário de Notícias   33, 39
DocLisboa (film festival)   226
documentary (film genre)   1, 11–13, 15, 16, 23, 24, 27, 29, 38, 43–5, 48, 50,

51, 60, 88, 101, 108, 111, 112, 115, 116, 121, 129, 130, 131, 133–44, 147, 148, 152, 153, 154, 156, 159, 162, 171, 172, 175, 216, 220, 223, 224, 226
domesticity   99, 178, 183, 223
Doomed Love (Amor de perdição)   49
double minority   3, 4, 9
Durão, Rita   179, 180

Easter   98
Eastern Europe   117
East Timor   54
eco-cinema   108, 109, 111, 113, 118
eco-feminism   109–10
eco-feminist   14, 121
ecological footprint   107
Edinburgh (film festival)   16
…*E era o mar*   24
Eldorado XXI   16, 212, 215, 218–21, 224, 227, 228
embodiment   68, 89
emigration   26, 103, 120
environment   14, 27, 82, 107–12, 114, 117, 118, 120
Erin Brockovich   108
essay film   15, 169–84
Estado Novo (also New State)   10, 25, 141
ethnographic (film genre)   24, 27–9, 131, 223
ethnography   28, 218
EU   4, 116, 213
EURIMAGES   218
European cinema   3, 4
Euro-zone   88, 213
exile   15, 154, 169, 177
experimental (film genre)   148, 169, 215
Exterminating Angel, The (El Ángel Exterminador)   73

family   9, 14, 47, 49–53, 56, 59, 66, 68, 69, 88, 93–7, 101–3, 147, 153, 156–8, 176, 202, 206, 225–7
Fantasporto (film festival)   53
Far From Poland   175
Faria de Almeida   24, 37, 38
female gaze   195, 196, 198

femininity   47, 67, 89, 96, 99, 113
feminism(s)   4, 5, 10, 14, 17, 65, 83, 99, 103, 207, 208
  feminist address   89, 96, 101, 102
  feminist film (feminist cinema)   5, 101, 116, 131, 192, 194, 196, 203
  feminist film scholarship   6, 7, 9, 110, 193
  feminist geography   96
  feminist theory   80, 194
Ferreira, Joana   214
FICA   213, 214
Figueiras, João   214
Filmes do Tejo   214, 223
Fonseca e Costa, José   24, 31
Foucault, Michel   150, 154
found footage   15, 130, 173
Frágil como o Mundo   170
France   14, 193, 218, 220, 226
Francisca   49, 170
Freire, Raquel   1, 10, 11, 12, 14, 66, 73
FRELIMO   133–5, 137, 138
French New Wave   38

gender   1–10, 14, 59, 68, 75, 80, 89, 92, 96, 99, 101–4, 107, 110, 115, 116, 130–2, 146, 153, 183, 194, 203, 224
  gender (in)equality   9, 47, 102, 112, 227
gentrification   90, 92
geography   89, 96, 176, 216
Germany   116–18
Gil, Margarida   1, 7, 10, 12, 13, 43–57, 60
Godmilow, Jill   174, 175, 184
Gomes, Miguel   2, 3, 8, 102, 194, 195, 218
gothic   66, 73, 83
gothic horror (film genre)   67, 69, 70, 78
Greece   178, 183, 213
Green, Eugène   219
Griffith, D. W.   134
Grupo Zero   45
Guardian Angel, The (O Anjo da Guarda)   13, 44, 53–5, 58
Guattari, Félix   3
Guerra, Maria do Céu   53, 58
Guerra, Ruy   133
guerrilla   133
Guinea-Bissau   162
Guterres, António   66

Harlan, Thomas   25
Hespanha, Tiago   215
Hestnes, Pedro   54
Hollywood   3, 69, 108, 193
Holy Family   69
Holy Girl, The (La niña santa)   196, 206, 207
Homem, Luísa   215
home movies   225
horror (film genre)   5, 67–71, 73, 77, 78
Horta, Maria Teresa   36

Iberian   8, 9
ICA   32, 212, 213, 218, 221, 223, 224
immigrant(s)   59, 214
immigration   14, 117
imperial   151, 155
INC (Instituto Nacional de Cinema (Mozambique))   133–8
IndieLisboa (film festival)   57, 217, 226
Indonesia   151
intersectionality   10
IPACA/ICAM   53; *see also* ICA
IPC (Instituto Português do Cinema)   31, 33, 34
Italy   116, 193, 213

Japan   5, 222–4, 227, 228
Jeusse, Herman   199
Jonaze, Francilia   199
Jorge, Lídia   66, 133, 204
Jornal de Letras   46
José, Herman   55

Kintop   152
Koretzky, Aya   224
Kuxa Kanema   134
Kuxa Kanema: The Birth of Cinema (Kuxa Kanema: o nascimento do cinema)   12, 15, 129, 132–41, 143, 147, 148, 203

Lamas, Salomé   1, 16, 212, 218, 219, 227, 228
Letter from Siberia   172
Letters to a Dictator (Cartas a uma Ditadura)   12, 15, 152–5, 159, 160, 164

Lisbon   7, 10, 14, 23, 37, 43, 44, 56, 57, 68, 72, 73, 88–93, 95, 97, 102, 104, 223, 226
literature   5, 12, 30, 36, 44, 54, 76, 107, 170, 176
   minor literature   3 (*see also* minor cinema)
Locarno (film festival)   16, 50, 51, 170, 217
Lopes, Fernando   32, 45, 193, 214
Lopes, Nuno   60
Los Angeles   107
Luiza, Natália   53
Luz, Adriano   198

Mabjaia, Mário   198
Macedo, António de   25, 36, 37, 193
Machel, Josina   205
Machel, Samora   136
Madonna and Child   71
Malumbe, Samuel   199
Manja, João   198
Mar del Plata (film festival)   170, 217, 226
Martel, Lucrecia   16, 192–7, 199, 203–8, 219
Martins, Marco   102
Masks (Máscaras)   12, 13, 14, 23–33, 39, 107, 111–18, 121
maternity   14, 65, 75, 81, 88, 89, 98, 100, 104; *see also* motherhood; mothering
Matos, João   214, 215, 224
Mayer, Maria João   214, 223
Medeiros, Inês de   1, 12, 15, 150, 152–8, 160, 162
Medeiros, Maria de   8, 60
melodrama   101, 226
memory   5, 8, 13, 15, 129, 130, 136–48, 150–5, 159, 160, 165, 200, 215, 217, 226
Mendes, Murilo   140
Midas Filmes   214
Mind Loss (Perdida Mente)   13, 44, 56, 58
minor cinema   3
mise en scène   36, 72, 91, 92
Moçambique 65   24, 37
modernization   10, 11, 112

Mondlane, Gabriel   138
Monteiro, João César   44, 45
Moreira, Ana   57, 68, 116
Morning Light (Luz da Manhã)   223
Mostra: Realizadoras Portuguesas   10, 43
motherhood   60, 96, 98–102
mothering   96, 100, 101
Movimento Nacional das Mulheres Portuguesas   155
Mozambican   38, 133, 135, 136, 138, 140, 141
Mozambique   37, 132, 133, 136, 137, 141, 203–5, 217
Mozos, Manuel   171, 218
MUBI   221
Mudar de vida   24
Murmuring Coast, The (A Costa dos Murmúrios)   133, 136, 195, 196, 198, 204
museum   5, 13, 196–8, 204, 220, 221
Mutants, The (Os Mutantes)   14, 66, 68–73, 83

nationhood   2, 142
nature   14, 57, 82, 95, 107–21, 206, 216, 223
Neto Jorge, Luiza   46, 48, 50
New Portuguese Letters (also *Novas Cartas Portuguesas*)   65
newsreel   24, 133, 134, 136, 140, 155
New State (also *Estado Novo*)   10, 15, 25, 103, 121, 141, 152, 155–7, 162
New York (film festival)   217
Nichols, Bill   130, 153
Nicolau, João   218
Nobre, Susana   1, 12, 88, 95, 98, 101, 215
Noivo, Leonor   215
non-fiction   130, 131, 171, 221
Nordlund, Solveig   1, 14, 45, 65–7, 78–81, 83
Noronha, Isabel   139–40
Nothing Factory, The (A Fábrica de Nada)   90
Notre Mariage   170
Novas Cartas Portuguesas (also *New Portuguese Letters*)   65
Nuevo Cine Español   193

Obscure Light (Luz Obscura)   90, 152, 153
Olivais   91
Oliveira, Alexandre   214
Oliveira, Manoel de   2, 3, 24, 49, 170, 214, 219
Once There Was Brasilia (Era Uma Vez Brasília)   217
O'Neill, Alexandre   31
Onwurah, Ngozi   174, 175, 184
OPTEC   214
Ordinary Time (Tempo Comum)   12, 14, 88–92, 95–102, 104
Ornatos Violeta   12
O Som e a Fúria   218–21
Others Will Love the Things I Have Loved (João Bénard da Costa: Outros Amarão as Coisas que Eu Amei)   171

parenthood   14, 88, 92, 97, 98
Paris   14, 25, 31
Parque das Nações   91, 93
Partido Socialista (also Socialist Party)   65
Pássaros de asas cortadas   24
Passion (Paixão)   13, 44, 49, 58, 59
Past and Present (O passado e o presente)   24, 49
Pato, Octávio   153
Patraquim, Luís   135, 136
patriarchy   110, 112, 194, 196
Pereira, Benjamim   28
Periferia Filmes   214
pérola do Atlântico, A   24
Peru   5, 219, 228
photograph(s)   15, 30, 129, 141–7, 152, 153, 156, 159–62, 176, 196–8, 204
photography   57, 217, 222, 223
PIDE   15, 25, 33, 141, 152, 153, 160–5, 183
Pimenta, Joana   1, 16, 212, 215–18, 227, 228
Pinho, Pedro   90, 102, 215
Poe, Edgar Allan   73
Portas, Paulo   79
Porto   34, 73
Portugal Film   90, 226

Portuguese Cinemathèque   11, 44
Portuguese Farewell, A (Um Adeus Português)   132
Portuguese New Cinema (also *Cinema Novo*)   24, 31, 32, 36, 40, 131
Portuguese Woman, The (A Portuguesa)   170
post-colonialism   5
post-crisis   101, 102
post-feminism   10
posthuman   14, 67, 68, 75, 78, 80, 82, 83
postimperial   155
postmaternity   96
postmodern   80, 150, 175
Pousada das Chagas, A   24
POV   71, 76, 77, 119, 177, 198, 224
PREC   25
prisoner(s)   141–7, 152, 153, 160–2

Que Amor Não Me Engana   72
Queirós, Adirley   217

race   10, 151
Rainer, Yvonne   174, 175, 184
Ravache, Irene   191, 205
Red line (Linha vermelha)   90
Rego, Paula   66
Reis, António   12, 25, 28, 113, 131
RENAMO   134
Rending (Rasganço)   12, 14, 67, 73, 75, 83
re-territorialization   2, 17
Rhodesia   133, 138
Rhoma Acans   226
Ribeiro Chaves, Abel   214
Rocha, Paulo   24, 25, 32, 193, 214
Rodrigues, Amália   57
Rodrigues, João Pedro   11, 195
Rose King, The (Der Rosenkönig)   170
Rotterdam (film festival)   90, 98, 217
Rouch, Jean   31
RTP   29, 30, 31, 43, 45, 46, 53, 132, 213
RTP2   29, 45
Russia   117, 120
Ruth, Isabel   57

Sachs, Ira   219
Saint Petersburg   116, 117
Salaviza, João   214
Salazar   15, 141, 152–8, 160, 194

Schengen   112
science fiction (film genre)   5, 36, 67, 68, 78, 217, 218
Sea (Mar)   13, 43, 44, 59, 60
Seixas Santos, Alberto   45, 219
Sena, Jorge de   15, 35, 169, 171, 173, 177, 178, 180, 182, 183
Sensory Ethnography Lab   215–17
Serralves   221
sexist   10
sexuality   75, 146, 157
sex worker   117, 118
Shakespeare   56
Shostakovich   95
Silva Melo, Jorge   45
Simões, Rui   25
small nation(s)   2, 3, 5, 89, 195, 207
SNI   31
Socialist Party (also Partido Socialista)   152, 213
Sócrates, José   65
Soderbergh, Steven   108
Som da Terra a Tremer, O   170
Sousa, Camilo de   135, 142
Sousa Dias, Susana de   1, 8, 10, 12, 15, 90, 129–31, 140–4, 146, 147, 150, 152–4, 159–64
Sousa Santos, Boaventura de   4
Sousa Tavares, Francisco   183
South Africa   133, 204
Soveral, Laura   54
Soviet Union   25, 139
Spain   8, 9, 10, 103, 193, 213, 217, 220
spectatorship   70
Still Life (Natureza Morta)   141, 152, 165
Sugimoto, Takashi   224
Super 8   171, 178
suture   70, 71, 75
Swamp, The (La ciénaga)   196, 206

Tagus (river)   68, 91, 94
Tanner, Alain   90
Tavares, Manuela   66
Teles, Leonor   1, 10, 12, 16, 90, 212, 224, 225, 227, 228
television   13, 23, 24, 29, 30, 31, 32, 39, 40, 43–6, 48, 49, 54, 55, 66, 137, 181, 212, 213, 214, 222, 224
Tempest, The   56

teoria dos cineastas 23
Terratreme 90, 214, 215, 217, 221, 224
These Are the Guns (Estas são as armas) 140
Tomás, Américo 152
Toronto (film festival) 217
Torre Bela 25
torture 59, 120, 145, 153, 159, 162, 165, 204, 206–8
tourism 51, 90, 92
Trabulo, João 214
Trance (Transe) 12, 107, 112, 116–21
transgender 11
transnational 2, 4, 8, 9, 15, 89, 112, 118, 121, 192, 194, 203, 204, 208, 212, 218, 221, 227
transnationalism 3, 4, 117, 118
Trás-os-Montes 23, 25, 26, 28, 30, 39, 40, 112
Trás-os-Montes 11, 28
Três Dias sem Deus 11
Tróia 78
Troika 213
Tropa, Alfredo 31
Trova do Vento que Passa 77
True and Faithful (Relação Fiel e Verdadeira) 13, 44–50, 55

Uma Pedra no Sapato 224
United States 154, 170, 193, 217
urban 12, 14, 25, 54, 73, 88–97, 101, 102, 104, 105, 111
Urbano, Luís 218, 219

Valles, Sita 133, 205
Varda, Agnès 174, 184
Varejão, Cláudia 1, 16, 90, 212, 221–4, 228

Vasco, Rosa 198
Velho da Costa, Maria 53, 56, 58
Venice (film festival) 16, 195
Verdes anos, Os 24
Vertov, Dziga 109
Viegas, Mário 52
Villaverde, Teresa 1, 12, 14, 65–70, 72, 73, 79, 88, 90, 94, 96, 101, 102, 107, 214
Virgínia, Bárbara 11
Visions du Réel (film festival) 224
VOD 212, 221

Waddington, Gonçalo 199
Wanting (Falta-me) 223
Weekend (Fim de Semana) 223
Wenders, Wim 90
What now? Remind me (E Agora? Lembra-me) 171
White, Patricia 4–6, 195, 203
Wolf's Lair, The (A Toca do Lobo) 90
Woman's Revenge, A (A Vingança de uma Mulher) 170, 171
Women in Iberian Cinema 7
Women on Waves 79
women's cinema 1–6, 8, 9, 13, 89, 111, 192, 196, 203, 207
Woolf, Virginia 197
world cinema 1, 3, 8, 17, 192, 194, 202, 203, 205, 207, 208, 228
world systems theory 4

year zero 212, 220, 223
Yvone Kane 12, 16, 133, 191, 196–8, 200, 202–4, 206, 208

Zama 203, 208
Zinebi–Bilbao International Festival 217